The Whole Parent

How to Become a Terrific Parent Even if You Didn't Have One

Debra Wesselmann

Foreword by

Foster W. Cline, M.D.

DA CAPO PRESS

A Member of the Perseus Books Group

Library of Congress Cataloging-in-Publication Data is available.

ISBN 0-7382-0876-0

Published by Da Capo Press
A Member of the Perseus Books Group
http://www.dacapopress.com

Da Capo Press books are available at special discounts for bulk purchases in the U.S. by corporations, institutions, and other organizations. For more information, please contact the Special Markets Department at the Perseus Books Group, 11 Cambridge Center, Cambridge, MA 02142, or call (617) 252-5298.
First paperback printing, December 2002

7 8 9 10—06 05 04 03

To my mother and to my late father, Phyllis and Vernon Bellows,
who gave me the precious gift of unconditional love

To Vince, Maddie, and Hannah, who bring joy to each day
with their enthusiasm for life,
and to Doug, who has worked a miracle in his

Contents

Foreword

A trained foster parent worked with a child while the birth parent watched behind a one-way window. As the parent watched, tears glistened in her eyes: "She *is* a professional and makes relating to Angie look so easy. I wish I could relate to her that way . . . Foster, you just don't learn this parenting stuff from TV, no matter how many family sitcoms you watch, do you?"

No, you don't!

Parenting is even tougher when a parent's childhood was dysfunctional. As Deb Wesselmann so eloquently points out, those ever-waiting ghosts of times past sneak out of our mouths, and attempt to control our behavior. Then, out of the mouths of babes come words we shouldn't have said in the first place. And we find ourselves saying, "My mother said that, and I told myself, I would *never* say anything like that!

One mother, after suffering utter frustration at attempts to control her ghosts, had a unique way of coping with them:

> "When I was a kid, all we ever did was fight at the dinner table. It was anger city. My dad turned it into an inquisition. He was not interested in wondering about how his kids' day went, but gave us a probing angry, intrusive, and critical type of cross-examination. Somehow it was obvious that all of us kids were somehow falling far short of his expectations. I hated dinner times when he came home.
>
> "Then, one day, I noticed out of the blue that my kids avoided dinner times! I had no idea why! So when dinner time came, I began my inquisition about that! And Teddy said, 'Mom, you just make it no fun!' I was shocked. I couldn't believe this kid was saying the same thing to me that I had thought for years about my dad. At first I had no idea what I had been doing. But it suddenly became all too clear. So I decided, 'this has to end.' But I couldn't end it! No matter how hard I tried, I realized I just felt angry sitting down at the table with

those beautiful kids. Awful! And the worse I felt, the worse I was, and the worse I felt. You get the picture!

"That's when we started eating dinner in front of the TV. This is a transition, Foster, and we *will* get back to eating at the table. But eating on TV trays in front of the TV, sick as it sounds, is my interim gift to the children! I'm developing a new head-set and new emotions. This is a way station to a happy dinner time of relating. But it's a whole new experience for this mother, I can tell you."

Leaving the differences outside our skin aside for the moment, our parenting is based on four factors: personality, attitude, belief systems, and our use of learned tools and techniques. Three of the four are straight out of our childhood! And most people ignore learning tools and techniques. No wonder parenting can be difficult!

I talked with a wonderful father who grew up in an alcoholic home. He said,

"Foster, you just gotta see, that for me, nothing in *Love and Logic Parenting* comes naturally. I have to think before I say anything to the kids, because if I go on my gut reaction, it will come out destructive. So I have a four-step process:

1. If I don't know what to say, I don't say anything.
2. If I do know what to say, I don't say it before asking myself how I would feel if my dad had said it to me—which eliminates about two thirds of the things I want to say to the kids!
3. Finally, I have found that I can almost always turn statements into questions, and that helps. Instead of yelling at the kids for fighting, I can more easily say, 'Hey, kids, what problem are you causing my ear drums right now?'
4. It's been like magic to talk about my feelings and how I am handling things, rather than what they are doing wrong; and what I want them to do and how they are behaving. It's starting to be second nature now to say, 'Hey guys, this behavior is hassling me,' instead of 'quiet down, now!'
5. I have learned to use Choices and Consequences rather than 'Rant, Rave, and Rescue' on almost all occasions. I still slip occasionally. I find I now have to say 'no' a lot less!"

This is an essential book, for the destructiveness of a difficult parental childhood can be hidden. *When the kids are small, frankly, any type of parenting works!* It's true! Even if one has no effective parenting tools at all, but the children are loved, they will appear to be turning out well in elementary school. At that age, it doesn't matter whether a parent yells to his kid to "get up there and start studying those spelling words *now!*" or says, "Honey, I hope you are prepared for that spelling test tomorrow." The child will probably be equally ready for the spelling test. But the latter statement leads to an adolescent adults want to be around, and the former to an adolescent who will probably rebel.

One needs to understand that small children almost always unquestioningly accept their parental value system and behavior and the responses of the adults in the environment. Therefore, if the parents are ecologically aware, so are the children. If the parents are Democrats, so are the children. If the parents are Republicans, that's the way their child votes in the school election. But suddenly, in adolescence, tacky parenting techniques that were so useful in the child's early years simply do not work. And parents are in for a rude shock. *The real goal of parenting is to handle children when they are small in a way that leads to their becoming adolescents who are responsible, respectful, and fun to be around. As children grow into adolescence, parents should be able to continue seamlessly using the very same effective consequential but nonjudgmental parenting techniques that they used when the children were younger.* Adolescent rebellion is common, but not necessary!

The truth is, great parenting techniques serve adults well in many different nonparenting situations. The correct techniques work on spouses, in the classroom, at work, and in all management situations. How often have I heard, "I tried those techniques you gave me for little Bobby on my husband, and they worked like magic!" Or a CEO will tell me, "Once I started giving people choices and consequences at work, my life has been so much easier!"

The more dysfunctional the childhood, the more easily folks can slide into "Rant, Rave, and Rescue" as a management technique—for children or employees. In fact, many of the family "games" in dysfunctional families revolve around worry and rescue. As one client noted:

> "I grew up in a home where mom worried about what dad was doing; dad worried about the kids and mom; the kids worried about

the parents and the marital situation, and everyone worried about someone else while their own life went straight down the tubes.

"Taking good care of *yourself* was a whole new process for me! I grew up thinking that all loving people just naturally and always put *everyone* else ahead of themselves. And I didn't realize what an awful model I was giving the kids—'always put yourself last.' No wonder my kids had self-image problems, and of course, the more I did for them, and the more I ranted and raved when things went wrong, the more their self-images suffered, and the more their self-image suffered, the more I rescued, and we had a very ugly little cycle going here for a few years!"

The earlier one starts on the journey of correct parenting, the easier the journey. At our clinic in Evergreen, Colorado, we always taught that real change takes about one month for every year that things have gone wrong. That means if an 11-year-old is irresponsible and unhappy and has been parented in ineffective ways for nine years, it will take at least nine months for change to be locked in and for the change to be easy and semi-permanent. That is not to say it takes one month per year for life to *improve.* But change takes time.

Human behavior—the behavior of children or the behavior of their parents—can be likened to a freight train with cars filled with coal. There are four cars of coal for every year that things have gone wrong. So a 20-year-old with a lifetime of difficult experiences is like a train 80 coal cars in length. That's a *lot* of momentum. And the more extreme the dysfunction, the faster the train is moving. So, speaking metaphorically, a 30-year-old person who grew up in a very difficult environment for 20 years will parent with the tenacity and momentum of an 80-car train, zinging 80 miles per hour down the track. So change is not going to be quick, but with loving, consistent application of new ideas, change is possible, and many, if not most, come to live new and richer (and much easier!) lives.

I remember well a young teacher who first came to one of my classes for educators. I taught teachers many of the same effective techniques that you will read about in this work. At first this young lady sat in the back, and obviously disagreed, or had a hard time coping, with much that I said. But she continued to come, and was progressively more interested and accepting and understanding of the message. In the later classes, she was downright enthusiastic. This was reflected in her moving progressively toward the front rows of the class. One day after class she came to me and said, "Foster, I am 30 years old. I've been taking these classes for nearly three years. You are right! It takes one month per year of life to really 'get it.' Now I've got it! Goodbye!" I never saw her again, and I wish her well!

And my best wishes go with all the brave young parents who are now on the parenting journey.

Enjoy reading this book. Take things seriously, but keep your perspective and have fun. Lots of things that seem so serious in childhood are flat-out forgotten and not that important only one year later.

Your children will know you as an adult, hopefully as a friend. And that time of adult friendship lasts four or five times as long as their childhood with you! You want them to have nice memories, right? Of course, the way you raise your children will, in large part, effect the way your kids raise your grandchildren . . . and on and on through the generations. So raising children is an important and generally enjoyable task when you know the right tools and techniques.

God Bless.
Foster W. Cline, M.D.

Preface

Several years ago I moved my private practice across town to join a group of professionals whom I both liked and respected for their dedication to continued learning and professional growth. Soon after I moved into my new office I discovered that one of my colleagues down the hall, Debra Combs, was doing some interesting therapy with children who had severe character disorders. Many of the children had been adopted and had experienced abuse prior to placement. They had been brought in for treatment by distraught adoptive parents after coping with fire setting, cruel treatment toward animals and people, and an unnerving ability to remain emotionally disconnected from any other human being. Debra described these children as "unattached" or "severely attachment disordered" and treated them with "holding therapy." I asked her if I could sit in and observe. I was invited instead to participate actively in this very intensive attachment therapy. I was very touched as I watched the walls come down and witnessed these children releasing overwhelming feelings of rage and sadness and connecting with other human beings on an emotional level for the first time.

Meanwhile, I was working intensively with parents, children, and depressed and traumatized individuals. I found that because of my exposure to attachment therapy I began to view my clients' problems from a new perspective. Although my clients were not severely attachment disordered like the kids in Debra's office, I began to speculate that early attachment experiences were at the root of many of the problems. I began an intense study of the literature in the fields of attachment and infant psychiatry and attended workshops around the country. I discovered there are many types of attachment problems with varying degrees of severity. I began to understand more clearly how the attachment problems my clients had experienced in their early lives had affected their core beliefs about themselves, about closeness, and about trust. The transmission of attachment problems from generation to generation became apparent.

From a new perspective I began listening more closely to what parents were telling me. A mother came in with debilitating panic attacks and extremely high anxiety about the safety of her four-year-old daughter, causing her daughter to become anxious and insecure. It became clear that the source of her anxiety was rooted in her earliest experiences as she began describing how *her* own world had fallen apart at age four when her parents divorced and her mother started drinking. A couple entered my office on the verge of divorce. The wife had run out of tolerance for her husband's temper and harsh treatment with their children. As I asked more questions I discovered that he had suffered much worse treatment at the hands of *his* father. The impact of his earliest primary relationships seemed all too clear. Another client was distraught because she found herself exploding in anger at her child in the same way her own mother had exploded toward her. She had been determined to give her child a happier childhood than the one she had experienced. I had worked with these types of problems in families for years, but through my studies I began to truly understand the process by which early attachment experiences were infiltrating present-day families.

Most of the moms and dads in my office shared the same desire to give their children a better start in life than the one they had had. Most shared feelings of frustration and inadequacy because they were having problems in their parenting that they hadn't expected and they couldn't seem to control, even after learning the proper parenting skills. Parents were eager to learn about attachment and it soon became clear that insight into how their earliest relationships had affected their ability to be close, to trust, or to connect emotionally with others seemed to be the first key toward change.

Meanwhile, the clinicians' study group that met weekly at Therapy Resource Associates was actively seeking therapeutic methods that could be used to help people reprogram their deepest core beliefs as well as techniques for helping people manage their emotions. As we found some very helpful new methods for changing core beliefs, resolving trauma, and teaching emotion management skills I discovered that these methods, along with inner child therapy, could help parents change the entrenched beliefs that had become barriers to healthy relationships with their children and others. Changing core beliefs and healing the wounds of the past appeared to be the second important key to help parents change their relationships with their children. Through workshops with the Association for the Treatment and Training in the Attachment of Children (ATTACh), my association with Debra Combs, and attachment research literature I gathered methods my clients were able to use to actually mend the bonding breaks and strengthen the parent–child attachment. These techniques became the third and final key to help parents repair and recreate their relationships with their children.

I couldn't imagine anything more important than helping parents form secure attachments with their children and break old patterns of relating that had been passed down in some cases for generations. With the support and help of many others I began creating this book as a guide to parents everywhere who would like to overcome the effects of their difficult pasts and create the happy, healthy families they were meant to have.

Acknowledgments

I wish to thank all of the clients who have come to my office and shared their stories with me and who have allowed me to be a part of their healing and their families' healing. I have learned so much from these many courageous people. Special thanks to those clients who allowed me to share their stories in this book so that others could benefit from their experiences.

I am indebted to my editor, Frank Darmstadt of Insight Books, for believing in my project and offering most valuable suggestions for improving the manuscript.

Thank you to my agent, Rhonda J. Winchell, for her enthusiastic support throughout, and for sharing my vision even in an early stage of the manuscript.

I am indebted to all my colleagues at Therapy Resource Associates. This very special group of clinicians has been a tremendous support to me both personally and professionally. I would like to give special thanks to all of the members of the T.R.A. study group, which has been a very important part of my own professional growth.

A heartfelt thanks to Ann Potter, Ph.D. Not only has she been personally supportive, but her book and her guidance in the area of inner child healing and trauma resolution have had an enormous influence on my clinical skills. She also read parts of my manuscript and offered some invaluable suggestions.

Thank you to Eric Ridgeway, who found out about my efforts and cheered me on from across the country. He also took time to read much of the manuscript and offered many very valuable suggestions. Thanks also to Charlotte Kasl, Ph.D., and Anne Stirling Hastings, Ph.D., for reading and offering helpful feedback.

Thank you to all my colleagues who read parts of my manuscript for me: Bette Tarrant, LCSW, Ardyce Schoonover, LPC, Anne Marquardt,

LMHP, Susan Smith, LCSW, and Dale Battleson, Ph.D. They have all been personally supportive, and I would like to thank Barb Detlefsen, LCSW, Karen Stacey, LCSW, Mary Glassman, LCSW, and Shane Kotok, MS, for their encouragement and support.

I would also like to acknowledge Debra Combs, LCSW, now Director of the Attachment and Bonding Center of Nebraska, for introducing me to the topic of attachment and sharing her knowledge with me. She also took the time to read parts of the manuscript for me.

Thanks go to the board of ATTACh for the work that they do in the area of educating professionals and parents, and for the education I have received at their annual conferences.

I wish to thank Lou Shilton for her many ideas, suggestions, and resource materials that led to my decision to write a chapter especially for adoptive families, and for reading some of the manuscript.

I am very grateful to Foster Cline, M.D., who offered enthusiastic support, many helpful comments, and informational material.

Thanks go to Jana Smith for helping locate materials for me.

Thank you to Marleine Bernstein for giving me advice on preparing the final manuscript.

I wish to give a heartfelt thank you to my mother, Phyllis Bellows, for all her help in preparing the final manuscript and locating materials, as well as helping out in countless other ways.

I am deeply grateful for my husband, Doug Wesselmann, who was extremely supportive of my efforts from the very beginning and took over many extra jobs in the management of the household as I prepared the final manuscript. I also would like to thank him for reading my early manuscript and insisting that it be "reader friendly."

I am very grateful to my sister, Robin Griess, for contributing the beautiful cover art and an inside piece as well.

Thanks, too, go to my brother, Kent Bellows, who gave me much needed motivation early on.

I am grateful to my son, Vince Wesselmann, for his expert help with our computer. Thank you to all of my children, Vince, Maddie, and Hannah, for being so patient as I finished up the final manuscript.

A special thanks to Hannah, who said, "Mom, make sure you write in your book that all the moms who are writing books should remember that their seven-year-olds still need lots of attention." I thank her for helping me keep my priorities straight and for asking for what she needed.

Introduction

The information in this book is equally important and relevant to mothers and fa-
thers, and is intended to address both; however, for the sake of simplicity and read-
ability, unless gender is specifically relevant, "she" and "he" will be switched in
alternating chapters in referring to both parents and children.

All names of parents and children have been changed throughout the book to
protect anonymity.

The Whole Parent is completely different from any parenting book that you
may have read before. It is a guide for all moms and dads who would like
to heal and overcome the effects of their difficult pasts in a way that will
help them become more effective, nurturing, and responsive "whole" parents in the present.

If you have been unhappy with your own responses and interactions
with your child and have felt powerless to make things better, you are not
alone. If you have always desired to give your child a better foundation for
emotional health than you were provided, but have found yourself struggling to create a happy, healthy family in your present life, be assured that
your struggle is common to many. This book was written for you and for
the thousands of other parents out there who want to heal the past and improve the quality of their relationships with their children. If you are a
therapist and you want a book that you can use as a tool in therapy to help
the parents you are working with break free of generational patterns in
parenting, this book was also written for you.

As a psychotherapist who works with parents and families, the problem of how I could more effectively help parents began to preoccupy me
several years ago. Some of the parents I work with come to me specifically
because they are having difficulty with the behavior of a child or due to
feelings of inadequacy as a parent. Other parents come in because they
have symptoms of depression, anxiety, or stress or because they are struggling with addictions or relationship problems. But often these parents,

1

too, admit to feelings of frustration, shame, or hopelessness related to their relationships with their children. When I began exploring parents' childhood histories more thoroughly I found that many of the parents who are struggling experienced inadequate emotional nurturing when they were young. Frequently parents remember one or both of their own parents as emotionally distant, depressed, or suffering from addictions or other emotional problems. Some recount frightening explosions of anger or verbal, physical, or sexual abuse that was either overt or covert in nature. Often there is evidence of these types of problems going back to previous generations.

The majority of the parents I work with love their children deeply, and when they first became parents held very high hopes and ideals for creating a family that was healthier and happier than the family they grew up in. They desperately wanted to give their children the emotional foundation in life *they* did not receive. Many parents did not expect to experience problems with parenting their children, and subsequently struggled with feelings of shame, frustration, and inadequacy. As I began to listen to the parents in my office more carefully, these are some of the concerns I found common to many:

> I can't seem to trust my automatic responses with my child.
> I know *how* to use the "right" parenting techniques, but I when I get upset I end up just "reacting!"
> I feel totally helpless in dealing with my difficult-to-manage child.
> I can't seem to stop myself from screaming at my child.
> I feel the need to control everything, and yet I can't seem to control anything!
> I feel like I don't have the right kind of "parental instincts."
> I'm just not a nurturing type of person!
> I'm uncomfortable being affectionate or physically close to my child.
> I feel disconnected from my child emotionally.
> I have trouble talking with my child.
> I just don't have a close relationship with my child.
> I fear that my child doesn't love me.
> Sometimes I think my child is acting out just to hurt me.
> I seem to feel more anxiety about my child than most parents.
> I do O.K. until I get stressed out and then I just lose control!
> Others tell me I expect too much from my child.
> I can't seem to set limits for my child.

I just get so mad at my child!

When I lose my temper I end up spanking, and then later on I feel badly about it.

Something is wrong with my relationship with my child, but I don't know what it is!

When parents describe problems with their children and then talk about their own childhoods it often becomes apparent even to the parents that their childhood experiences are somehow affecting their relationships with their children in the present day. Often parents can even see generational patterns to parent–child problems. But what isn't obvious is exactly *how* this is happening and what can be done about it!

These types of problems are not exclusive to gender, race, socioeconomic class, or any other specific situation. Dads and moms experience identical struggles. Parents who are married, never married, divorced, remarried, Caucasian, African-American, Asian, wealthy, middle income, and lower income, gay, or heterosexual can all experience common problems in their parenting. Some of the parents I work with are only in their teens. Others have teenagers themselves, and some parents are attempting to repair relationships with grown children or want to develop healthier relationships with their grandchildren than they had with their kids.

Many of today's parents are also dealing with tremendously stressful circumstances that sometimes arise in modern life such as divorce and single parenting, relocating, financial difficulties, marital problems, or job problems. Many parents lack a support system they can rely on for help or respite. These types of stresses can hamper parents with the most *ideal* backgrounds, and they most definitely compound the difficulties for parents who are already struggling with the effects of their difficult pasts.

I became determined to find some way I could more effectively help the parents I work with stop the generational cycle of problematic parenting and give their children a healthier environment than the one in which they grew up. However, my determination might never have proved fruitful had I not learned about "attachment," the all-important bond that develops between parent and child that forms the foundation for emotional well-being. My education in the area of attachment began quite accidentally when I became curious and started observing the work of a colleague who was doing a type of therapy called "holding therapy" with children she referred to as "unattached" or "severely attachment disordered." I observed how these unattached kids, with histories of severe abuse and abandonment, had hearts that seemed to be made of stone and thick protective walls of rage which effectively kept anyone else from getting too close to them. The importance of our earliest attachment experiences to the development of core beliefs affecting our ability to connect emotionally to others lifelong became clear to me as I observed these rageful children.

As I thought about the severe damage these children had suffered during their early attachment experiences I knew I had to learn more about the effects of early bonding problems of a less severe form. I began researching the literature on attachment as well as the related literature in the field of infant psychiatry, and began attending lectures around the country. I began to understand more clearly how our earliest experiences with our caregivers determine core beliefs about closeness, trust, and self-worth and how those early years affect our ability to manage emotions for our entire lives. I began to understand more clearly how our early attachment experiences affect our later emotional responses and perceptions when we become parents. I realized that this knowledge had never been made available to parents or to many clinicians in a way that could be helpful. As I began conceptualizing parents' problems from the attachment perspective, I began sharing what I had learned and helping parents sort out exactly *how* their early attachment experiences were intruding into their current relationships with their children. I became very excited when I found that the insight and understanding parents gained into their own responses and reactions with their children seemed to be a vital key to helping them overcome the effects of their difficult pasts.

I also began a quest for specific techniques to help parents heal their "broken instincts." I searched for tools that might help parents change the negative core beliefs they had formed as young children, make up for deficits in nurturing, and learn the skills they didn't receive as they grew up for managing emotions and forming healthy relationships. In addition, I sought techniques to help parents make up for any deficits in their attachment relationships with their children, repair the bonds, and give their children the secure emotional foundation *they* did not receive growing up. I discovered that all of these components together gave parents the critical combination they needed to help them unlock the door and break free from the old unhealthy patterns. I observed parents finding genuine, ongoing success in their parenting experiences, enjoying time spent with their kids, and discovering their present-day families to be safe and healthy environments for themselves and their children.

I wrote this book for all of the parents who didn't experience emotionally healthy attachment relationships in childhood and for the professionals who may be helping them. However, after reading my manuscript, author Anne Stirling Hastings encouraged me to think of my audience as ALL parents and potential parents. She commented, "This information isn't about a few or a lot of people, it is about every single one of us. No one got a good parenting model, the culture won't allow it." I agree that there are few of us who haven't been wounded in our early relationship experiences in some way, if not in our families, then in our neighborhoods and in our schools, and through what we heard and observed in our communities and in our broader culture. The stresses on families from the culture are not becoming any less problematic. As a mother of three, two of whom are teenagers, plus two older stepchildren, I can attest to the fact that parents today are severely challenged in terms of outside influences from the media and from peer groups.

The Whole Parent is not a typical parenting book. Part One of this book takes parents on an in-depth journey that will help them thoroughly understand how their early life experiences unconsciously affect their perceptions and responses with their children. This part gives parents the key of enlightenment that seems to be so important to breaking free from the unhealthy patterns rooted in the past. Part Two gives parents the tools they need to heal their broken instincts. Parents are guided through a process of creating a new wellspring of nurturing experiences to heal their own inner child upon which they may draw to nurture their own children. Parents are given tools to help them make up for skills they may not have gained in childhood for managing their emotions and coping with stress. Additionally, parents are helped to revise core beliefs and make new, healthy connections with others. Part Three gives parents the third and final key—specific steps to strengthen the parent–child bond, create a healthier relationship, and teach children responsibility at the same time. If you are a parent who would like to overcome the effects of your own difficult past, I would like to acknowledge the courage and honesty I know it takes to be willing to take this journey into self-discovery. Consider sharing what you are reading with someone you trust, like a counselor, therapist, or Twelve Step sponsor. Your journey may become more meaningful if it is shared.

There will be some information and stories in this book that you will relate to and there will be other information or examples that will not fit you at all. Although there are always many commonalities, every parent's story and every parent's needs are a little different. Take what fits for you and leave the rest.

Several helpful exercises are included throughout this book that will help you to gain further insight into your own personal situation and make some real changes in your life. I recommend that you buy a notebook so that you can keep all of your written exercises together and take notes when you run across something that feels especially important to you.

Good luck to you. You may be just beginning your healing journey for you and your children. Or you may be reading this book at a time when you are already in the midst of great changes in your life. Either way, I believe you are on the most important journey you will ever take. You *can* overcome the effects of a difficult past and become the parent you always wanted to be. This journey will benefit not just you, but your children, and your children's children.

Part One

The First Key

Understanding Your Broken Instincts

You begin this journey now because you care. Please remember along your journey that this book would not exist if it were not for parents like you who obviously care so much that you are willing to invest both time and energy in reading this book and facing the challenge of change.

I invite you now to unlock the first door on your healing journey as you gain an in-depth understanding of exactly how your earliest experiences in life may be affecting your perceptions and reactions as a parent today. This knowledge and understanding will be the foundation for the healing work in Parts Two and Three.

Chapter One

Enter: The Uninvited Ghosts of the Past

1. THE HAZARDS OF GROWING UP INSECURE

Almost all parents desire to see their children grow up to be healthy, secure, and happy adults. In my therapy practice I find that those parents who were abused or neglected as children are often the most anxious about their children's well-being because they know from their *own* experience the hazards of growing up in this world without the benefit of a consistently nurturing relationship with one's parents. If you were once a young person lacking a sense of security at home you may remember well how it felt. Like a man without a country, you may have felt a rootlessness, an insecurity, and a desperate need to belong. You may have looked for that sense of belonging in all the wrong places. Perhaps you looked for it in unhealthy relationships, in bars, or in a group of adolescent rebels.

At the same time, having learned not to trust in relationships with people, you may have kept your relationships with people superficial. You may have turned to relationships with alcohol, drugs, food, sex, or gambling, or obsession with appearance, money, or power to replace genuine relationships. Unfortunately, these kinds of interactions are not deeply and genuinely fulfilling. Therefore, as individuals become involved in the behavior even more frantically in an attempt to get their needs met emotionally, the obsession can develop into an addiction. These relationships with substances or activities eventually cause harmful consequences and create barriers to real intimacy. You may have experienced or may still be experiencing a struggle with some type of addiction.

As an adult who grew up without security in a home base you may have also discovered yourself to be extremely vulnerable to stress, struggling to cope at times with even ordinary problems and obstacles in your life. You may have also found yourself suffering from symptoms of depression or extreme anxiety. If your childhood was difficult, you are familiar with the hazards of growing up without a secure home base. You are probably well aware of how hazardous the world is today for someone who feels insecure on the inside. The social pressures kids and young adults face are tremendous. For a child looking for a sense of belonging the easy solution may be to join a peer group which is ready to welcome him complete with alcohol, drugs, or criminal activity. Unhealthy relationships seem to be all too easy to find. To walk away from a welcoming group or relationship based on one's principles or values takes an inner sense of security and self-confidence that is difficult to develop without a secure relationship at home. It is easy to see why kids with a solid relationship with parents grow up happier and more assertive and have healthier relationships.

2. BROKEN INSTINCTS

As a parent who may have experienced inadequate emotional nurturing in your own upbringing, you may have discovered a gap between the secure relationship you sincerely want to provide your own child and the reality of what is happening in your home. You may have been vaguely or even acutely aware of problems even when your child was still quite small, but you may have hoped things would get easier as your child grew older. Instead, you may have discovered the problems only increased. Or, you may be a new parent, or even a prospective parent, already aware that you may be missing the so-called "natural instincts" for healthy parenting that others talk about. You may find yourself feeling more confused and anxious about your new role as parent than you would like.

Psychoanalyst Selma Fraiberg, one of the pioneers in the study of infant/parent attachment, wrote an essay entitled "Ghosts in the Nursery." From her extensive studies of parents and infants, Fraiberg observed, "In every nursery there are ghosts. They are the visitors from the unremembered past of the parents; the uninvited guests at the christening." Fraiberg adds, "Even among families where the love bonds are stable and strong, the intruders from the parental past may break through the magic circle in an unguarded moment, and a parent and his child may find themselves reenacting a moment or a scene from another time with another set of characters."[1] The ghostly influences of the past are carried into present-day parent–child relationships by the unconscious minds of parents. As they interact with their children, memories, feelings, and beliefs rooted in childhood experiences can influence the actions of parents without their conscious awareness. Any nursery, whether small and sparsely furnished, or spacious with furnishings that are shiny and brand new, is vulnerable to these ghostly phantoms. The phantoms can be as immovable as a broken-down truck, and immovable despite mountains of parental love and the best parental intentions.

On the positive side, if the caregivers from their early years were loving and nurturing, the friendly phantoms from the past may be helpful to parents, enhancing their instinctive responses to their children. Warm, loving feeling memories of the past can make parents feel as if they are in touch with their own natural parental instincts—although their "natural instincts" are in actuality a "ghostly" gift from their loving parents.

The ghosts in the nursery may be primarily good natured, with just a few bothersome gremlins, perhaps in the form of occasional self-doubts or fears picked up here and there along the way. Or the ghosts may be rudely invasive and hostile. They may take the form of intrusive and frightening memories or overwhelming feelings beyond the parent's control. These monstrous ghouls may be so powerful that they consistently haunt the parent–child relationship, distorting perceptions, impairing responses, and contaminating a relationship that means so much to both parent and child.

The most frightening part of this whole thing is that the demons don't leave because the baby has become too big for the nursery. In fact, they don't leave when the child starts elementary school . . . or junior high or high school. In fact, by the time the child leaves home, he has his very own demons that will move in to *his* child's nursery . . . and on and on it will go, generation after generation.

3. THERE IS HOPE

And yet—you *can* be a terrific parent even if you didn't have one! Many parents *have* found a way to heal and overcome the effects of their difficult pasts. Courageously, these parents have thrown out the monsters and the demons. These parents have reclaimed their lives for themselves and for their children. *It can be done.* This is in fact the sole purpose for the writing of this book—to give more parents the keys that will help them unlock the nursery doors and throw out the unwanted phantoms . . . no matter what age the child is now. All parents deserve to become "whole parents"—to have the opportunity to break the generational cycle and find a better life for themselves and for their children . . . and for future generations not yet born.

The first key is *understanding* where these ghosts come from. The first step is to become acquainted with the ghosts in your nursery, the friendly and the not so friendly, and to learn which memories, emotions, and beliefs these ghosts entered through.

The stories in this chapter are composites of many clients I have known. They are not meant to represent specific individuals. Like an investigator in a haunted house, the reader can begin looking for the ghostly shadows lurking between the lines of these pages. The characters in these stories will introduce the reader to several types of phantoms commonly encountered in the early months of the parent–child relationship, from helpful to destructive. The reader will also gain insight into how emotions and beliefs rooted in childhood experiences allow these ghosts entry into present-day nurseries.

4. MARY AND MARTHA; FRIENDLY GHOSTS

It was Friday, and Mary was on her way to the sitter's to pick up her daughter, Martha. This had been Mary's first week back to work since her maternity leave. It had been even more difficult returning to work than she had expected it to be, as she had missed Martha terribly every minute she was at the office. Mary was visualizing Martha—her large brown eyes, and her adorable smile, as she turned up Pam's driveway. Mary smiled to herself as she noticed the familiar tingling in her breasts as her milk "let down." She thought it amazing how her body responded to just the anticipation of seeing Martha. Mary felt grateful for Pam, who was more than just a sitter; she was a long-time friend and a support to her. Pam had watched Mary's son, Mack, from infancy until he started school last year. She had encouraged Mary to go ahead and nurse Martha right there at her house after work each day. Pam had nursed her own kids, so she understood the urgency of both mother and baby after a day apart.

As Pam greeted Mary at the door, Mary could see Martha lying on a quilt in the middle of the living room. Martha looked up, and Mary saw her face visibly brighten as Mary entered the room. Martha smiled and gurgled as Mary reached down and lifted her up. "Hey, squirt! Mom missed you today!" Mary carried Martha to the back bedroom to the rocker that Pam had used to nurse her own babies. Martha was beginning to fuss now, as if the sight of Mary had reminded her that she was hungry. She found her fist and began sucking loudly on a knuckle. As the two settled in, Mary could feel Martha's little body relax as she began nursing. Martha looked up and her eyes locked on her mother's eyes. Mary felt her own body relax as well as she gazed down at Martha and cradled her closely. Neither Mary nor Martha paid any attention as the other day-care children ran through the hallway just outside the bedroom door. As Mary rocked slowly back and forth holding Martha in her arms, images and sensations floated in and out. The memory of holding Mack when he was a baby floated into consciousness. She could see the same big brown eyes but that head *full* of dark hair . . . and then it was Martha in her arms again, more petite and delicate. In her mind's eye, but not quite a part of her conscious awareness, Mary also imagined herself *as* Martha, warm and content in her own adult arms. As her mind continued to wander, Mary became herself again, but now very small, snuggling on her mother's lap. She could feel and smell her mother's skin. And there were other images . . . just fleeting—Dad's whiskers against her cheek, Grandma's cooking smells. And then she was her *own* mother, looking down on herself as a baby in her arms. As Mary continued to rock, and Martha nursed contentedly, Mary did not consciously take notice of her mind's wanderings. And all at once she was Mary holding Martha, looking up at Pam in the doorway. "She's such a good-natured little thing," Pam was saying. "She doesn't even mind all the noise and activty around here."

"I'm so grateful this is working out." Martha, satiated, had fallen asleep, and Mary and Pam giggled as together they tried to put her limp body into her snowsuit. "Do you have to go home and cook dinner now?" asked Pam.

"Monty has been actually making dinner each night since I went back to work," said Mary. "Sometimes I'm not sure what I'm eating, but trust me, I don't say a word! I'm just grateful I don't have to cook!" Mary was holding the sleeping Martha, strapped in her infant seat now. The bulky diaper bag was draped over one shoulder, her purse over the other. Suddenly, Mary realized she was exhausted from the week. It would feel very good to get home.

In Conclusion . . .

All parents would be able to rely on their natural instincts each time they interacted with their children if their ghosts were as friendly as Mary's. Her warm, loving feeling memories from her own past create feelings of security and love as she interacts closely with her new baby.

5. HELEN AND HENRY; GREMLINS IN THE SHADOWS

Helen switched off the vacuum cleaner only to find that Henry was crying loudly from his crib. Helen unplugged the cleaner, wound the cord, and parked it in the corner of the tidy living room. Helen and Hank had moved into this house just before Henry was born. Hank was hard working; a postman, quiet, like Helen. Helen had worked as a secretary before Henry was born, but she had never enjoyed it that much. She had told Hank that after the baby was born she intended to stay home. Luckily, Hank didn't mind that money was tight. Neither Helen nor Hank cared for going out to dinner or movies anyway. Neither really had any outside friends. They liked staying home and watching television. Helen did crossword puzzles and embroidered. Hank enjoyed puttering around his shop in the basement. Occasionally they would have Helen's sister and her husband over for dinner, or Hank's brother and his wife.

As Helen entered Henry's room he stopped crying and began staring intently at the activity center hooked to the side of the crib. Helen silently picked up the six-month-old. With a serious expression on his face, Henry soberly looked down at his little red socks. The short blond fuzz on top of his head stood up evenly like a military cut. Helen quickly and efficiently changed the wet diaper, carried him to the playpen in the living room, and moved to the kitchen to warm his bottle. Henry was sitting up now, but staring intently at his socks again. Helen shook the bottle and carefully tested the milk on her wrist. It was warm; but not too hot. She picked up the sober baby and laid him on her lap, his head propped on a cushion. She offered Henry his bottle. He grabbed it from her and began sucking methodically, holding the bottle and staring off into space.

Helen looked down at the baby on her lap. He was only six months old, and yet—he seemed to not need her very much. *He's going to be very independent*, Helen thought . . . *just like me*. As she leaned back and closed her eyes, with Henry's small body tucked comfortably in her lap, Helen's mind began to drift. Images and feelings began floating through her mind as

Helen drifted, somewhere between sleep and waking consciousness. Helen wasn't consciously aware of the memories and images—her mother's face . . . her father's face . . . tired faces . . . angry faces. The faces of her three younger siblings were looking up at her . . . looking to her—to wipe their noses and clean their faces. Suddenly she was very small. She was trying to pull herself up onto her mother's lap. She could hear words. *I'm tired. Leave me alone.* She could feel the sting of rejection—the loneliness—the disappointment. And then *she* was her mother. Looking down at herself. Helen roused herself and felt an immediate repulsion as she saw her child self in her mind's eye. *Scrawny. Ugh.* Helen suddenly became aware of Henry's warm, soft body on her lap. She opened her eyes, and for a brief instant his eyes looked up at hers expectantly. Suddenly, Helen felt very uncomfortable. She felt like she was suffocating. She needed some fresh air. She hastily set Henry down in his infant seat on the floor and handed him his bottle.

Helen stepped out on the back porch, still within earshot of Henry, and lit up a cigarette. *I hate this habit,* she thought. Her brow furrowed, as she wondered to herself, *Why do I sometime feel so uncomfortable holding Henry? Is there something wrong with me?* She looked at Henry through the screen door, lying there in his infant seat so small and alone. Again, memories of her own feelings of smallness and loneliness as a child were stirred, but this time they found their way into her conscious mind. Her chest ached. *Enough of this!* she thought. She tossed her head quickly, as if to shake off her troublesome thoughts and feelings. She focused on the taste of the last drag of her cigarette, and except for the queezy feeling in the pit of her stomach she only felt numb.

In Conclusion . . .

Apparently, Helen's early needs for nurturing and closeness were rejected when *she* was young, and she also experienced overwhelming responsibilities toward younger siblings. It seems that her feeling memories are intrusive ghosts in her relationship with Henry.

6. JAKE AND JANIE; HOSTILE PHANTOMS

"Hey you kids! I told you to stop that fighting! Now knock it off!" Jake was yelling down the basement stairs at Margaret, age six, and Sam, age four. It seemed to Jake he just had no control over those kids anymore.

And now he could hear the baby, Janie, crying in the bedroom. "Damn! Now the baby's awake! Where the hell are you, Beth?" Beth had left to go shopping with her friend. That had been two hours ago, and Jake could feel his blood pressure rising. She knew he wasn't comfortable taking care of the baby! And he could feel that little nagging paranoia that always ate at him whenever she stayed out too long. He hated that feeling!

He went into the nursery and lifted Janie out of the crib. Janie stopped crying, but her little face looked sober and worried, and she stared at the buttons on Jake's shirt. "Damn! This means I'm gonna have to change your diaper!" Jake mumbled under his breath. "Thank God you're only wet!" He threw the diaper in the trash and fumbled with the Velcro tabs on the clean diaper. He picked her up under her arms and carried her awkwardly out to the living room to put her in her infant swing. "Here, play with this." He picked up a rattle off the counter and placed it in the tray in front of Janie. Janie silently fingered the rattle as she swung quickly back and forth. Jake paced from the living room to the kitchen and back again, stopping only to rewind the swing every few minutes or so. Suddenly he stopped and stared. His father used to pace like this—back and forth, back and forth. In his mind's eye he could see his father, wearing that damned belt. He never knew when he was going to get it with that belt. Jake began pacing again. *Where the hell did Mom go during those beatings. It seemed like she just disappeared! She was never around!* Jake stopped and stared at Janie, who was silently turning the rattle over in her hand. *Why the hell am I thinking about this? Jesus! They're both dead now! Let it go!*

Jake was rewinding the swing when he heard the car pull up. He sighed with relief and sat down in his chair. Beth burst through the door, piled with packages. "The mall was a nightmare! But there were some great sales!" She set down her packages and turned to Janie, who was swinging soberly. Suddenly Janie's eyes lit up. She smiled widely as her mother lifted her from the swing. She gurgled happily and began sticking her fingers in Beth's mouth. "M-m-m-m! Good fingers!" Jake felt a pang of envy watching the two interact so comfortably together. Beth was so close to all the kids.

"Did you guys have a great time together? What's the matter, Jake?"

"Huh? Nothing! Yeah, we had a great time." He grabbed his jacket off the hook and opened the door. "I'm gonna go work on the car."

As he opened the hood of the old Chevy Jake could hear the sounds of laughter through the kitchen door. He could picture Beth at the counter cheerfully making sandwiches for Margaret and Sam, and all three of them entertaining Janie with noises and funny faces. *What the hell is wrong with me? This is my family, too! Why don't I feel like I belong? Why do I feel like such an outsider? What am I so goddamn mad about?* Jake slammed the hood of the car and stood there silently, contemplating the feelings of despair and alienation wrapped tightly around his chest.

In Conclusion . . .

From Jake's story, one can surmise that he did not feel much security in his earliest attachment relationships. The abuse from his father and lack of protection from his mother are troublesome ghosts interfering in his ability to trust and enjoy those he loves the most—his wife and his children.

7. NANCY AND NATE; THE LITTLE MONSTER

Nancy sat on the sofa staring at *Donahue*. The show had something to do with weight loss, but she couldn't even concentrate enough to follow exactly what it was about. She felt tired, defeated, and helpless. Three-year-old Nate had covered the carpet with blocks, action figures, and Hot Wheels. He was now pulling out a huge box of Legos. "No, Nate. *Please* don't get out the Legos!" Her voice sounded weak and pleading. Nate turned deaf ears to his mother and began dumping the box of Legos onto the floor. "Nate *please!* Now don't get out anything else!" As if in response, Nate turned and ran into the kitchen. Out he came with a big box of Ritz crackers. "I want crackers!" he shouted.

"No, Nate. It's too close to dinner time." Her voice was barely audible now.

"I want crackers!" Nate screamed louder.

The doorbell rang. Nancy looked around the room frantically. "Oh, no!"

She was relieved to find Sarah at the door. "Thank God it's just you. The house is a mess."

"Just me? I'm not sure how to take that!" Sarah laughed. Then she caught her breath. "Wow! Did a hurricane hit?"

"Oh, no! Not the crackers!" Nancy put her hands to her mouth as she saw Ritz crackers sprinkled everywhere. Nate was sitting peacefully in the middle of the floor stuffing his mouth full of crackers, watching the end of *Donahue*.

"I'm sorry if I came at a bad time." Sarah looked embarrassed.

"Any time is a bad time anymore. Nate was a difficult baby and a terrible two-year-old. But now he's a monster! He's a complete monster!" Nancy started to cry.

Sarah looked embarrassed. "I'm sorry, Nancy. Tell me what I can do to help."

"There's nothing anyone can do." Her chin was trembling as she looked over at Nate who was happily chomping down crackers.

"What, Nancy?" Sarah was looking at Nancy intensely now. "What is it? There's something you're not telling me. I know you too well. Is something wrong with Nate? What is it?"

Nancy hadn't spoken the words ever—to anyone. She didn't know if she wanted to say them. It might make her fear more real. The words suddenly tumbled out. "I can see my brother in him, Sarah!" There they were—those awful words. She sat down on the sofa and crumpled, her head down in her hands, sobbing silently.

"Your brother?" Sarah sat down next to Nancy and gingerly touched her shoulder. Sarah's face reflected her confusion. She glanced over at Nate, who had fallen asleep in front of the T.V., crackers in hand. He looked quite angelic and peaceful right at this moment. "He does look like your brother, Nancy. But how is that a problem? He's a darling little boy!"

"You don't understand!"

"Help me understand! What are you talking about?"

"My brother was a monster, Sarah! He used to . . ." Nancy put her head in her hands, crying silently.

"What did he do, Nancy?"

"He used to . . . hurt me! He'd lock me in the closet and he wouldn't let me out! One time he tied me up and left me in the basement for hours! He was a sadist, Sarah!" Nancy lowered her voice so that it was just a whisper. "And *Nate's* father—I didn't even *know* him, Sarah! He was a one-night stand! For all I know *he* may have been a monster like Luke! I think it's hopeless, Sarah! I'm scared to death. There's nothing I can *do.*"

Sarah sat down next to Nancy. "Nancy—look at me. Now listen. Nate is *not* a monster. He is *not* a psychopath. He is *not* abusing you. He's just a little *kid*, Sarah. He's a normal, highly active little boy. You're having a bad day and you're just not thinking rationally."

"No, Sarah, I've been thinking this for a long time—not just today. But every day it gets worse. I just feel so *scared and helpless.*"

"Nancy, how can you be scared of your own son? Look at him! Look how cute he is! Nancy, Ed and I have baby-sat for him. We even had him for the weekend last summer, remember, when you went to the wedding? Nancy, he's a normal kid! We had to be firm with him of course. But that's true for a lot of kids! Look! What does the day care say about him? Do they say he's a monster—lock him up before it's too late?"

"No, they say he's active—bright—needs firm limits."

"See, there you have it."

Nancy looked at Nate, sleeping amid the clutter and chaos. She looked skeptical. "I don't know, Sarah. I hear what you're saying, but I just don't *feel* it's true. I know you mean well, but I think you just don't understand the situation. I don't think anyone *could*. Just forget it, O.K? I'm sorry I lost it in front of you. You just caught me at a bad time."

Feeling overwhelmed now with shame, Nancy tried to gulp down her anxiety and put on a calm facade. The swallowed fear felt like a lump of coal stuck in her throat as she bent down and began picking up the crackers scattered across the carpet. Sarah watched her friend with a look of concern on her face. She sighed as she shook her head and kneeled down to help.

In Conclusion . . .

Sarah, it seems, did not experience a safe, secure environment as a child. The feeling memories of the abuse by her older brother have become intrusive ghosts, interfering with her ability to see her little boy in a rational way and with her ability to respond effectively to his needs for limits.

8. LYDIA AND LAURA; OVERWHELMING GHOULS

Lydia opened her eyes. The baby was crying. *I can't do it*, she thought. *I just can't handle it today. It's too much.* She closed her eyes and tried to ignore the baby's cries and bury herself in sleep. But the anxious knot in the pit of her stomach could not be ignored. *Please, please, Laura! Just quit crying and go back to sleep. Please quit crying. I can't handle it today.* She couldn't figure out why Laura's cries made her feel so overwhelmed. She loved Laura more than anyone else she had ever loved in her life. But depression and anxiety had been part of Lydia's life for as long as she could remember, and since Laura was born the panic attacks had been relentless and the depression had made her feel like she had sludge in her veins. She wondered what time Luke left for work this morning—and what time he would be home. Luke couldn't cope either—with her. His words from last night rang in her ears. "Just snap out of it, Lydia!" His tone had been sharp. "Your problem is, you just like to feel sorry for yourself. You have everything you could want—clothes, a beautiful home, a beautiful new daughter. I just don't get you, Lydia!"

I don't blame him, she thought to herself. *He should have married someone else, instead of . . . damaged goods.*

Lydia gathered all of the energy she could muster and crawled out of bed. As Lydia approached her, Laura screamed more loudly. "I know, I know." Lydia said aloud. "You hate me too, don't you? Well, I don't blame you. I wouldn't want a screwed-up mother like me either." She lifted Laura out of the bed and began bouncing her nervously up and down in her arms. Laura continued to cry. Lydia finally laid her down on the changing table, still feeling like she had sludge in her veins. As she pulled off the soaking wet diaper, Lydia did not notice that Laura's sobs were subsiding. Laura was staring now, wide-eyed, at Lydia's face. Lydia was wiping Laura's bottom with a disposable wet cloth, her thoughts immersed in the pictures flashing through her mind. The pictures were very familiar to Lydia. They had played themselves in her mind many times before. She was aware that it was happening again, and yet once they started she couldn't seem to stop the movie. In her mind's eye, she was five years old and she was taking a bath. Daddy was rubbing her, down there, with a washcloth—too hard. "Stop it Daddy. That hurts." Suddenly, the wash cloth was gone. She could feel his rough hand, and smell the familiar alcohol smell on his breath. Lydia shook her head, squeezing her eyes tightly. "Stop, stop, stop," she chanted to herself. She looked down at the wet cloth in her hand. She threw it in the trash with more force than was necessary and quickly diapered up the baby. She looked at Laura—and suddenly realized Laura wasn't crying anymore. In fact, Laura was looking at Lydia, right at her eyes—smiling—and making those cute babbling noises. "Oh, so you want to play, huh? Are you my big girl? Do you love mommy?" Lydia picked Laura up and raised her quickly in the air. Laura looked suddenly startled, then smiled. Lydia held her close. "Don't leave me, Laura. Don't ever leave me, O.K.?" Lydia grabbed a little outfit for Laura and took Laura in on her bed to dress her. She sat cross-legged in front of her on the bed. "This little piggy went to market . . ." Laura laughed delightedly as Lydia wiggled each little toe and then reached the final tickle. But as quickly as it had come, her brief surge of energy drained away and she felt overcome once again with the dark cloud of depression. Staring straight ahead, numb, and listless, she didn't notice as Laura tried to make eye contact again. Laura batted at her mother's arm and kicked her legs. And then slowly, Laura's little smile faded. Her sparkling eyes grew dull. She became very, very quiet. Her legs and arms grew still. Laura's little face resembled Lydia's then—sober, with lifeless, staring eyes.

In Conclusion . . .

Lydia experienced trauma in her relationship with her father when she was a child. The memories and her depression have become the disquieting ghosts interfering in her ability to stay emotionally connected to the little girl she obviously loves so much.

9. KATE AND KARL; MONSTERS LURKING

"I can't believe it. There is nothing in the paper again today!" Kate said angrily to 18-month-old Karl, who stared at her wide-eyed, as he stood next to the couch, motionless. "We can't live on welfare forever. We'll starve! And I never have any money to do anything fun!" She threw the paper down. She could hear her mother's words reverberating in her head in response. *You made your own bed, now you have to lie in it.* Kate had heard that statement a hundred times. "But it's not fair!" Kate almost screamed. She put her head in her hands, but there were no tears. She suddenly thought of Michael as she looked over at Karl, still standing motionless at the sofa. He had Michael's dark eyes. And his square jaw. Suddenly she had a picture of Michael in her mind, lounging around some dormitory joking with his friends. She knew so well his gestures and his facial expressions. She pictured him at a party, flirting and joking with a faceless college girl. Kate could feel the anger welling up inside of her. Just a year and a half ago she and Michael had been seniors in high school and in love—or so she believed. They had spent endless evenings driving around and looking at houses—big two-story houses with wide front porches and porch swings. He would say, "That's the kind of house I want you and I to live in someday." But Michael was going off to college in the fall. College had never been part of Kate's plans. As summer progressed Michael had seemed more and more distant and aloof. And then she told him the news—she was pregnant. "I'll help you pay for an abortion," was his reply. And that was it. No more drives. No more long phone calls into the wee hours of the morning. It was like none of it had ever happened. The first words her mother had to say were, "I know where you could get it taken care of and no one will ever have to know."

She had screamed at her mother, "That's all you care about, isn't it? What other people will think!" And she had made a decision right then and there to have the baby and hold her head up high. No one will be ashamed of her baby! And she had begun dreaming of this baby. She had pictured a little girl, cute and smiling, all dressed in pink and bows. She had imagined taking her to visit her friends and how they would "ooh" and "aah." But when Karl was born he was six weeks early. He was scrawny and red. He spent two weeks in intensive care, and when Kate finally brought him home he was colicky. He was impossible to comfort. She had to keep the rooms dark and quiet. Any noise or activity around made him fuss more. She and her mother had fought constantly over what was wrong with Karl and what *she* was *doing* wrong.

"You're holding him too tight. You need to burp him more often. You need to stand up, he doesn't like it when you sit down." It seemed like all her life she could never do anything right. But when she was younger and she tried to defend herself against her mother's verbal barrage, her mother would slap Kate's face so hard it used to make her head spin. One day, holding Karl in her arms she had had all she could take. She had screamed at her mother, "I hate you! You make me sick! I won't live here for one more day!" She had bolted out of the house, Karl still in her arms, and had found this apartment that same day. She looked down at Karl's wide staring eyes again and tense little face. When he looked at her that way Kate could swear those were her mother's eyes looking at her. *Disapproving* of her. *Criticizing* her. *Maybe he hates this apartment as much as I do,* she thought. Her whole apartment was the size of a bedroom. She wanted a job. She wanted to get off this welfare. But there was nothing. Nothing out there. Kate pounded the sofa and cursed loudly.

Karl had been leaning on the sofa staring intently at his mother. He jiggled with the sudden movement and lost his balance. He landed on his bottom with a thump. His chin began to quiver and he began to wail; a whining, pitiful wail of sadness. "I'm doing the best I can!" Kate shouted. "It's all your fault anyway!" Karl's cries grew louder. His eyes seemed to be boring a hole right threw her. Kate grabbed him by the shoulders. "Shut up! I'm sick of your screaming at me!" She shook him. One shake—but hard. He stopped crying suddenly and seemed to be holding his breath. "Oh, God, I'm sorry!" Kate drew Karl to her and held him. His little body shook as he began to cry again. "I'm sorry, I'm sorry," she whispered. "God, I don't know what to do!"

In Conclusion . . .

It appears that Kate did not receive the emotional nurturing she needed as a child and also experienced a painful rejection in her relationship with Karl's father. Her deep hurt, as well as the stress of her situation as a teenage mother trying to make it on her own, have become the ghosts interfering with her ability to interpret Karl's feelings accurately and respond to his emotional needs.

10. BEN AND BARRY; TERRIFYING DEMONS

Ben was watching an old *Gunsmoke* rerun in the family room after dinner. It had been a long day at the garage. He had his feet propped up, a six-pack of beer in front of him, and a plate of chocolate chip cookies on his lap. For the first time all day he felt like he could relax. The only annoyance was that Mary Pat was running the vacuum upstairs. It was causing a lot of static on the screen. It irritated him that Mary Pat had waited until after dinner to vacuum. *She was home all day, for God's sake! Why did she have to do this right now?* Ben thought about how he had had to put up with the guys at the garage all day, putting off work, making mistakes, not listening. He was sure they were purposely trying to annoy him! Some days it felt like he didn't have any control at all. Suddenly the irritation became just too much. He stood on the ottoman and pounded on the ceiling. The vacuuming continued. "God damn her!" He heard a thumping coming down the steps and two-year-old Barry entered the family room pulling his teddy by the ear. He walked over to a can of Tinker Toys and dumped it upside down. "Jesus, Barry! Look at the mess you just made! Pick up those Tinker Toys and take them to your room!" Barry began obediently, methodically, picking up the Tinker Toys and putting them back in the can. "Jesus! You are so slow!" Barry froze. "Just leave them and go to your room. I'll pick them up! Get out of here!" Ben began scooping up the toys and Barry quietly turned to go. "Here. Have a cookie." Ben held a cookie out to Barry, and Barry turned and smiled as he reached for the cookie. Just as his hand touched the cookie, Ben jerked it away. "What do you say?" Barry smiled tentatively.

"Please?" He reached for the cookie again. Ben jerked it away.

"Say 'pretty please.'"

"Pretty please?" His small hand just touched the cookie and again it disappeared.

"Pretty please with sugar on it!" It became too much for Barry, and he started to whimper. He reminded Ben of a little weakling, puny and pale. Ben felt a sudden gush of repulsion toward the small boy. He threw the cookie back on the plate with disgust. "Oh, you big baby!" Barry was crying louder now. Ben's voice boomed. "Babies don't get cookies! Only big boys get cookies! You're a little wimp! Go sit in your room and cry!"

As Barry ran out of the room sobbing, Ben looked up to see Mary Pat standing in the doorway. Her long dark hair was disheveled. She was crying, too.

"Now what's your problem!" Mary Pat said nothing. "For God's sake, Mary Pat! I was just playin' with him! He's gotta grow up and quit acting like such a baby! He's gonna turn into a wimp!"

"He *is* a baby, Ben. He's only two!" She shook her head. "My God, don't you realize what you're doing?" Mary Pat walked over to Ben and looked him straight in the eye. "Ben, we need to go talk to someone about this." Ben looked stunned. She paused and then blurted out, "Ben, yesterday your aunt told me more about your mother."

Ben's voice boomed again. "My mother was a nut! We all know that! She hasn't been around in 20 years. What's your point, damn it?"

"Ben, the day your aunt took you in she found you, two years old, hungry, wet, and locked in a closet! And do you know what your mother said to your aunt? She said to leave you there! She said you had acted like a baby and she was teaching you a lesson!"

"Shut up, Mary Pat! I don't need to hear this shit! What's past is past! I don't even remember it! What are you bringing it up for? Just leave me the hell alone!"

"My God, Ben! Can't you see it? I've seen it for months. You're starting to treat Barry the way your mother treated you!"

Mary Pat slammed the door as she left the room. Ben sat down and stared at the television set. He didn't move. He didn't think. He didn't feel. There was only emptiness. Several minutes passed. Suddenly he blinked several times, rubbed his face in his hands, and shook his head. He got up and began pacing. He stopped. His hands clutched at his chest. He suddenly had the familiar sensation that he could not breathe. And his heart was beating so hard it was going to beat right out of his chest. So many nights he had awakened clutching at his chest in panic until Mary Pat was able to calm him down. "Mary Pat!" he whispered hoarsely. He made his way up the stairs and reached the top just as he heard the car pulling out of the drive. He sat on the sofa for what seemed like an eternity, until at last the panic attack began to subside. He looked around. Mary Pat had pulled the suitcase out of the closet, knocking the coats down onto the floor. "Shit!" He punched the wall with all his strength, punching right through the drywall. He felt a momentary sense of satisfaction as he looked at the hole in the wall and felt the pain in his right hand. Now *this* was a pain he could deal with.

In Conclusion . . .

Ben learned that it was shameful and unsafe to have needs as a child. These ingrained beliefs have become intrusive ghosts as he unconsciously transfers his own feelings of shame from childhood onto Barry.

11. LET US ASK THE RIGHT QUESTIONS

Parents who experienced painful circumstances as children cannot control the feelings that surface unexpectedly. The next chapter will illustrate exactly why our interactions with our children are such a powerful trigger for emotional responses related to childhood, and will describe the unconscious mechanisms that create them.

It is important to remember that parents who were lucky enough to grow up in happy, healthy environments like Mary did will naturally interact with their children in ways that are instinctively more positive and effective. But any one of us with the same wounds to our sense of trust and self-worth and to our sense of belongingness as experienced by Jake, Nancy, Lydia, Kate, or Ben would struggle in similar ways.

As a society, we can be much more effective in helping our families if we can refrain from judging and blaming. "Who is to blame?" is not a useful question. Let us ask instead, "How can we better understand the problem?" and, "What will help solve the problem?" These are the only questions that lead to effective solutions, and, I hope, questions for which you will find answers in the pages of this book.

Chapter Two

The Ghosts Explained

Tapping into Feelings and Core Beliefs Rooted in the Past

What gives these ghosts their power? How do they find their way into our nurseries? Why can't we simply banish these phantoms of our past and raise our children the way we intend? Thank God there is a way you *can.* But you *must* have the *right keys* in order to accomplish the difficult task of unlocking the nursery door and casting out the ghosts. The first key is understanding—learning "who" or "what" your phantoms are, and understanding the workings of the mind. It takes tremendous courage to peek behind the nursery doors to get to know the ghosts who reside there. But you will soon come to understand how your own earliest experiences in life influence your thoughts, your emotions, and your actions in your present-day interactions with your children. Be sure to keep your notebook nearby to write down thoughts and complete the exercises that begin midway through the chapter.

1. HOLDING BABY: A PLACE FOR REMEMBERING

The relationship between a parent and infant is intensely close both physically and emotionally. When our children are infants they are completely dependent on us for their very survival. They require soothing, touching, holding, feeding, cleaning, and face-to-face and skin-to-skin contact on a consistent daily basis. We experienced the same intense intimacy we have as parents with infants only one other time in our lives, and that was when *we* were infants. When we hold our own child in our arms and experience our child's all-encompassing dependency upon us, memories and emotions stored in our brains related to *our* earliest experiences with closeness naturally get triggered. Dr. Daniel Stern, a researcher and Professor of Psychology at the University of Geneva, describes this experience of intense closeness with our infant as a "remembering context."[1]

Stern describes how he and his colleagues examined in minute detail the minds of mothers while the mothers were interacting closely with their small children. Mothers and their three- or four-year-old children first interacted freely for 15 to 20 minutes in the nursery of the center, which was familiar to the children. After the interaction, a "moment" was chosen. Stern used a method called "free association" to study what kinds of thoughts and feelings were going on in the deeper levels of the mothers' minds during the chosen moment in the interaction.[2]

Our minds are incredibly complex and can hold many layers of thoughts, memories, images, and feelings simultaneously. We are consciously aware of only the most surface layers of thought at any point in time. We are for the most part unaware of the content of the deeper layers of our minds, sometimes called the "unconscious." What Stern and his colleagues discovered by studying these very small moments in great depth is that during any small interaction with her child, no matter how insignificant, a mother may experience many different kinds of memories and associated feelings related to her own childhood (in the deeper layers of her mind) all at the same time.[3]

More specifically, a mother holding her child, on the most surface level experiences the moment in the here and now, in her role as mother to her child admiring and loving her baby. At the very same time, however, in a deeper layer of her mind, the mother very likely is imagining empathically what it must be like to *be* her baby lying there in her arms at that moment. Due to the closeness and intensity of the relationship, she unconsciously feels what she perceives her child is feeling, whether it is a feeling of distress or a feeling of being snugly held and comforted. A mother's feelings are unavoidably linked to her child's feelings in this way.

But this is not all! This experience of empathizing with one's own child automatically takes the mother back to her own past. At a deeper layer of her unconscious mind, empathizing with her child triggers feeling memories for the mother of actually *being* a child. If our feeling memories from infancy and childhood are warm, like Mary's memories in our very first story in Chapter One, the memories will connect us with the associated feelings of closeness, security, and happiness that we experienced in infancy. The warm feeling memories will naturally enhance our pleasure as we hold our baby in the present. Memories of feeling loved will also enhance our good feelings about ourselves in that moment.

But this is still not the end of the remembering experience. In yet another layer of her unconscious mind, as the mother is connected to memories of her own feelings in infancy, she may also imagine what the experience must have been like for *her own* parent holding her when she was an infant. If she imagines that her own parent was having warm, loving feelings toward her during this intimate experience of holding her when she was small, these imagined feelings enhance the mother's good feelings toward her infant. Imagining the nurturing, loving feelings of her own mother also increases the mother's self-confidence as a mother.

The child lying snuggled in the mother's arms benefits from his mother's warm, loving feeling memories as he senses the mother's pleasurable feelings while she holds him. The child picks up her good feelings, enhancing his pleasure. Snuggling with mom becomes associated with feelings of warmth and security for the child. It becomes something he looks forward to, and learns to trust and depend on for comfort.

When mother's feeling memories related to her own infancy are warm and her imaginings of her own mother are loving and good, these become the friendly ghosts in the nursery, enhancing the whole experience of motherhood. Mary, in our first story, was one of these lucky mothers. Her memory feelings were loving and nurturing, making her mothering experience pleasurable both for her and for her baby.

Although Stern's study focused on mothers, fathers undoubtedly experience the same remembering context created by the fatherhood experience and the emotions associated with it no differently than mothers. A father experiencing the closeness and intimacy of holding his own child will empathically imagine his child's feelings as he interacts closely with him. Additionally, in a deeper layer of his mind, a father will also tap into memories and feelings related to his experience of closeness with his own parents. As he goes back into time as a child, he will naturally imagine the emotions he believes his parents must have felt while looking down at him in their arms.

As the child grows, the relationship between the parent and child continues to be both intimate and intense, and continues to trigger feeling

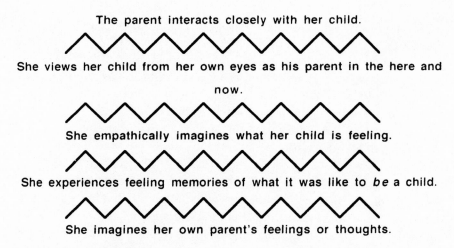

The parent interacts closely with her child.

She views her child from her own eyes as his parent in the here and now.

She empathically imagines what her child is feeling.

She experiences feeling memories of what it was like to *be* a child.

She imagines her own parent's feelings or thoughts.

Figure 1. The thoughts and feelings in the layers of the mind of a parent interacting closely with a child.

memories for the parent related to his own childhood feelings and his own parent's attitude toward him. As the child grows older, the parent will naturally be reminded of feeling memories related to the time period when he was the same age as his child. If the parent's feeling memories related to his childhood are warm and pleasant, this phenomenon will continue to enhance his experiences with his growing child. The friendly ghosts will continue to create positive feelings within the parent–child relationship at each age and stage of the child's growing-up years.

Figure 1 illustrates the typical layers of thoughts and feelings in the mind of a parent interacting closely with a child. Moving from top to bottom, the figure illustrates the thoughts and feelings at the most surface levels of the mind, moving to the deeper layers of a parent's unconscious mind.

2. BROKEN INSTINCTS

Unfortunately, for many parents the scenario is not always ideal. Imagine what happens when a new mother, trying to connect with the baby lying in her own arms, is unconsciously remembering her own past childhood feelings of rejection, anxiety, and unhappiness. The mother in this less-than-ideal scenario may suddenly find herself feeling depressed "for no reason" (that she can identify) as she holds her infant. The baby in this mother's arms may become suddenly aware that mother's smile has faded and her face has become flat and unresponsive to baby's cues. Her arms and body suddenly feel tense and hard. Baby doesn't know the words for what he is now experiencing, but he nevertheless may feel abandoned and alone as he lies in his mother's arms.

Even further, suppose that in a deeper layer of the mother's mind she is imagining herself as her mother, looking out of her mother's eyes with the feelings of indifference or even repulsion that she believes her mother felt toward her when *she* was a child. She may suddenly feel an urge to push away this sad little baby lying in her arms. Or she may simply feel a heightened sense of anxiety without conscious awareness of what may be causing it. These feelings seem to come from nowhere, and this mother finds these unbidden reactions very upsetting. She wonders, *Am I a bad mother? Does this mean I don't love this child?* Neither of these is true. But this mother's feelings from her own infancy and the apparent feelings of *her* mother have clouded and confused her own feelings in the present. Her earliest most intimate relationships are haunting her present closest relationship. Yet she may not think about this consciously, and therefore the ghosts remain invisible to her in the deeper recesses of her mind.

3. INFANT MEMORIES

As a parent holds his infant, the memories influencing his feelings and reactions may surface from as early as the parent's own infancy. This may be difficult to believe, because when most of us think about memories we are thinking of the kinds of memories that we stored after we acquired the ability to speak. The latter are like little movies in our brains, complete with picture, sound, and sometimes even smell and touch all rolled into one. Endel Tulving, a memory researcher with the University of Toronto, describes these types of memories as part of the "episodic memory system." At the moment of birth we have access to a primitive type of memory system that involves different brain processes than memories encoded after we have acquired speech. This memory system records perceptual sensory images and is referred to as the "procedural memory system." This primitive memory system is necessary for the survival of the infant. For instance, it is imperative that infants learn and remember what faces and voices they can depend on for protection. An infant can remember the touch and smell of her caregiver. She remembers how to suck, and how to position herself to get the most milk. An infant remembers what actions on her part are the most effective in getting the responses she needs from her caregivers. She remembers special objects such as teddies, pacifiers, and pillows that give her the security and comfort she needs in a sometimes overwhelming world. She remembers the things that are scary to her, and she remembers how to best avoid those frightening things. A third type, called the "semantic memory system," records verbal generalizations formed from our experiences upon which we make decisions about future situations and events.[4]

Dr. Lenore Terr, Clinical Professor of Psychiatry at the University of California, San Francisco, learned a great deal about the primitive memory system of infants through studying children who had experienced traumatic events. She discovered that children who were younger than 28 to 36 months old at the time of their trauma could not recount the trauma with words. Sometimes short verbal snatches or short phrases were recounted, but children who were infants and toddlers at the time of their traumas do not generally have access to the full memories of those events in such a way that they can describe them coherently. However, almost every child in her study who experienced trauma in infancy or toddlerhood had experienced their trauma in fears and nightmares, or had reenacted their trauma behaviorally. These children seemed to be unconsciously reenacting their trauma even though they had little or no conscious recall. One child in her study was traumatized between birth and six months old, and she, too, consistently showed reenactment of the trauma in her behavior.[5]

In his 1995 book for professionals called *The Motherhood Constellation* Daniel Stern recounted his viewing of a videotape of a patient being treated by psychotherapist George Engel. The adult patient's name was Monica, and Monica had been fed by tube as an infant due to an esophageal atresia. This tube feeding required the parent to use two hands, and so Monica had been fed in an unusual position; on her back, lying across her mother's knees. After age 21 months she was fed normally, as the problem was surgically repaired. However, at three and four years of age she was observed feeding her dolls in the same unusual position across her knees. Later, as Monica was an adult and became a mother, without apparently having any knowledge of how she was first fed, she went on to feed her own infant daughter in this same position. Furthermore, Monica's daughter began to feed her daughter in this same way, although she later switched to a more normal feeding position.[6]

Another example of the procedural memory system comes from my own life. My middle daughter, Maddie, joined our family at close to three years of age. Her first three years had been spent in Korea and immediately I recognized she did not like to be picked up and carried in the front-to-front fashion to which I was accustomed. She would, however, take advantage of a close-by chair or a step to scramble up onto my back whenever she could. I am quite sure this must have been the position in which Maddie was accustomed to being carried by her very busy foster mother in Korea. I was personally uncomfortable with this, however, and always shifted her around to the front position. Oddly enough, when Maddie was around seven and our youngest daughter Hannah was a baby, Maddie often insited on carrying Hannah on her back. This past year we were caring for a friend's baby in our home, and this youngster, too, wound up on our oldest daughter's back. I have never witnessed her carrying a child in the front position. Our Korean-born daughter has absolutely no memories prior to being carried off the plane onto American soil.

Our earliest experiences in this world may have included warm and comforting sensations of being held tenderly and closely, or fearful and lonely sensations of being held at arms length, left alone to cry, or even harmed. These feelings and sensations were recorded in our procedural memory system. Although we cannot consciously recall our earliest memories in the same way we can recall our later memories, the feelings and sensations related to the way we were welcomed into this world may still get triggered by environmental cues. They may be experienced as sudden emotions, body sensations, flashes of images, or even behaviors for which we may not have a conscious explanation. And one of the most powerful triggers for our earliest memories is finding ourselves welcoming our own child into this world.

4. THE INNER SELVES

There is no one who hasn't struggled with feelings and behaviors that after the fact seemed totally irrational, out of character, and way out of proportion to the reality of the situation. We have all said to ourselves, probably thousands of times, *Why in the world did I do that? What got into me? What on earth possessed me? What was I thinking?* Parents of young children often find themselves asking these kinds of questions quite frequently. Transactional Analysis (T.A.), originated in the 1960s by a well-known psychiatrist, Dr. Eric Berne, and the "inner child" therapy that has sprung from T.A. provide us with a useful framework for further understanding our feelings and behaviors in our relationships with our children.[7]

Transactional Analysis tells us that our personalities are divided into ego states. An ego state is a fancy word for a "state of mind." An ego state consists of the current state of our thoughts, beliefs, emotions, and behaviors. We all experience various ego states during our everyday lives. Think about the "state of mind" you are in when you are at work. This might be considered your "professional" state of mind. You take on certain mannerisms, you hold yourself in a certain way, you think in a certain way. Now compare that ego state to the ego state you are in when you are having a raucous good time with someone you are intimate with. Compare your mannerisms, your thoughts, your behaviors, and your emotions. Every human being operates from different ego states in different situations. But T.A. points out that there are three ego states that are basic, like the foundation building blocks, to every adult personality. These three ego states consist of the parent, the adult, and the child ego states.

5. THE ADULT SELF

The *adult* ego state is logically at the center of the adult personality—whether we are male or female. This is the part of our personality that is sensible, logical, and rational. When we respond to others from our adult part, we are basically responding from our present experience, without the overwhelming intrusion of thoughts or feelings from the past. We are behaving and thinking logically, and appropriately, for the current situation. When we are operating from our adult ego state we can problem solve and communicate effectively and reasonably with others. We can face difficult or precarious situations and "keep our head on our shoulders" or handle things without overreacting.

Let's look at a very common example of a difficult parenting situation. Imagine you are in the supermarket, and your child becomes entranced by the colorful picture and the free toy offer on a box of Sugar Yummy Cereal, but you have made a rule that you do not allow Sugar Yummy Cereal in your house. Imagine your otherwise wonderful child decides to throw the tantrum of her life in the middle of aisle eight. If you are fortunate enough to be able to stay in your adult ego state you will be able to manage the situation with aplomb. You will remain calm, yet firm, as you carry your screaming child out of the store, unperturbed by the stares and rude comments around you. Your adult self remains logical and sensible, composed and collected.

6. THE INTERNALIZED PARENT

We also have as part of our personalities an *internalized parent* part. "Internalized" means that as a child, we adopted as our own the thoughts, feelings, and beliefs of our parents and other care-giving adults such as grandparents and babysitters. (This happens whether we want it to or not.) The internalized parent part itself has two basic parts, equivalent to the two main roles our parents played in our lives.

6.1. The Nurturing-Parent Ego State

The *"nurturing parent"* is the part of ourselves that internalized our parents as they soothed, calmed, and reassured us when we were small. Like Mary in the first story, when our infant memories are triggered and we imagine how loving and caring our parent must have been with us, we connect with the nurturing-parent ego state and the wellspring of nurturing messages associated with it. When we are faced with an upsetting situation we can use our internal nurturer as a resource, tapping into the calming, encouraging messages to affirm and comfort ourselves. Children begin internalizing their parent's soothing messages from infancy on. An infant who has been nurtured and loved can be seen comforting herself with her blankie or teddy. This is the first step toward developing the nurturing-parent ego state.

I was only partly awakened by my five-year-old daughter, Hannah, jumping in bed with me one night. "I had a nightmare mom!" I heard her say. I think I mumbled something incoherent, and then I heard her, lying next to me, talking aloud to herself. "Don't be scared, don't be scared, don't be scared . . . ," she was saying gently. The next morning I thought about how nice it was that she had internalized my own words from the past, and could use those words to comfort her*self* when I was not emotionally available. Children who are developing an internal nurturer can also be seen caring tenderly for their dolls, their stuffed animals, and their pets.

The parent who had many experiences growing up of being nurtured will be quite comfortable operating out of the nurturing-parent ego state with his own child. When interacting with his child, warm feeling memories of childhood, and memories of his parent's loving messages, will naturally get triggered in the deeper layers of his mind. These loving memories become a wellspring of nurturing experiences from which the parent can draw upon in nurturing his own child. The parent who operates comfortably from the nurturing-parent ego state has an instinctual *knowing* about what his child is feeling and what his child needs. The parent with a strong internalized nurturer is comfortable touching, hugging, and holding his child. This comes naturally and feels normal to him.

The parent who did *not* receive adequate nurturing growing up has much more difficulty operating from the nurturing-parent ego state. After all, it is logically impossible for him to internalize something that was not a part of his experience. The parent who lacks this internal part has a scarcity of memories of loving messages stored internally. This leaves him without an adequate wellspring of loving, nurturing messages which he can draw upon to offer his children. When interactions with his child trigger feeling memories from his childhood, he may tap into painful feelings and memories of negative messages from caregivers. The parent who lacks an adequate store of internalized nurturing-parent messages may struggle to understand exactly what it is his child is needing from him, and may feel uncomfortable in the nurturing-parent role.

Adults who lack a strong internalized nurturer also, naturally, have more difficulty calming themselves under duress because they don't hear affirming or reassuring messages about themselves internally. They often don't take very good care of their health, don't allow themselves to rest, and they don't know how to manage their stress. Not only do they often feel unequipped to calm or comfort their own infants, but they feel unequipped to calm or comfort *themselves*.

6.2. The Critical-Parent Ego State

The other primary role our parents and other important adults played in our lives was one of guidance and structure. This internalized part of our caregivers is called the *"critical parent."* This part is equivalent to Freud's "superego" or the conscience. These internalized parental messages keep us from acting impulsively and doing things that would be unsafe or harmful to ourselves, others, or society. Internalized messages such as *it would be wrong to steal* or *it would be dangerous to run this red light* allow us to function as useful, healthy members of society. On the other hand, if our early experiences with our caregivers were filled primarily with experiences of criticism or even abuse, our internalized critic may be oversized, or even monstrous, filling our thoughts with messages of our own worthlessness and leaving us filled with self-hate. The parent with the oversized internal critic may replay shaming messages to himself, such as *I'm not good enough, I'm stupid,* or *I'm worthless,* leaving him with feelings of self-hate.

It is important to remember that the oversized internal critic does have a self-protective function. The logic of the inner critic, at an unconscious level, often goes something like this: *If I keep myself down, then I will have less far to fall. If I continually warn myself that I'm going to fail, it will prevent me from becoming overconfident and doing something wrong. If I beat myself up, I will be more prepared when others criticize me.* The oversized internal critic may also think negatively of others and direct the critical thoughts and feelings outwardly. This, too, serves a self-protective function. The logic is, *If I expect the worst from others, I won't feel hurt when they let me down. If I don't value others, I won't be hurt by their rejection of me.*

Remember the research by Stern and his colleagues that examined in minute detail a very brief moment between mothers and their infants. As a mother's feeling memories of infancy are triggered, she often imagines what it was like to be her own mother looking down upon herself as an infant. If she believes her mother admired and loved her when she was an infant, this will connect her to her nurturing-parent ego state with its wellspring of loving, nurturing messages. If, on the other hand, she believes her mother looked upon her with disappointment, she will tap into her internal-critical parent, and the associated negative thoughts and feelings. These negative messages may get directed both toward the unloved self and toward the infant in her arms. The mother, as a result, may feel like distancing herself from her infant, or she may simply become anxious and upset about her confused feelings.

Imagine you are back in the grocery store with the screaming child in aisle eight. In the back of your mind you remember similar interactions from your own childhood with your parents, and the critical messages you received in childhood get tapped into at an unconscious level. Instead of leaving the store unperturbed by the stares and rude comments, you will probably become overwhelmed with self-critical messages: *Now everyone in here thinks I am a terrible mother. I must be a terrible mother. I am worthless and hopeless as a mother. My child is a horrible child.* With your oversized internal critic in charge you may also find yourself directing critical messages toward your child, who becomes, in a sense, an extension of your filled-with-shame child self. You may shout, "You are a horrible child!" as you drag your screaming child through the store. As a result of the oversized critical-parent ego state, your self-composure and your ability to handle the situation rationally go right out the window. When we are in a critical-parent ego state that is gigantic in size we become disconnected from logic and reason.

7. THE INNER CHILD

We also have a child ego state. The child within can be a source of positive feelings, fun, and spontaneity. It can also be a source of hurt, fear, loneliness, and anger.

7.1. The Free-Child Ego State

If we have internalized memories from our childhood years of being playful and spontaneous, we can draw upon those childhood memories at times to feel playful and fun-loving in our current life. It can be fun to "feel like a kid" at times. This ego state is often referred to as the *free child*. When we are in touch with this free child part we have access to the free and playful "kidlike" feelings within us. This part allows us to find balance in our lives between a life of commitment and structure, and relaxation and play. If we don't have access to a healthy free-child ego state we can become really out of balance and depleted emotionally. On the other hand, if we stay in our free-child ego state too much we can lack balance in the other direction, avoiding responsibilities and commitments. Staying in the free-child ego state too much can become a coping strategy that can result in some serious consequences in the long run.

7.2. The Hurt-Child Ego State

Another part of the inner child is sometimes called the *wounded* or *hurt child*. We all have memories of having our feelings hurt as a child, or feeling sad, lonely, or vulnerable. When something in our adult life makes us feel hurt, angry, or afraid it can trigger memories of painful childhood feelings. Tapping into these childhood feeling memories may bring back the same kind of vulnerable feelings we felt as a child. Sometimes in the hurt-child ego state we may think or behave in "childish" ways that are not really effective in our adult life. This part of us might be hypersensitive, might hide, act pouty, whiny, or demanding. In the hurt-child ego state our emotions are in charge and we have difficulty thinking or behaving in a rational manner.

An adult who was abused or neglected as a child may have an enormous store of painful childhood memories. This adult's hurt-child ego state may be oversized, and he may be overwhelmed much of the time with the fear, hurt, or rageful feelings of childhood. These wounded child feelings may be so close to the surface that they are easily triggered by current adult-life situations. These feelings can be completely out of proportion to the actual present-day situation that triggered them, preventing the adult from being able to think or respond rationally, logically, or effectively.

Remember for a moment Kate, in our Chapter One story. She was a teenage mother, living on welfare in an apartment with her baby, Karl. Kate had experienced criticism and physical abuse regularly in her earliest attachment relationship. As a child, her hurt and rage were probably overwhelming, and yet there was nowhere for her to express those feelings or get the comforting she needed, because the person she would naturally run to—her mother—was also the *source* of her distress. Unfortunately, her childhood feelings of rejection were reexperienced in her relationship with her baby's father. Kate expects to encounter the same kind of rejection in her new relationship with her baby, Karl. Although Karl is only a few months old, Kate's internalized hurt child is oversized, and she imagines her mother's critical look in Karl's eyes. This in turn triggers a pent-up rage within Kate that by now has become monstrous in its size and force. This ghoulish rage belongs to Kate's wounded child, and is really completely unrelated to her baby. Nevertheless the rageful ghost of Kate's painful childhood past will continue to lurk in her new baby Karl's nursery until Kate's scared and hurt inner child is given some way to heal.

Figure 2 illustrates how the triggered feeling memories in the layers of the mind of a parent interacting with her child are linked to the inner child and the internalized-parent ego states.

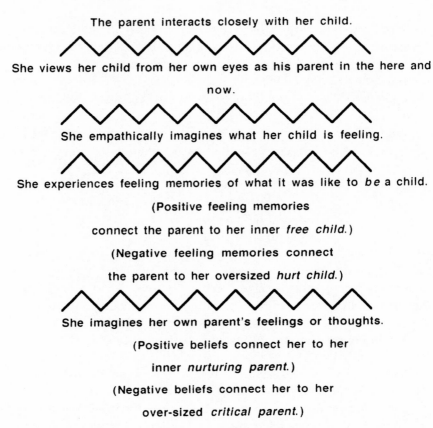

The parent interacts closely with her child.

She views her child from her own eyes as his parent in the here and

now.

She empathically imagines what her child is feeling.

She experiences feeling memories of what it was like to *be* a child.

(Positive feeling memories

connect the parent to her inner *free child.*)

(Negative feeling memories connect

the parent to her oversized *hurt child.*)

She imagines her own parent's feelings or thoughts.

(Positive beliefs connect her to her

inner *nurturing parent.*)

(Negative beliefs connect her to her

over-sized *critical parent.*)

Figure 2. The layers of the mind of a parent interacting closely with a child, along with the associated ego states.

8. THE EGOGRAM

The concept of the *egogram* was first described by John Dusay in his book, *Egograms: How I See You and You See Me.*[8] The egogram can help us get a visual picture of the different parts of our personalities and their relative sizes. Figure 3 shows a picture of the relative sizes of the different ego states in an adult who was raised in a healthy, loving family.

In this individual, the adult ego state is the primary ego state. The adult from a healthy family will think, feel, and behave the majority of the time in the adult ego state. When in the adult ego state his feelings will be related to what is happening in the here and now. His decisions and be-

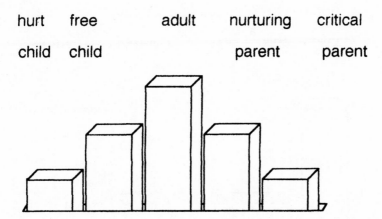

| hurt | free | | adult | nurturing | critical |
| child | child | | | parent | parent |

Figure 3. Egogram of an adult raised in a healthy, loving family. (From *Egograms* by John M. Dusay. © 1977 by Harper & Row. Reprinted with permission from HarperCollins Publishers.)

haviors in general will not be influenced by wounded child feelings or critical parent beliefs.

The adult personality pictured in Figure 3 also has an internal child, but when he experiences a child ego state, it is more often the internal free child as he decides to have some fun or get creative.

The adult raised by loving parents will also have internalized a good strong nurturing-parent part. Self-soothing and self-calming messages first heard in childhood will automatically kick in whenever this adult experiences painful feelings or circumstances. These soothing and loving messages will also be directed outwardly to others easily and naturally. The critical parent messages will also be there as needed, to sound a warning bell about ideas or behaviors that may have negative consequences, and to help set limits and boundaries.

Figure 4 illustrates how an egogram may look for an adult who was raised in an unhealthy family. The adult ego state is overshadowed by a powerful internal critic and an overwhelmed hurt child. The shaming and self-denigrating messages of the overpowering critical parent carry on the hurtful messages that this adult received in his childhood. These critical messages help fuel the painful feelings of the inner hurt child. Because the inner nurturer is relatively small, this adult has a limited capacity to self-soothe and give reassurance when the hurt child gets overwhelmed. The free child is suppressed by the internal critic or was never there to begin with if fun and play were not experienced on a regular basis in childhood.

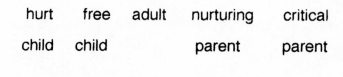

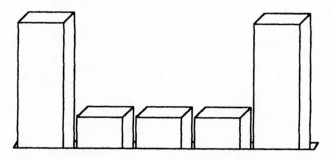

Figure 4. Egogram of an adult raised without adequate nurturing.

It is easy to see that this configuration of ego states can become en-trenched and lead to even more exaggeration of this hurt and critical pat-tern. As this cycle repeats over time it becomes even more difficult for the free child, adult, and nurturing-parent to play a larger role in this adult's life.

Exercise: Open your notebook and sketch your own egogram as you feel it would look right now. List the critical messages you hear toward your-self and others inside the critical parent part. List your wounded child feel-ings inside the wounded child part.

9. A CHILD'S LOGIC

ALL of our early experiences—whether they are locked in our brains as verbal or primitive memories—affect our *belief system*. Our belief system is the set of beliefs we carry around about ourselves, others, and the world. Alfred Adler was a cohort of Sigmund Freud's, but not a follower. Con-trary to Freud's view that sex is our primary need and motivator, Adler be-lieved that our ultimate need is to feel a sense of belonging and significance. He also believed, from his studies of children, that our beliefs about ourselves and our belongingness become firmly established by the time we turn five years old. This can be a problem for human beings because, as Adler pointed out, children are very good observers, but they are very poor interpreters. We see and hear everything around us when we are children. We do not miss much of anything. Our senses are acute—and we have an intense sense of curiosity and wonderment about the world around us. But the conclusions we draw from what we see and hear, from what happens to us, and from what we are told are often quite inaccurate and can be very misleading.

Children have their own kind of logic. Their logic is simple. Their logic is black and white. *I am good. Or I am bad. Everything happens for a reason. Adults know everything. Adults are all powerful. If bad things happen to me as a child, they must happen because I am bad. If I am bad, then no one could ever love me. If I am bad, then bad things will always happen to me. If an adult tells me I am bad, then I must be bad, because adults know everything. If I am rejected for needing someone, then I must never need others again. If others hurt me when I get close, then I must never get close again.*

10. CORE BELIEF SYSTEM

According to the way a child thinks, these conclusions make sense. These conclusions become part of the child's core belief system. Once these core beliefs become set around age five they can be very difficult to change. In fact, these core beliefs can become so ingrained that even after the child has grown and developed a more mature kind of logic and reasoning ability the old beliefs will often continue to affect her. As adults we should be aware that our core childhood belief systems are probably affecting our perceptions and reactions in relationships today with other adults and with our children.

Sometimes adults can *know* one thing on an intellectual level, but still *experience* the childhood beliefs to be true at an emotional level. Naturally, we are more vulnerable to the old childhood beliefs when we are connected to childhood feelings. Sandy was only affected by her negative childhood beliefs when she was operating from her child ego state. She stated,

"I know as I sit here in your office that I am safe in every part of my life now. There is no one in my life who would hurt me, and I can make choices now that continue to ensure I will be safe. And yet, when Ronnie and Susan start arguing over who will do the dishes after dinner each night, I suddenly feel just like a scared little kid again.

It makes me feel the way I felt when my mom and dad fought. When it happens I just do not feel safe no matter how illogical it is! And when I get anxious like that I start screaming, which only makes things worse!"

Some negative childhood beliefs are part of our critical parent messages. Dan described this kind of experience to me one day. He stated,

"When Ellen brought home a note from school the other day that she hadn't been turning in her homework, I suddenly felt so *guilty*. I felt like this rotten father—like the teacher had scolded *me*. I could just hear my Dad's voice saying, 'You are just worthless. You can't do anything right.' I felt like I was a failure as a father and Mrs. Green now knew it. As a result, I really overreacted with Ellen—like she had committed some terrible crime! And then I felt even more worthless because I had reacted like that!"

11. SELECTIVE MEMORIES

One of the reasons negative childhood beliefs tend to hang on even into adulthood is that our brains are computer-like in that we tend to be able to recall *only* information or memories that are *congruent* with our original belief system. None of us remembers every moment of our childhood. Many events are lost from memory simply because, at the time the events occurred, they did not create much of an emotional impact. However, many events are not recalled because they do not *fit* our belief system, or if they are recalled they are immediately dismissed. Trying to recall something that disputes our embedded belief system is like trying to call up information from a Macintosh program on an IBM. It just "does not compute." Therefore, if you have a deeply held belief that you are unlovable and not worthwhile, your positive memories such as Aunt Jane telling you that you were her favorite niece or getting that math award in the fourth grade will *not* be readily recalled. It is a very common experience for people to suddenly have access to more positive memories *after* they begin to change their core negative beliefs. With a revised belief system these positive memories now "compute" and can be accessed from the memory banks.

Core beliefs color perceptions of events both past and present. We all view the world wearing tinted glasses, unaware that our vision is colored and assuming our perceptions are completely accurate. A parent's negative perceptions of himself, others, or life can become very nasty gremlins lurking in the nursery. These beliefs are forces beyond the parent's conscious control or awareness, and yet they are very powerful. They can affect the parent's ability to feel safe with his child, to feel safe with closeness, to believe his child loves him, or to trust himself as a parent.

12. I AM UNLOVABLE

Do you remember the Chapter One story about Lydia and Laura? Young Lydia had been sexually abused by her father. The overwhelming emotions and the negative beliefs belonging to Lydia's hurt child were the ghosts haunting Laura's nursery. They were depleting Lydia emotionally and impairing her ability to respond to Laura, even though she obviously loved her very much. But Lydia's love for Laura did not change her deeply embedded belief that she was not lovable, and that others could not possibly really care about her, including her young daughter and her husband. Her memories of abuse confirmed her lack of self-worth according to her own private logic from her childhood. This logic said, *if the people who are supposed to love me abused me, then it must mean there was something unlovable about me.* In her child's mind it could not have been the *adults* who were wrong, because adults are all-knowing and all-powerful. Furthermore, if Lydia did have some experiences of being loved and cared for by some adults in her life, these experiences did not fit her belief system, and therefore would not likely be recalled. If she does recall some loving experiences, she may dismiss them until she begins to challenge her overriding negative belief system. Right now she is immobilized by her inner child feelings of anxiety and depression. She lacks a strong inner nurturer to self-soothe and self-calm. Lydia's husband may be feeling frustrated and confused about Lydia's actions, and he may unwittingly confirm her expectations of rejection. This cycle can repeat itself many times, further reinforcing Lydia's beliefs that she is unlovable.

13. I CANNOT TRUST

A child may also conclude after experiencing many frightening experiences in early life that the world in general is dangerous. As an adult he may remain forever hypervigilant and anxious, ready for harm to befall him at any moment. The child who could not trust his caregiving adult to respond when needed or to keep him safe when there was danger is likely to grow up to be an adult who feels powerless to affect the world around him. At the same time he may become obsessed with trying to gain power or control in his life to compensate for that awful helpless feeling.

Do you remember Jake from Chapter One? He was watching daughter Janie while his wife went shopping. He was unable to relax and enjoy his young daughter and therefore had apparently never developed any closeness to her. Jake's hypervigilance and anxiety were intruders in his relationship with his youngest child, stemming from his deep-seated fear that he will be abandoned and hurt by those he loves. His inability to trust and his fears of abandonment haunt his otherwise peaceful home, making it difficult for him to relax and enjoy any of his relationships, even though they *are of the utmost* importance to him. Unfortunately, like Lydia, the hypervigilance, anxiety, and anger of Jake's inner child puts a big strain on his relationships.

If hurt or rejection became associated with closeness with others as a child, the now grown adult may become hypervigilant and controlling in his close relationships in an attempt to feel safe. This had become Jake's way of coping with the fears. Some adults, on the other hand, have learned to turn off their needs for closeness or affection in order to feel safe: *If I don't need closeness and affection, if I keep a buffer zone between myself and my significant others, never asking, never needing, then I don't have to endure that anxious, unsafe feeling.* This is almost always an automatic, unconscious response that one is not aware of in a conscious way.

If you remember the story of Helen and Henry, you may remember that Helen seemed to be a woman who had not received much nurturing as a small child. As she was growing up it seemed that her brothers and sisters depended on her to help take care of them, but she had no one to depend on for herself. She was rejected for having emotional needs of her own. Helen had probably learned how to turn off her own needs for closeness and affection early on in order to avoid rejection. As an adult Helen still maintains a buffer zone between herself and others in her attempts to feel safe. Her husband, Hank, may have a similar background and so the two may be able to be together without either one making too many demands for closeness on the other. In addition to avoiding closeness with others, Helen also unconsciously avoids closeness with herself. She avoids knowing her own feelings and memories. The ghosts are lurking there, but Helen looks away from them. Henry, however, was born with his own needs for closeness and affection still intact. Helen is uncomfortable with the intensity of closeness her baby requires. It may get easier for Helen as Henry begins to learn that the best way to keep Mom nearby is to give her plenty of space and he begins to turn off his own needs in the same way that Mom did when she was growing up. In this way, sadly, the cycle can repeat over many generations.

Exercise: Write down the negative beliefs from this list that you believe affect you emotionally (even if you know on an intellectual level that they are not really true.) Note those beliefs that you think may be negatively affecting your parenting in some way.

I am worthless.
I am inadequate.
I am insignificant.
I do not deserve to be loved.
I do not deserve good things in my life.
I am unlovable.
I cannot do anything right.
I am not good enough.
I do not belong.
Things will never go right for me.
Others are unsafe.
It is not safe to be vulnerable.
It is not safe to be close.
I will always be rejected.
I cannot trust others.
I cannot trust my judgment.
The world is dangerous.
I am powerless.
I am shameful.
I am bad.
I am stupid.
I am alone.
I will always be alone.
I am defective.
I am a disappointment.
I am a mistake.
I am a failure.
I cannot succeed.

When we are feeling vulnerable due to some kind of stress or conflict in our lives, or when our internal hurt child or critical parent has been triggered, we are especially vulnerable to any negative core beliefs rooted in childhood. Our childhood logic can distort the lenses through which we view our relationships with our own children and with other significant people in our lives. This distorted perception will usually manifest itself behaviorally and will likely affect how we respond and interact with others.

14. TRAUMA AND POST-TRAUMATIC STRESS DISORDER

Experiencing neglect or abuse as children almost always affects one's beliefs about self, life, and others, and leaves one with leftover feelings of helplessness, powerlessness, anger, and shame. For many parents, childhood experiences of abuse were so overwhelming that they were left traumatized. Without skilled professional help, these individuals can experience symptoms of what is called *post-traumatic stress disorder* (PTSD) for the rest of their lives. One of the symptoms of PTSD is living in an ongoing state of hypervigilance. This hypervigilance can cause feelings of anxiety or agitation, difficulty concentrating, difficulty falling asleep, and, in a more extreme form, panic attacks. The hypervigilance, although problematic, has a purpose. The unconscious mind is trying to remain hyperalert in an effort to identify any kind of threat in the environment in order to prevent getting hurt again. Individuals suffering from PTSD feel chronically unsafe.

Another symptom traumatized individuals experience is feeling intensely overwhelmed by the memories of their experiences and by their inability to avoid them. Seemingly insignificant events, people, places, sounds, or smells can trigger traumatic memories, and sometimes the memories come back as vivid *reexperiencing* of the events. This is called a *flashback,* which means the memory is so vivid, either in image, sensation, smell, or sound, or all of these that it feels as if it is actually happening right now, in real life. Sometimes the reexperiencing of the trauma takes place at night in the form of nightmares. These nightmares, for traumatized people, can be relentless and terrifying. They are much more intense than typical nightmares.

This reexperiencing, whether daytime or nighttime, may actually be the result of a well-intentioned unconscious process gone awry. Our unconscious minds are always striving to help us feel masterful, in control in life, and safe. And so, the mind of the trauma victim begins the process of reworking what happened when he was victimized, in an attempt to develop mastery over the traumatic event. In other words, unconsciously he is attempting to relive it so that this time he can *get it right*, so that this time he can find a way to *come out on top*. Unfortunately, due to the intensity of trauma, as he tries to work through it emotionally the trauma victim becomes overwhelmed and shuts down so that he never completes the working-through process. The unconscious mind has to keep trying again and again. Instead of getting relief from the past traumatic event, the trauma victim winds up being *revictimized* by the reexperiencing because it feels so close to a real-life reliving of the event.

Unfortunately, one of the most common triggers for the remembering or reexperiencing of traumatic events is when one's child, especially a same-sex child, reaches the age that the parent was when the traumatic event occurred. Many parents are forced to seek help at this time, although typically they do not have a conscious understanding of the reason they have so suddenly become *so* overwhelmed. Naturally, the overwhelming feelings interfere with the parent's ability to effectively parent the child. This is a situation in which professional help by someone skilled in trauma work is an absolute necessity.

15. DISSOCIATION

Dissociation is a skill we all have to some extent. If we have a slight headache we are able to dissociate from the nagging ache, or block it out, in order to complete a task we need to do. If we get bored in church, we dissociate or space out and then feel guilty when we find ourselves unable to recall a word of the sermon. We dissociate by necessity when we are studying for an exam by "tuning out" extraneous noises around us. Individuals who suffer from PTSD often dissociate more than the average person, because the unconscious mind wants to protect the individual from experiencing the overwhelmingly painful feelings. Often individuals report feeling "spaced out" or "in a fog" and appear to others to be "in a day dream." Sometimes individuals report feeling "numb," or remote and unfeeling until the emotions break through like an erupting volcano. Sometimes individuals have dissociated from the entire memory of the trauma, or have amnesia to certain parts of the trauma. Sometimes dissociation can cause an individual to "lose time" in their current life either occasionally or frequently. In some cases of severe trauma, an individual may function as a separate personality during these periods. This was previously called multiple personality disorder. The official diagnosis is now dissociative identity disorder.

16. RELIVING THE TRAUMA AS VICTIM

Sometimes the unconscious mind attempts to rework a trauma in order to gain mastery and control over it through unconsciously reenacting the trauma in present life. One form of this reenactment is reliving it as the victim of some kind of abuse all over again. The unconscious motivation is, *I'll relive this event, but this time I'll find mastery. This time I'll have power.* Unfortunately, this form of reenactment usually results only in further revictimization. The situation resembles the original abusive situation too closely. The individual becomes overwhelmed with the old feelings of powerlessness and helplessness and becomes trapped once again and unable to get away. The unconscious mind's attempt to find mastery through doing it again, "but this time getting it right," results in yet another traumatization.

17. SWITCHING FROM VICTIM TO PERPETRATOR ROLE

Sometimes victims of abuse have a compulsion to reenact the abuse by actually repeating the abuse, but this time in the role of the perpetrator. This is one way that the unconscious mind can rework the abuse and guarantee mastery over it—by reenacting the same play with the same script, but taking the other role—the role that holds all the power and control. Often children who are abused will be seen acting out the abuser role with their dolls or with pets. If you have ever seen a child reenacting abuse in her play, you would have been struck by how little her play resembles play. It's serious business and often the rituals are performed with an agonizing compulsiveness. In fact, the unconscious drive can be so strong that the child is unable to stop doing what she is doing. She often looks like she is in a trance—and she is. She is in a dissociated state. She is dissociated from the present reality and from her feelings. Unfortunately, even the child who reenacts her abuse as the perpetrator often does not find relief from her traumatic experience, but is instead retraumatized by the feelings of intense shame and powerlessness she has over her own behavior. A 22-year-old I will call Emma came to see me with severe symptoms of post-traumatic stress disorder. She suffered from dissociative experiences which she described as "just going away somewhere in my head." She would lose minutes or sometimes hours of time. She was also severely depressed. She had memories of physical abuse by her father, which, thankfully, she was able to resolve through intensive therapy. One memory, however, was more difficult for Emma to work with than all the others and it caused her severe distress. It was a memory of being four or five years old, trapped in a compulsive ritual of abusing her beloved cat in the same way she was being abused by her father at the time. She remembered how powerless she had been over her actions, and the feelings of shame were overwhelming to Emma. Eventually Emma was able to work through this painful memory and forgive herself for actions over which she had no control at the time. With help, Emma was able to become free of the dissociative symptoms.

Some children who are abused reenact their abuse with younger siblings. Some children grow into adults who find themselves compulsively reenacting their abuse with others or with their own children. In the final story in Chapter One, Ben was ridiculing and rejecting his son Barry similarly to the way he had been ridiculed and rejected by his mother. Unconsciously, he was reenacting his abuse, but now he was experiencing the more powerful role. In addition, his son, Barry, had become an external representation of himself as a child, triggering Ben's internal offender. The message "You wimp!" directed at Barry was unconsciously meant for Ben's inner child, whom he detested for having been small and vulnerable. However, when Ben realized that his treatment of his son resembled the treatment he received from his mother he was overcome by remorse and by the familiar wounded child feelings of self-hate, fear of abandonment, and powerlessness.

Donna, a 24-year-old mother with whom I worked, came to see me after her four-year-old daughter had been removed from her home when a preschool teacher reported evidence of abuse to the Child Protective Services. In our first session Donna recounted briefly how she had been removed from her mother's care when *she* was four years old. Her mother had been emotionally ill and had neglected her. She had a very painful memory of workers tearing her away from her mother's arms, associated with tremendous feelings of despair and abandonment. Following her removal from her mother's home she was placed with a foster mother who beat her cruelly for the next 14 years. When Donna was 20 she gave birth to a daughter. She described to me how happy she had been to "finally have someone to love and to love me back." Tearfully, she went on to describe how when her little girl reached age four, she had suddenly experienced very aggressive feelings toward her. "I wanted to hurt her," Donna remembered. "I wanted her to feel the pain that I had felt." She reenacted her own abuse, but this time in the powerful abuser role with her daughter as the helpless victim. Donna shook her head in amazement, and then cried with overwhelming feelings of shame and guilt. "Why would I want to do that? I don't understand why I would want to do that. Can you help us?" Thankfully, Donna was very motivated. She was willing to accept responsibility for the pain she had caused her daughter. She began working both on herself and her relationship with her daughter. These were very difficult tasks, but eventually Donna and her daughter were reunited.

I would like to acknowledge that there will be some readers who will read the story about Donna and feel very angry. If you are one of these readers, you may be thinking right now, "Who cares why she did it? There is no good reason for ever abusing a child." To these readers, I would like to say that I empathize with how you are feeling right now. I am not *excusing* child abuse. It is very important that parents take responsibility for their actions. That is part of getting better. But it can be very helpful to better *understand* what happens in the minds of abusing parents so that those parents and others who may be at risk of abusing their children can use the key of *understanding and insight* to help them *not* abuse. I think it is very important that we as a society try to stay focused on effective solutions that can help families heal.

I would also like to acknowledge that there will be some readers who are reading this section who are feeling very much like Donna as she sat in my office. You may be feeling so overwhelmed that you may have an urge to throw the book away right now. *Please read on.* The best amends you can make to your own child is to overcome how you were hurt, understand with compassion how that hurt has affected you as an adult, and change your behavior so that your actions will more closely reflect the kind of parent you want to be. But to do so you will need to make a commitment to face these challenging issues head on.

18. IN CONCLUSION . . .

You are now beginning to understand how difficult childhood experiences can impact a parent's present-day interactions with her or his child through feeling memories, negative core beliefs, and the hurt-child and critical-parent ego states. The next two chapters will help you understand attachment, the parent–child bond that evolved for the purpose of our survival and our emotional well-being. You will learn how our earliest attachment experiences can affect our ability to form secure bonds with others, including our children, lifelong. Later you will learn what you can do to improve the quality of those bonds.

Chapter Three

"I Belong"

The Secure Attachment

In the 1950s, a British psychiatrist named John Bowlby became very concerned when he heard reports about changes in children's personalities following institutionalization or long hospital stays. Prior to the 1960s, children were often allowed no contact with parents for weeks or months during hospitalizations, due to fears of cross-infections. John Bowlby began studying these children, and witnessed intense despair, anger, and withdrawal during the separations. Even after reunification with their parents he observed that the children continued to have problems with trust and anger for months and even years afterward.[1]

At about the same time, Harry F. Harlow, a researcher with the University of Wisconsin in Madison, began publishing his studies of baby monkeys separated from their mothers at birth. In one study he supplied the baby monkeys with two types of substitute mothers: one made of wire with a nipple that supplied milk, and the other of soft terry cloth, but without milk. Surprisingly, the baby monkeys clung desperately to the terry cloth mothers despite their lack of milk. When fearful, the baby monkeys ran to their terry cloth mothers and upon reaching her they appeared to immediately relax. As adults, these same baby monkeys, raised only with fabricated terry cloth mothers, had severe problems both with socializing and with parenting their own young.[2]

It became obvious to John Bowlby, when he heard about Harlow's monkey experiments and compared them with his studies of children, that attachment between infants and parents is a phenomenon that has evolved in all primates, both for the purpose of survival and as a vital foundation for emotional development. Bowlby recognized that attachment is not simply a conditioned response to being fed, but is an inborn system with strong significance of its own.[3]

To use a simple metaphor, attachment is like an invisible elastic cord connecting the child to the parent. If the attachment is good and strong, the child and parent feel a profound connection, one to the other, soul to soul. The invisible cord between them is thick and strong, but elastic and flexible, so that even with physical distance between them the cord will simply stretch. It will not break.

As you continue to read about attachment you may feel a sense of sadness and grief because a secure, strong attachment may have been missing in your own childhood. It may even be missing to a greater or lesser degree in your relationship today with your own child. But I think you will find that gaining a clear understanding of attachment is an important part of understanding how our instincts can become distorted. Through understanding attachment you will have a better understanding of your relationship with your own parents and a clearer idea of what you are working toward in your relationship with your child, and why. You will better understand the rationale for the steps and exercises in Parts Two and Three. And when all *three* keys are in place you will have the power to *strengthen* your own attachment status—and the security of the connection between you and your child.

1. WHAT MAKES IT HAPPEN?

Several important factors form a basic foundation for attachment in the very beginning between a parent and child. They are touch, eye contact, shared movement, and the sharing of positive emotions. Right after birth a new mother feels her baby's skin, touches his small hands and cheeks, and strokes his soft hair. As a baby nurses he feels his mother's warmth. He explores her soft skin and studies her face. As the baby grows more alert and feels sturdier with each passing day, he becomes a more active participant in these critical early interactions. He babbles silly sounds, and his mother babbles back. She moves him rhythmically, back and forth, up and down, and side to side. The baby giggles in response to his mother's silly actions. Mother gazes into her baby's eyes, and the baby gazes into his mother's eyes with wonder. He is amazed by a dawning awareness that *he is not alone* in this universe he finds himself in. He has emerged from a place of total oneness with his mother within the tranquility of the womb, to discover that his mother's face, her voice, and the arms that are holding him belong to a separate other. He feels her separate skin and he looks into her separate eyes. But most amazing of all is his discovery that she sees *him*, she feels *him*, she hears *him*, and she responds to *him*. His mother is almost as amazed to find that a separate little personality exists inside this small baby. He has emotions. And he, too, sees *her*, feels *her*, hears *her*, and responds. He is saying no words, and yet they are communicating exquisitely. Their desires are communicated clearly. He is aware that she understands him, and she knows he is aware of her understanding. They are linked one to another emotionally. The baby cries and Mother feels distressed. The baby smiles and gazes happily into Mother's eyes and she gazes back with contentment. Mother frowns and looks away and the baby feels forlorn and alone. Mother smiles and gazes into her baby's eyes and he feels joyful and connected. As the baby and Mother become attuned, one with the other, there is a touching of the souls, an inextricable linking of two hearts. She falls in love with him and he with her.

"I never imagined myself a mother, before," said Alicia, a new mother. "Even while I was pregnant I had a hard time visualizing myself actually holding a new baby. And yet now, I have difficulty being away from Tara for more than a short time. When I'm away from her I can only think of her. When she's crying and I pick her up, she snuggles in close and my heart just melts." During our conversation six-month old Tara was studying her mother's face. She was ignoring me as if to say, "You are not important to me. This woman here—she's the one I love."

A baby's attachment to his mother includes a physical and emotional *dependence* upon her. Mother is not dependent upon baby in this way, but nevertheless, as she touches her baby and makes eye contact she may develop a strong, powerful need to be *with* her baby—to keep him close to her. A baby's attachment to his mother and a mother's attachment to her baby are part of the same built-in "attachment system."

Although mother was used as an example, fathers and their babies develop attachments no differently. Through touch, eye contact, and the sharing of positive emotions, babies and fathers can form deep and lasting attachments to one another. Depending on their level of involvement, a baby may form a primary attachment to both parents or a primary attachment to one and a secondary attachment to the other. Although the attachment with parents tends to be the most crucial to the child's well-being, a child also will often form secondary attachments to grandparents or other substitute caregivers. These additional attachment figures can play a very important part in a child's emotional development.

As described in Chapters One and Two, the intense physical and emotional intimacy between a parent and a baby may trigger positive memories and feelings for some parents and uncomfortable or painful feelings for other parents. If you feel the "ghosts" in your nursery interfered with your ability to establish a secure attachment through touch and close contact, don't despair. You will find keys for healing yourself and your relationship with your child later in this book.

2. THE CYCLE OF TRUST

It is a scary thing to be completely dependent on other human beings in order to live—when the fear of abandonment equals fear of complete annihilation in this world. Imagine what it would be like for you if right now you suddenly lost your ability to speak, to walk, or to feed yourself. Imagine if every time you needed something you could ring a bell, but then it was up to your caregivers to try to guess what it was you needed.

Every time a baby feels distressed, whether due to hunger, physical discomfort, or an outside threat, he is completely dependent on his parents for help. Each time the parent lovingly gives the baby what he needs, and comforts and soothes the upset baby, the parent is completing what is called the *cycle of trust*.

Each time the cycle of trust is completed, an infant learns: *Maybe I can trust mom or dad to be there for me. Maybe they will not abandon me in this scary world. Perhaps I really am safe with them. Maybe I am important enough to them that they will take care of me.* As a baby's trust deepens, the imaginary cord which connects him securely with his parents grows stronger and stronger. He knows he is not alone in this world. He feels a safe and secure connection to a parent who is all-powerful and all-loving—who will protect him from all threats to his safety, from pain, and from hunger.

3. THE WARNING SYSTEM

In just the first few months of life, an infant's trust becomes attached primarily to just one or two caregivers, usually parents, whom he is able to recognize and distinguish from other caregivers. The attachment system evolved early in the evolution of human beings because it allowed babies a greater chance of survival against predators, starvation, and cold. The attached parent wanted to stay near the helpless baby. And the baby, firmly attached to the protective parent, developed a built-in warning *system*. Just as a town's tornado siren sounds a warning if a nearby tornado is threatening the town, baby's internal sirens begin to blare causing him to feel frightened when his trusted parent moves too far away.

4. THE SIGNALING SYSTEM

When a baby becomes frightened, he automatically has a desperate need to bring his attachment figure closer. When the warning sirens go off, he feels, *I will not survive without her*. There are many kinds of *signals* that babies use to bring the parent back. When the baby's anxiety is still low level, he may attempt to keep his parent near with some low-intensity signals. He may coo sweetly to her, call "ma-ma!," or catch her eye and give her an endearing smile. But as his parent moves farther away or some external threat presents itself, the baby's internal sirens sound more loudly. As the baby feels more frightened, his attachment signals become very intense. This behavior usually first becomes apparent around eight months of age. A baby may cry or scream, and as a toddler may even kick or hit. A baby may crawl after his parent, and as a toddler may run after her and cling to her. This is called *protest behavior*.

There is a picture that will always be embedded in my mind of my son, around age two, clinging to the chain link fence in our yard one day sobbing in despair as I was pulling out of the driveway. I can still remember how awful I felt about leaving that day, and the feeling I was left with ensured that I did not leave any more often than I had to. Protest behavior is not bad behavior. The child is in survival mode and he is biologically programmed to react in this way. It is a good sign in that it means he is forming an attachment with his parent, as he should. When his parent responds to his protest behaviors, giving the baby the reassurances he needs, the baby knows he has been heard. He feels significant. He has a voice and his voice matters. The older a baby becomes, the easier it will get for him to understand, remember, and trust his parent's reassurances. This will lessen the anxiety that the child feels upon separation from the primary caregiver.

5. THE SECURE BASE

As mentioned earlier, one of the reasons it is believed that attachment evolved in humans is that human babies needed a way to make sure mom or dad would hang around and protect them from predators or from starvation. It became clear to Bowlby and other attachment researchers that children who trusted their parents to meet their needs had a sense of a secure base in the world.[4] When the imaginary cord between parent and child feels secure to the child, that imaginary cord can *stretch*. The stronger the imaginary cord, the further it can stretch without the child fearing that it will break, because it is both elastic and strong. As the child gets older, more curious, and more mobile, he begins to stretch that elastic cord and he begins to explore his environment. The older he gets, the more he needs to move away from mom in order to fully explore his surroundings. As the child becomes more independent and self-sufficient he begins to meet and interact with others. Because of the stretchy cord he can do this and still feel safe. The stronger and more elastic the cord, the more self-confident and secure the child feels as he moves out into the bigger world.

Having said all that, I must also make clear that not everything about a person is determined by his or her early attachment experiences. We all have personality traits that affect the way we approach the world that seem to be a result of our own unique genetic makeup. Some of us are naturally more extroverted—others are more introverted. Some of us inherited a tendency to approach new situations and people with ease. Some of us inherited a natural tendency toward shyness and we typically approach novel situations with caution and care. These traits are not good or bad—just different in different people. You will learn how to assess your child's inborn traits and learn how to deal with them in Part Three of this book.

6. ATTUNEMENT

Think for a moment about one of your closest friends. What is it about this friend that makes you feel so connected, so bonded? Many people would respond, "I hardly have to speak. He just knows what I am feeling," or, "She really listens to me—and she understands. She knows exactly what I am saying." When we feel this kind of *attunement* to another human being it creates a powerful bond between us. We are no longer alone. There is another person who knows us, who truly understands what we are feeling and thinking. All human beings are striving to not feel alone in this world.

Attunement of the parent to the child greatly strengthens the security of the attachment. The more attuned the parent is to the baby, the more secure the baby feels that his parent truly understands. *She is connected to me. She knows what I am feeling. She knows what I need to feel better.* The baby can sense his parent's attunement, not only when she knows what he needs, but also when she plays with him. When the parent understands which toy her baby wants to look at or when she matches her singsong voice to her baby's rhythmic bounces, the baby senses that his parent is in sync with him. *She hears me. She sees me. We are communicating.* When a baby becomes overstimulated and feels nervous and fussy, his parent may use a calm, slow voice and the baby feels better. When a baby is cranky with boredom and his parent offers an exciting toy or game, his parent again knows what the baby needs to feel better. The baby senses that his parent knows him, hears him, sees him, and knows what he needs. Internally the baby is developing a clearer sense that he and his parent are attached in a secure way.

As a baby gets older, a good attunement between the parent and the child continues to be an important quality of their relationship, strengthening the connection between them. The more "tuned in" the parent is to the older child, the more the child *feels understood* by the parent, resulting in a stronger, more secure attachment between them.

Attunement comes more easily and naturally to the parent who grew up with attunement between herself and her own parent. If there are troublesome "ghosts in the nursery," this can interfere with the parent's ability to perceive the baby's needs, and subsequently with the degree of attunement between parent and child and their degree of attachment. Chapter Five will help you more clearly identify any parental misperceptions that may be interfering with your attunement to *your* child.

7. THE HOLDING ENVIRONMENT

An English psychiatrist and world renowned psychoanalyst, Dr. Donald W. Winnicott, emphasized the importance of the *holding environment*. He wrote, "In an environment that holds the baby well enough, the baby is able to make *personal development according to the inherited tendencies.*"[5] In a secure holding environment a baby feels enveloped by the reliable steadfastness of his parent. He feels safe with his parent and he knows he can count on her. The security of his attachment to her is strengthened because he trusts she won't leave or fall apart in response to his needs or strong feelings. The child feels safely "held" emotionally because he knows that no matter how fearful or rageful he becomes his parent will remain relatively steady and give him the support he needs. The holding environment allows the child to feel safe with his feelings. Even his rageful or fearful feelings become safe, normal, and acceptable. This is very important to the child's self-esteem, because his emotions are an integral part of *who he is* as a person. If he grows up believing his feelings are O.K., it really helps him to realize that *he* is O.K., feelings and all. If he believes his feelings are acceptable, then when he experiences feelings he can allow himself to identify them, to feel them and work through them, and to express them if necessary. In other words, he can handle his feelings in a healthy way and then go on.

Often the most difficult time for the parent in maintaining that holding environment is when the child's rage gets directed *at* the parent. It can be a scary thing to be the target for someone's rage, even if that someone is only two and a half feet tall! Often the parent becomes the target for the child's overwhelming feelings of frustration because it is the parent who most often has to frustrate the child in what he wants. That, of course, is part of being a parent, too—setting limits. In addition, the child is more likely to direct his feelings of rage toward his attachment figures because they are the people he feels safest with. When the child gets angry with mom or dad and they remain steady the child learns his anger is not a monster to be feared. He learns he can get angry and he won't be abandoned. When the parent also maintains safe limits for the child such as, "I won't allow you to harm me or to harm yourself," the holding environment provides *containment* for the child's anger so that it does not become dangerous. The child's anger is *not* given more power than it really has and the child is able to safely feel his feelings until they have run their course.

Many children attach to what Winnicott called *transitional objects.*[6] These are objects that substitute for mother or father at those times when parents are not there. Many children attach to "blankies," "teddies," or "pillows." There are two main requirements of these transitional objects. One requirement is that they be soft, silky, or cuddly, supplying a substitute for the parent's warmth and nurturance. The second requirement is that the transitional object be strong and firm. Like mom and dad, the blankie or teddy must be able to withstand becoming a target for the child's rage without "coming apart at the seams!" This is the real test for a transitional object, as well as for the holding environment.

A child who grows up in a calm holding environment will eventually *internalize* that holding environment. Even without the calming influence of his parent, as an adult he will internally sense he is safe even when he has strong feelings of rage or fear. His internal holding environment will give him a greater capacity to soothe and calm *himself*. The internalized holding environment increases his sense of a secure base within himself.

A parent who was lucky enough to have experienced a safe and nurturing childhood will empathize with her child when she becomes distressed but will have the capacity to manage her own emotions so that she can supply the calm, secure holding environment her child needs. If, however, she lacked a secure holding environment *herself* as a child she is more likely to become overwhelmed with anxious feelings when *her child* is distressed, interfering with her ability to provide a secure holding environment for him. The healing steps in Parts Two and Three of this book will help you to better provide a holding environment for yourself and for your child, from infancy through adolescence.

8. THE GOOD ENOUGH PARENT

It should be a great relief to parents to find out that there is no parent who can respond to a baby's needs every time, or be attuned every time, or provide the perfect holding environment every time. Winnicott coined the term *good enough mother.*[7] The good enough parent is *for the most part* caring, responsive, and attuned, but she is also *human*. Sometimes she is not there. Sometimes she misunderstands what her child needs. Sometimes she makes mistakes. Yes, *all* parents make mistakes. Even *terrific* parents have limitations. Over time the child learns, *my parent is not perfect.* The child of the good enough parent also learns, *my parent doesn't have to be perfect for me to trust him or her.* And although the good enough parent doesn't say no or deny her child things to be mean or for just no reason at all, the good enough parent does have to set limits for her youngster. She cannot give him what he wants all of the time or allow him to do what he wants all of the time. Through the limits that the loving parent sets the child learns, *she won't give me everything I want or let me do everything I want, but I can still trust her.*

9. PRIVATE LOGIC

A baby begins developing his private logic during the very first years of life. The first few years are the formative years for the child's core belief system. Remember the cycle of trust: If a parent responds to a baby with attunement and gives him what he needs when he is distressed, in that very first year of life he will begin developing the core belief that *I can trust others.* If his parent's touch is gentle and loving, he learns that *touching and closeness are good.* If his parent acknowledges the child's feelings, and his feelings and needs are understood and accepted, then he will begin developing the core belief that *my feelings are O.K. and therefore I am O.K.* If the parent sees the child and through her gaze, smile, voice, and touch reflects back to him her feelings of love and enjoyment of him, it will be much easier for the child to believe *I am lovable.*

Each time baby signals his caregiver that he is in need and his parent responds and helps him, he learns that *I do have some power and control in my life. I am not totally helpless.* This empowering belief increases the baby's sense of security and lessens his feelings of anxiety at being in the world.

If his parent is playful and fun, baby learns that *I can enjoy others and others enjoy me.* If the baby's world is consistent, responsive, and safe he also learns in general that *the world is a pretty O.K. place all the way around—somewhere that I want to be.* He learns that it's a good thing to exist—*to be.* The baby with a loving parent who is also human learns, *I can't expect others to be perfect, but that's O.K.* The child with a loving parent who sets limits also learns, *I can't get everything I want in this world, but I can live with that.*

As I mentioned in Chapter Two, once a human's private logic has been formed, which happens in the first few years of life, it becomes pretty stable. It then affects our expectations and our reactions to everything and everyone the rest of our lives. The private logic described above is typical of a child with a good, secure attachment—a good, strong cord between himself and his parent. He believes *I can trust, I am loved, and I am worthy of love.*

Private logic that is negative is also pretty ingrained after the first few years of life, but with the right keys it *can* be changed.

Core Beliefs of the Securely Attached Child

I can trust others.
Touching and closeness are good.

My feelings are O.K. and therefore I am O.K.
I am worthy of love and I am loved.
I can enjoy others and others can enjoy me.
I do have some power and control in my life.
I am not totally helpless in this world.
The world is a pretty O.K. place all the way around.
I can't expect others to be perfect but that's O.K.
I can't get everything I want in this world but I can live with that.

10. AS THE CHILD GROWS

When it comes time for school, the child with a sense of a secure attachment at home has a better chance of learning at his potential. To understand this, remember a time when you were feeling anxious or stressed out. Remember how difficult it was to concentrate, to make decisions, and to problem solve. A child with a secure base believes, *I can trust others. Others will respond to me positively. I have power in this world.* This child has very little to worry about! He can move out into the world of school with a sense of safety, trust, and self-confidence. He can concentrate and use his senses to take in everything that he can hear and see and touch around him.

The child with a secure attachment at home is less likely to be fearful as he makes new friends in this bigger world of school. He will tend to be more outgoing because he assumes others are basically trustworthy, and he assumes others will find him acceptable. His first experiences with other children who are hurtful or unaccepting of him will be difficult, of course. But he will view these experiences with people as the exception rather than the rule. He will gravitate away from peers who treat him cruelly because his internal working model says, *I am worthy of being responded to positively.* He will generally give others the benefit of the doubt unless the evidence proves otherwise. He will tend to see the good in others, instead of focusing on the faults. Consequently, he will be more easy-going and will not be easily provoked to anger.

It is important to note here that these are generalizations. The securely attached child will be *more likely* to get along well socially than children who do not have a secure attachment at home. There are innate differences between children directly related to personality temperaments that also affect many areas including social life. Personality temperaments will be discussed further in Chapter Thirteen.

Children with a secure attachment tend to hold a basically positive view of themselves, but do not perceive themselves as all-good. They tend to have a pretty balanced, realistic view of themselves. *I am basically a good person, but I do have faults.* In other words, these children are able to admit their faults without feeling worthless because of them. This capacity is a big help in their social relationships. After all, it is much easier to get along with someone who can say, "I was wrong. I made a mistake."

11. ATTACHMENT IN ADOLESCENCE

Teenagers, with all the effort they make to show us they don't need us, still very much do need a secure strong attachment with their parents. Teens with a secure attachment tend to view themselves and others more positively. They tend to avoid others who treat them badly because they don't believe they deserve to be mistreated. They are better able to admit to their faults without feeling worthless. Just like the toddler, they are more able to stretch that cord and go out into the world to try their wings. The securely attached teen isn't burdened with a sense of desperation to fit in, to *belong* somewhere. Therefore he is less vulnerable to pressure from peer groups. Because of the security he feels in his relationships the securely attached teenager has a better buffer against stress and emotional problems.

Of course, even teens with a secure attachment to their parents have to complete the very important developmental task of separation and individuation. Part of this process includes the trying on of different values and behaviors from that of parents. Having a secure attachment at home won't prevent the drive for weird hair colors, strange attire, and different music. This is a normal response to the separation stage which all teens must go through as part of the development of their own identity. In addition to the security of his attachment, the ease with which a child moves through adolescence is also affected by his inborn temperament and personality, and the multitude of external stresses and pressures in his environment over which parents have no control. Nevertheless, a secure home base is very helpful to a child trying to get past the hurdles of the teen years.

12. THE STRONG CORD IN ADULTHOOD

One of the developmental tasks of the young adult is finding a significant other who will eventually replace the parent as the primary attachment figure, although the attachment to one's parents never becomes insignificant. After all, the loss of a parent, if we had a close relationship, is a painful loss at *any* age. But our attachment to our parents becomes secondary as we become adults, even though the attachment to our mate differs from the attachment to our parent in that it is also a sexual relationship. There is also a give and take in our attachment with our mates. Sometimes we supply the comfort and security for our mate, and other times our mate supplies the comfort and security for us.

Adults who grew up with a fairly secure attachment to their parents as children developed positive core beliefs about self-worth, closeness, and trust. Adults with a secure attachment style tend to expect and to feel a secure connection with mates, friends, and children. The adult with an imaginary strong cord connecting her with others will have a sense of a secure base inside. Even though she no longer lives at home, she holds a feeling of home within. In a sense, she "feels at home" wherever she is and whomever she is with.

The adult with a strong cord *will*, however, typically feel uncomfortable with others who mistreat her. She will tend to be drawn more toward others who meet her positive expectations. The adult with a strong cord will overlook minor transgressions in others. She will tend to give others the benefit of the doubt and will not be easily angered. The securely attached adult will also be able to admit her own faults while still viewing herself as basically good.

The adult with a strong cord is more likely to marry another adult with a strong cord and the research shows these relationships last the longest. It's not hard to see why, as both adults will tend to see the good in one another, to trust one another, and to own up to their own character defects.

Just as the attached infant has a warning system that alerts him when he feels his attachment figure has moved too far away, the adult in an attachment relationship has an internal warning system. If a man's wife takes on a project that suddenly keeps her at work for long hours, the warning system will become aroused, perhaps for both spouses. In response, the signaling system will kick in. Phone calls between them will probably increase and the couple may spend more time together during off-hours and hug and touch more often. Thus, the warning system and the signaling system are both helpful to the stability of the couple in that they help to keep them feeling connected in spite of long separations.

13. ATTACHMENT AND GRIEF

It becomes very evident how extremely important our attachment relationships are to our emotional well-being when an attachment relationship is lost. When we lose a primary attachment figure at any age our reaction is a deep and profound sense of grief. Whether we are a child losing a parent or a parent losing a child or a spouse, this kind of loss is akin to losing a limb from one's body. Paradoxically, the very person we want to turn to for comfort is the very person who is not there. We may eventually pick up life and move on, but the sense of something missing may remain with us indefinitely. Additionally, when a marriage ends through separation or divorce, one or both spouses may experience the grief of a lost attachment. The person who once was there for them and to whom they turned to for comfort and security is no longer there for emotional or physical comforting.

Infants and children suffer profound grief reactions at the permanent loss of an attachment figure or a separation that is so long that the child has lost hope of the attachment figure returning. In Bowlby's observations of hospitalized children the grief reactions he witnessed included feelings of profound despair, increased aggression, and withdrawal. Later, Bowlby observed that the children's interactions with others were superficial, as if they were afraid of becoming to close to anyone again. Bowlby noted that the effects lasted long after the parents and children were reunited.[8] Children who have the most severe long-term effects from the death of a parent are children who do not have another good, secure attachment figure to turn to for comfort.

14. STRESS BUFFER

Having a secure attachment status as an adult appears to lessen a person's chances of suffering from depression or anxiety. This is not a 100% guarantee, but having a sense of a secure base within naturally increases self-confidence and self-esteem, and creates in general a more optimistic expectation of what life has to offer. If life handed me a fair bill of goods when I was an infant, I am likely to look forward to what life has to offer me now. Occasional bad experiences are seen as the exception to the rule, not the norm.

In addition, the adult with a secure attachment status will gravitate toward supportive types of people who fit her expectations of how people should be from her experience with relationships in childhood. When her supportive others show themselves to be imperfect, she will tend to view their imperfections as the exception and not the rule and will continue to perceive her relationships as positive overall. After all, even her usually attuned and responsive parent made mistakes and couldn't be there every time she needed her. Yet, the overall trend was positive, so that as a child she could forgive the occasional blunder of the loving mom or dad.

The adult with a secure attachment status who perceives her relationships as generally positive and supportive will therefore also have the "holding environment" of caring relationships with others to buffer her against the stresses of the world. Additionally, she will have internalized the secure holding environment of her childhood, enabling her to self-soothe and self-calm in the face of strong emotions. Her ability to comfort herself will also lessen the impact of stress upon her well-being and help carry her through the tougher times.

15. BECOMING A PARENT WITH A SECURE CORD

You may have wondered how parenting can come so easily for some parents you know. It is as if they were just "born with" natural instincts about parenting. You may have felt "less than" because parenting came less naturally for you. The truth is, most parents for whom parenting comes easily were fortunate as children. They most likely descended from generations of securely attached people and therefore developed a secure attachment status of their own. Parents with an internal "strong cord" naturally experience less of a struggle with new parenthood. With positive expectations in general about their relationships with other people, the expectant mother with a secure strong cord will for the most part have positive expectations about the upcoming new person in her life. She will optimistically assume that her new child will love her and that she will love her child. With an internal secure base and a strong internal nurturer, she will generally feel pretty self-confident about becoming a new mother, guessing that what she doesn't know she will learn. As in the story of Mary and Martha in Chapter One, the intensity and intimacy of the experience of holding her child will trigger positive feelings related to memories of being held, as well as positive feelings about mothering. Her own internal nurturer, as well as the supportive others in her life, will supply her with a buffer against the stresses of new motherhood. The mother's own holding environment will allow her to provide a soothing holding environment for her distressed infant. Expecting her child to love her, the mother who was herself securely attached as a child will not feel rejected by her infant's rage or her toddler's tantrums. And she will not have unrealistic expectations of having a perfect child or being a perfect mother.

The same, of course, applies to the new father who has a secure attachment status. He, too, will tend to feel optimistic about the experience. He will feel held by his own internal nurturer and the people in his life as he in turn holds and calms the infant in his arms. His own holding environment will give him a greater capacity to supply a holding environment for his child.

Dr. Bertrand Cramer, Professor of Child Psychiatry at the University of Geneva, uses a wonderful metaphor in his 1989 book, *The Importance of Being Baby,* that illustrates this concept well. We have all marveled at those beautiful Russian dolls that open up to reveal a smaller doll held inside, which in turn opens up to reveal an even smaller doll inside of that one, and so on. This is a perfect visual picture of how the calm, loving, holding environment of the parent holds the child securely, allowing that child to eventually supply the tender holding environment his child needs, and so on down through the generations.[9]

16. IN CONCLUSION . . .

The attachment system is a wonderful thing when it works according to nature's grand evolutionary plan. A secure parent/child attachment in the present helps to ensure closer, loving relationships in the same family generations later.

Unfortunately, this generational quality of attachment is a double-edged sword. Many, many families have become caught in a generational trap of *insecure* attachment relationships. If, as you read this chapter, you felt a sense of sadness for what you missed in your own early life you will probably find the next chapter more descriptive of your own childhood experiences and perhaps your own experiences as a parent. Remember— you are far from alone.

Chapter Four

"My Cord Is Frayed"

A More Tenuous Connection

Do you remember Raquel Welch, reduced to the size of a germ, and injected into a scientists's bloodstream? Like the 1966 movie, *The Fantastic Voyage*, we will continue our microscopic examination of the brain, not on a physical level, but on a level of thoughts and feelings. If you did not identify with the description of the secure-cord parent described in Chapter Three, you may find the frayed-cord parent described in this chapter to be more recognizable.

1. RELATIONSHIP CORDS OF VARYING STRENGTHS AND ELASTICITY

The child or adult who did not experience a consistently responsive and loving caretaker in the first months or years of life may develop an imaginary thin, frayed cord connecting her with others. This imaginary cord has lost its elasticity, and it is feared that any stretching or testing of this frayed cord will cause it to snap. The child or adult with a frayed cord has what is called an *insecure attachment status*. The private logic says, *I must be extra watchful in every relationship or I will be abandoned*. It is important to remember that the internal model of the strong cord versus the frayed cord is not a black/white, either/or, situation. If you could magically visualize the imaginary connecting cords belonging to each individual in any population, you would see a whole range of cords—from the thickest, strongest, and stretchiest cords possible, all the way down to the thinnest, most frayed threads. In the middle range you would see cords that were only slightly frayed or lacking in elasticity.

Many adults whose cords are frayed see themselves as the cause of their tenuous connections to others. The core belief is, *I am not lovable or worthwhile enough for others to care about.* An adult with this frayed cord may tolerate what would normally be called "intolerable" behavior from significant others because he considers himself lucky to have *anyone* in his life.

Other adults see their imaginary frayed cords very differently: *I am O.K. But other people are not trustworthy.* This adult fears others will hurt him. He views their untrustworthiness as responsible for his flimsy connection to others. The adult with this type of a frayed cord may require others he comes into contact with to pass some very stringent tests. These are often pass/fail tests. When the other person being tested makes a mistake, she or he may be immediately discarded as one of those "untrustworthy ones."

The thinnest, most fragile cords belong to adults who see it both ways: *I am not lovable or worthwhile and others are not trustworthy either.* These adults may vacillate between clinging to significant others and then pushing them away, giving the double message, "Come here, go away."

A world where I cannot depend upon others, where I am left adrift to make it alone, can be a pretty scary, unsafe world. If early experiences taught me that *It does no good to ask for help, no one will meet my needs anyway,* I logically come to believe *I have no power or control over what happens to me.* I may try to compensate for this belief by going to extreme measures to regain a feeling of control and power in my life. Or I may be stuck in feelings of helplessness, powerlessness, and depression.

2. NO SECURE BASE

An ambassador who is sent by a strong, dependable government to travel to other countries can do so safely and with confidence. He knows that if he runs out of supplies he will be given what he needs. If he runs into trouble in some negotiation, his country will back him up. However, an ambassador traveling from a small, unstable country that is in political turmoil will surely be more tentative in his negotiations. He will be careful not to take risks because he knows that if he looks to his country for help, he may find no one there to effectively back him up.

The adult with a frayed cord is likely to venture into life very much like this insecure ambassador. He may lack a sense of a secure base *internally*. And *externally*, he may have no one he can really count on to back him up. This may be due to his general mistrust of others, or he may have chosen relationships that resembled the insecure relationships he was familiar with from childhood. Without a secure base, not only will he avoid taking risks, but he may feel the need to maintain a state of hypervigilance: on guard at all times, ready lest disaster strike. On the other hand, he may compensate for his lack of a secure base by throwing caution to the wind and living on the edge as if he had no future to worry about anyway. If external pressures become too great or difficult to handle he may give way to hopelessness and powerlessness, defeat, and depression. Although not all adults with a frayed cord become anxious or depressed, there is definitely a relationship between the frayed cord (i.e., insecure attachment style) and increased vulnerability to these types of struggles. Without a secure base there is little to help buffer him against the stresses of life: *I'm on my own and there's no one I could really depend on to back me up.*

3. ATTACHMENT AND ROMANCE

3.1. The Overactive Warning System

Adults who have a frayed cord have more problems in their romantic relationships. Sometimes a partner is chosen who resembles a neglectful or abusive parent. But sometimes the problem is unwarranted mistrust. To understand this more clearly, remember the description of the attachment warning system of the infant in Chapter Three. Every time the infant senses that the attachment figure is too far away the internal sirens sound. When the sirens go off the infant becomes anxious and the signaling system kicks in. At this point the infant will attempt to bring the caregiver back in any way she can. As adults, our sirens sound in the same way if we sense some sort of threat to our romantic relationship. We may sense a threat due to emotional or physical distance, or the intrusion of a third party. Unfortunately, an imaginary connection cord that is thin and frayed can cause the sirens to sound far too often. Whether or not the core belief is *I am not lovable, Others are not dependable*, or both, the expectation is that

I will be abandoned. It's like living in a town where the tornado sirens sound every time there is a high wind.

3.2. The Overactive Signaling System

The adult who has an internal *strong* cord and senses some threat to the security of his attachment relationship in terms of either emotional or physical distance will probably respond by attempting to reach out to his mate in some way or entice her to get closer to him. He might talk to his mate about his feelings, plan a romantic evening, or call her and tell her he loves her. These are called *attachment signaling behaviors.*

However, the adult with an overactive signaling system, when feeling threatened by either emotional or physical distance in the relationship, may express his needs for his loved one to get closer with *more intensity* than the situation warrants. He may have learned to signal his needs intensely when he was a child and he discovered that he could not get the response he needed from his caregiver without becoming loud and forceful. Subsequently, when he becomes anxious in his adult relationship he may attempt to get more closeness by crying, coercing, or pleading. He may become controlling or move into angrier kinds of signaling behaviors such as shouting, threatening, or explosions of anger. Unfortunately, the effect of the overly intense signaling tends to be opposite to the desired outcome. Loved ones often naturally draw further away due to hurt, anger, or fear. In response, the anxiety may intensify and the signaling behaviors may become even more forceful! It is easy to see how the situation can spiral out of control. Kim Bartholomew, a researcher at Simon Fraser University in British Columbia, has labeled this type of frayed cord the *"preoccupied attachment style."*[1]

Laura came to therapy after a suicide attempt. Prior to her attempt, her fiancee had broken off their engagement. He had complained that he felt suffocated in the relationship. Laura explained tearfully, "The frustrating thing about this is that I knew all along I was driving him away but I couldn't stop myself. I was so afraid he was going to meet someone prettier or smarter than me. Every time he went out without me I became nearly hysterical! Now I've really lost him. I just want to die and escape these feelings." As it turned out, Laura had felt this same way at an earlier time in her life—when her mother had married and moved out of state leaving her to live with her biological father whom she barely knew.

3.3. The Shutdown Signaling System

Another problematic type of signaling is just the opposite of the previous one. Instead of intensifying the signaling behaviors in an attempt to bring the loved one closer, the signaling behaviors are *switched off*. This is often a learned response to experiences of rejection in childhood. In other words, the child who was ignored or rejected when he signaled to his caregiver that he needed her may grow up to believe, *If I let someone know I need them, I will only be ignored.* Therefore, when his warning sirens go off, he learns to ignore them. He avoids reaching out to others. He still has anxiety deep inside, but he blocks it from his awareness, and he convinces himself that he doesn't need to be close to others. He doesn't trust others to be there for him, so he builds walls around his feelings. He holds a core belief that says, *This way it won't hurt when I get rejected.* This type of attachment style has been called the *"dismissive attachment style"* by Bartholomew.[2] The dismissive attached adult who avoids reaching out and builds walls around his feelings often has difficulty maintaining relationships. The walls prevent real closeness or intimacy and the significant other tends to feel cut off and isolated, creating a very tenuous attachment at high risk of dissolving altogether.

Janet, an attractive woman in her early 30s and five months pregnant, had been married for less than a year. She came to therapy alone, but asking for help with her marriage. She stated, "I've never felt so alone. I'm totally frustrated because I feel that by now my husband and I should have achieved more closeness in our relationship." She described how she had been intrigued by Stan when they had started dating. He seemed "mysterious"—and she had wanted desperately to know more about him. When after just a few months Stan asked her to marry him Janet stated, "I jumped at the chance. I thought that I would finally get to know my mystery man! Besides, we share the same profession, and we seemed to share some of the same interests." Janet looked very sad as she went on to say,

> "Unfortunately, marrying Stan didn't change anything. We can talk about the legal profession and we can talk about golf. But he still doesn't tell me what he feels about anything, including me. I don't think *he* even knows what he feels! I only know that *I* feel lonely. Instead of viewing him as mysterious, now I see him as distant, unemotional, and unaffectionate. He won't come to therapy with me

because he thinks this is my problem. He says he is the way he is and that's that. I just have to learn to deal with it."

Janet tried to lessen her expectations of Stan and she tried to look to her friends to get more of her emotional needs met. But in the end, Janet concluded she was never going to be happy with Stan and she sadly filed for a divorce.

3.4. The Vacillating Signaling System

Sometimes adults with a frayed cord alternate between preoccupation with relationships and the opposite approach, dismissing and denying needs for closeness. Bartholomew calls this adaptation the *"fearful attachment style."*[3] Although deep-seated fear of hurt and rejection lies at the root of the fearful attachment style, the adaptive behaviors can damage or destroy relationships.

Edward, a postal worker, came into therapy feeling hopelessly depressed and lonely. He had just gone through his second divorce at age 35. He had had one child in each marriage. He was very honest with me about what the problems had been. "I have sabotaged every relationship I've ever had," he stated.

> "I get intensely jealous and controlling. In my last marriage every time my wife left the house I was certain she was having an affair. I demanded she account for every second of her time, and if I didn't feel satisfied I turned into a raving maniac. And yet, each time she tried to get close I pushed her away. I would find myself saying, 'Give me space, I'm tired.' Or I'd stay out all night with my buddies. Yet the whole time I was doing this I was scared to death of losing her. And that's exactly what happened—strike three."

Eventually, I learned more about why Edward had such an overactive warning system. Edward described to me how his mother had been addicted to prescription drugs since Edward was a small child. He had always tried very hard to get close to her, but she had been preoccupied with her medications and she had consistently pushed Edward away. Edward's father had left when he was only two. Edward had tried to make contact with his father as a teenager—but all of Edward's letters had been returned, unopened. It was no wonder Edward expected rejection. Edward had to change his core beliefs before he could have a healthy relationship.

4. SUMMARY OF THE FOUR ADULT ATTACHMENT STYLES

Judith Feeney, Patricia Nollen, and Mary Hanrahan, researchers at the University of Queensland in Australia, describe Bartholomew's four adult attachment styles as follows:

"*Secure*   It is relatively easy for me to become emotionally close to others. I am comfortable depending on others and having others depend on me. I don't worry about being alone or having others not accept me.

"*Preoccupied*   I want to be completely emotionally intimate with others, but I often find that others are reluctant to get as close as I would like. I am uncomfortable being without close relationships, but I sometimes worry that others don't value me as much as I value them.

"*Dismissing*   I am comfortable without close emotional relationships. It is very important to me to feel independent and self-sufficient, and I prefer not to depend on others or have others depend on me.

"*Fearful*   I am somewhat uncomfortable getting close to others. I want emotionally close relationships but I find it difficult to trust others completely, or to depend on them. I sometimes worry that I will be hurt if I allow myself to become too close to others."[4]

5. ATTACHMENT AND PARENTHOOD

5.1. The Unsafe Holding Environment

The adult who has a secure cord (i.e., a secure attachment) most likely grew up with a safe, secure holding environment for his feelings. Because mom or dad helped him calm his anxious feelings as a child he didn't have to feel frightened of his own feelings and he didn't have to fear losing control. He felt safe having feelings and expressing them. He was able to internalize this holding environment for his feelings and therefore as a parent he can remain relatively calm in the face of his *own* child's distress and respond in a way that helps his child feel safe.

Conversely, the adult with a frayed cord (i.e., an insecure attachment) probably lacked an adequate holding environment for his feelings as a child. Thus, his feelings didn't feel safe or controllable. As a result he has a weak internal holding environment to help him calm his own feelings in adulthood. As a parent, he may become anxious handling his child's strong emotions and therefore less able to offer his child the calm holding environment *the child* needs to feel safe.

Beth, a young, first-time mother, began to have panic attacks after the birth of her son. Every time she picked up her crying infant her heart began to beat wildly and her throat felt like it was closing up. Her son seemed to feel his mother's distress and as a result became increasingly more distraught. The only solution Beth found was to hand him over to her husband for calming. Beth came in to therapy desperate for help when her husband informed her he could take no more time off from work. She agreed that there might be issues from her past she didn't fully understand that were interfering with her ability to care for her son. Beth began healing wounds from her childhood that she had not even clearly remembered.

Unlike Beth, some frayed-cord parents have learned to cope with feelings by pushing them away. This parent may distance himself from his child's emotions because the child's feelings will trigger his own painful feelings. When his child becomes distressed the parent may become mechanical—meeting his child's physical needs, but lacking any emotional connection with the child. He cannot provide the soothing and reassurance the child needs.

Tara was only 21. Her mother had left when she was a baby. Her father was an alcoholic and drug-addicted. He had left her in the care of a succession of girlfriends. As Tara sat on my couch for our first session, her bangs almost covering her eyes and her head down, I found myself imagining how she must have been left to cry, lonely and alone, as an infant. Her one-year-old daughter, Annie, had a stuffy nose and congestion in her chest and obviously did not feel well. Annie sat curled up behind the corner of the couch, crying quietly. Tara showed no apparent awareness of her daughter's distress. With no emotion on her face, her honest response to every one of my questions related to her feelings was, "I don't know." To cope with her early life Tara had had to learn to shut down her emotional and physical needs. Tara needed help to learn to feel again—so that she could *really hear* her daughter's cries for the first time.

5.2. Misattunement

As mentioned in Chapter Three, one of the qualities of the parent–child relationship that creates a strong, firm cord is attunement between parent and child. Attunement means that the parent is *tuned into* the child's feelings and needs. As the parent calms the overexcited infant, enlivens the bored infant, or feeds the hungry infant, the infant feels connected to and safe with the parent. The infant senses the emotional connection between herself and her parent. She knows she is not alone in this world. There is another who is tuned in to her, who understands her feelings and her needs.

If a parent becomes fearful and overwhelmed or shuts down emotionally when faced with his child's feelings and needs, then attunement will suffer. These strong emotional responses prevent the parent from being able to tune in to his child. As a result, the child is not able to sense and experience a connection between them. Instead of a strong cord, the child develops a sense of a cord that may snap at any moment. She senses that the parent is not fully tuned into her, that the parent does not truly hear her or understand what she is feeling. She does not securely trust that her parent will respond and give her the reassurance that she needs. She cannot see herself clearly, accurately, and lovingly reflected in her parent's gaze.

6. THE CHILD'S SIGNALING SYSTEM GOES AWRY

Because of the misattunement, the parent may not accurately perceive or respond to the child's signaling behaviors. As a result, the child's warning and signaling systems may go haywire as the child attempts to get her needs met.

6.1. Overactive

As described in Chapter Three, a child's signaling system kicks in when she becomes anxious and needs her parent's closeness and reassurance. If, due to his own anxiety, the parent is not able to provide the child with the reassurance she needs, she will become even more alarmed—especially if she senses that the parent to whom she is turning for comfort is fearful himself! As a result, the child's signaling behaviors may intensify in an attempt to get the reassurance she needs. This may in turn trigger even more distress in the parent, creating a vicious circle between the parent and child. The child's inner warning and signaling systems can become chronically hyperaroused in this situation: easy to set off and difficult to settle down. Using the analogy of the tornado sirens, one might say that the oversensitive sirens get set off by a high wind, and then continue sounding even when the wind has calmed. These children may become highly anxious and intense in their attempts to get their needs met.

6.2. Shutdown

Conversely, the parent who felt rejected as a young child may have learned to shut down his own attachment system in order to avoid the disappointment and hurt of rejection. When this parent is faced with his child's strong feelings, his childhood memories of rejection get triggered. His automatic response is to shut down emotionally, just as he had learned to do as a child. Unfortunately, as he distances himself from his childhood distress he may also distance himself from perceiving and responding to

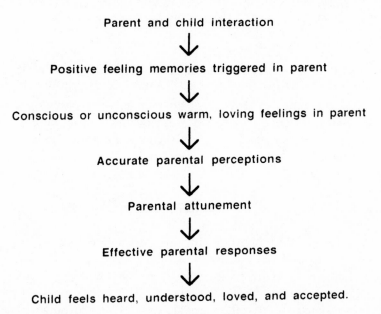

Parent and child interaction

↓

Positive feeling memories triggered in parent

↓

Conscious or unconscious warm, loving feelings in parent

↓

Accurate parental perceptions

↓

Parental attunement

↓

Effective parental responses

↓

Child feels heard, understood, loved, and accepted.

Figure 1. Passing a secure attachment from generation to generation.

his *child's* emotions. The child observes that her parent pulls away from her each time she signals her needs and so she, too, learns that the best way to keep her parent close by is to shut off her signaling system and make very few demands. Now both parent and child have learned to deny their internal sirens and shut down their signaling systems, although the sirens are still sounding on the inside. They learn to stay distant from others and hide their feelings of anxiety and stress.

7. ATTACHMENT THROUGH THE GENERATIONS

Attachment styles are often handed down from generation to generation right along with the family heirlooms. Figure 1 illustrates the chain reaction that takes place in the type of parent–child interaction that results in a secure type of attachment between a parent and child. The more often the child experiences this type of interaction, the *more securely attached* she will become. The foundation for the child's self-esteem is being laid.

Figure 2 is a simple illustration of the type of parent–child interaction that can leave the child with a feeling that either something is wrong with

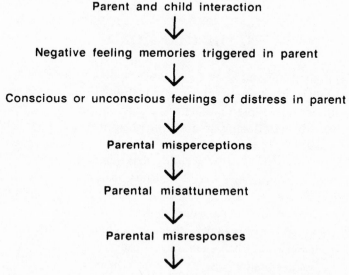

Parent and child interaction

↓

Negative feeling memories triggered in parent

↓

Conscious or unconscious feelings of distress in parent

↓

Parental misperceptions

↓

Parental misattunement

↓

Parental misresponses

↓

Child feels unheard, misunderstood, hurt, or rejected.

Figure 2. Passing an insecure attachment from generation to generation.

her or that it is not O.K. to trust others, or both. The more often this chain reaction takes place, the *more insecurely attached* the child will become. Fortunately, if the misattuned parent becomes more attuned, the child can then move toward a more secure attachment relationship instead.

8. ATTACHMENT AND ABUSE

Infants and children who experience physical or sexual abuse by their parents are in a real double bind. The parent is the attachment figure—the one to whom the child naturally wants to go to for reassurance when distressed or threatened. Yet, when the expected source of comfort is *at the same time* the source of the child's fear the child is left in a terrible predicament. Children in this situation generally become very confused and disorganized in their thoughts and behaviors, especially when they become fearful or stressed. When observed with their parent, these children sometimes look frozen: they are afraid to make a move either toward or away from the parent. These children are usually extremely anxious and angry, although out of fear they often have learned to suppress their strong feelings. Children of abuse or neglect have been found to have thoughts of suicide and homicide as young as age four.

9. THE TORN CORD

Alicia Lieberman and Jeree Pawl, researchers and clinicians with the Infant Mental Health Program at the University of California in San Francisco, identified three types of attachment problems: insecure attachment, disrupted attachment (losing an attachment figure), and the problem of the *nonattached child.*[5] Many centers specializing in treating severely disturbed children now refer to these children as *unattached children.* The unattached child has an internal cord that has been completely or almost completely ripped apart. She is no longer capable of attaching to *anyone* because her first few months or years deprived her of any hope she once had concerning relationships with other human beings. Many unattached children are foster or adoptive children, either due to removal from the birth family by the state or due to a voluntary placement situation. Many unattached children have experienced multiple moves within the foster care system resulting in multiple disruptions in their attachment relationships. Some unattached children live with birth families, but experienced severe bonding breaks due to long illnesses and hospitalizations, or severe early abuse or neglect by parents whose actions were guided by their own horrendous early experiences.

Experiences of severe abuse or abandonment do not cause a child to become unattached in every instance. Some children who undergo severe bonding breaks or abuse still retain the ability to form at least tenuous attachments with others. The outcome probably depends on the resiliency and the makeup of the individual child, as well as the specifics of the situation.

A child is recognized as unattached by specialists when she seems to have completely given up on human relationships altogether. The unattached child sees other human beings as objects to be used to meet certain needs. She appears incapable of forming a meaningful relationship with another human being. The unattached child is full of tremendous rage and hostility. Lieberman and Pawl identify the unattached child as impaired in cognitive functioning and in the ability to control aggressive impulses.[6] Dr. Foster Cline, adult and child psychiatrist and founder of the Attachment Center at Evergreen, Colorado, also describes the unattached child as frequently superficially charming and affectionate with strangers. In addition, he describes extremely manipulative and controlling behaviors, lack of eye contact, lack of friends, and a frequent preoccupation with fire, blood, and gore. The unattached child frequently has abnormal eating and speech patterns, and always shows lack of a normally developing conscience. Unattached children are at extremely high risk of becoming adult sociopaths.[7] These are the children we read about in the horrifying news stories of young children beating or murdering other children, animals, or even adults.

Fortunately, there is hope for these children. There are several centers in the United States that specialize in treating unattached children (see Appendix D). Often the children brought to these centers are adoptees who gave up on human relationships prior to joining their new families. Some of the children are brought in by birth families due to earlier severe bonding breaks. Unfortunately, there exist many adoptive and birth families who are raising unattached children and receiving no help.

10. ATTACHMENT ON A CONTINUUM

Most individuals do not fall neatly into one category of attachment status. I conceptualize attachment on a continuum, as illustrated in Figure 3, with the most securely attached individuals on one end of the continuum and

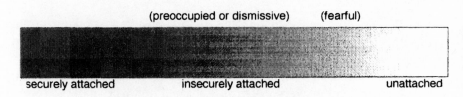

Figure 3. A continuum of attachment styles.

the most completely unattached individuals at the other end of the continuum. Bartholomew's preoccupied, dismissive, and fearful categories of attachment lie somewhere in the middle. Attachment problems that are the most severe are closest to the unattached end of the continuum. The individuals found *closest to the unattached end of the continuum* will exhibit *more of the severely disturbed behaviors* described earlier in this section.

11. THE UNATTACHED IK TRIBE

Anthropologist Colin Turnbull wrote a book in 1972 entitled *The Mountain People*. The book describes his nightmarish year-long stay with the Ik tribe of Uganda. Once a nomadic band of hunters and gatherers, the government had moved the Ik to a barren mountain region in northern Uganda sometime before World War II. Turnbull describes the Ik as an example of how human social structure can completely break down when a society is under overwhelming survival stress.[8] The story provides evidence that when children are raised in a society that must focus solely on staying alive the meaning of human relationships may be forgotten. In attachment terms, the Ik show us what happens when the hardship of chronic hunger and fear of death are so severe that they interfere with parents' ability to form attachment bonds with their offspring. This painful story describes what can happen when survival stress is pervasive throughout an entire society—and over time, what can happen as unattached or barely attached offspring grow up and bear their own children and the problems multiply.

Turnbull told hair-raising tales of the Ik mothers, who after grudgingly nursing their infants until age three, kicked them out of the family compounds to fend for themselves and join the bands of roving children who survived on roots and berries. He told one very sad story of a little girl who wouldn't leave her compound. She kept sneaking back in to be with her parents. Her attachment to them resulted in her demise as her disgusted parents finally left the compound, locking her in. A few days later they reentered, throwing her dead body out into the bushes. Turnbull told another baffling story of an Ik mother who laid her baby down at the watering hole only to turn around and find a mountain lion had snatched her child. The mother's response was to run to the village and excitedly alert the others that there would be a lion sleeping off a meal in the area very soon, and they must not miss this chance to kill him and get some meat.

By the time that Turnbull came to live with the Ik each member of the Ik tribe was living and breathing the message from birth on that human relationships were useless and that others were not to be trusted or cared about. Each generation was faithfully passing this message on to the new generations following. Over the generations the message had very likely become more and more severe as the attachment cords in the young were more severely ripped apart and destroyed. One wonders about the first generation of births after the Ik had been shuttled off to the mountains. Did they still maintain some semblance of attachment between parents and young? Did the bonds become more frayed as parents became more preoccupied with keeping themselves alive? Did the children of those parents not only learn that others can't be trusted to meet their needs, but that others can't be trusted to stay alive from one day to the next? At what point was there nothing left of human bonds whatsoever? It is interesting to note that the Ik maintained an interest in sex and continued to couple and procreate. Perhaps sex provided them with a temporary diversion from the reality of their lives. There appeared to be virtually no emotional attachment between sexual partners, however, as the death of one member of a couple appeared to have no emotional affect on the other.

12. IN CONCLUSION: THE CONTINUUM AND SOCIETY

Turnbull writes, "The Ik teach us that our much vaunted human values are not inherent in humanity at all, but are associated only with a particular form of survival called society, and that all, even society itself, are luxuries that can be dispensed with. . . . The Ik have relinquished all luxury in the name of individual survival, and the result is that they live on as a people without life, without passion, beyond humanity."[9]

The tale of the Ik made me wonder about what might be happening in certain pockets of our society where the emotional needs of infants and children take a backseat to just surviving one day at a time. Can parents who must fight each day just to get enough food to feed their families and keep a roof over their heads have enough energy remaining to invest in their relationships with their children? What happens to the attachments in families where life is so harsh it loses its meaning? What happens to the bonds in families of any socioeconomic group when it is all parents can do to endure overwhelming stress related to finances, marital conflict, divorce, and lack of social support? What happens to the parent–child bonds when parents find alcohol or drugs to be the only escape from the harshness of their lives? What are the children growing up in this kind of survival mode learning about the meaning of human relationships, and how will their beliefs play out in their relationships with their own children?

The more children we raise on or near the unattached end of the continuum in our society, the more Ik traits we will find in our own cities, towns, schools, and neighborhoods. On the other hand, imagine how different our society would look if more of our children were raised toward the secure end of the attachment continuum. We would see less crime, violence, mental illness, and child abuse. More of society's energy would be freed up for greater advances in medicine, space exploration, and technology. The more children we raise on the secure end of the continuum, the greater the benefit to our society. It is vital that we support and help one another as parents in learning how to cope with modern life and break damaging generational cycles and raise securely attached children. Enlightened professionals and parents must spread the word to all parents that a secure attachment is the best insurance that a child will grow up with good emotional health, a well-developed conscience, and a sense of compassion for other human beings. Many parents are unaware that they are not forming adequate bonds or are unaware of how to change the situation. Instead of blaming, adults who have the awareness must reach out to parents in need with understanding and support so that more parents can have the opportunity to heal themselves and help their children.

Chapter Five

"My Vision Is Blurred"

Identifying Your Parental Misperceptions

My husband and I took our children to Disney World last year and one of our favorite experiences was attending the show, *Honey, I Shrunk the Audience*. Through the magic of 3D glasses, we screamed and ducked as a hovercraft flew toward our faces, and shrieked in horror as rats appeared to pour off the screen. We would have looked ludicrous to an outside observer who couldn't see the images that floated in front of our eyes!

Similarly, all parents wear their own "magic" glasses. Depending on their past experiences and the images that dance in their minds, some lenses are even more distorting and blurring than others. Due to these distortions parents frequently misperceive and misinterpret who their children are, what their actions mean, and what they need.

Dr. Bertrand Cramer explains that the reason it is difficult *not* to misinterpret the actions of infants is that babies have no words to help their parents understand them—only actions.[1] In my own view, even as children get older it is very easy to misinterpret and misunderstand both their actions and their words. Older children remain extremely limited in their ability to communicate accurately their feelings, needs, and motivations. And why shouldn't they? Even adults find it difficult to identify and express their feelings accurately!

A parent with a frayed cord, an overwhelmed hurt child ego state, or a powerful inner critic is at greater risk of misperceiving and misinterpreting her child's behaviors in many different ways. In addition, she will be

89

more vulnerable to these misperceptions when under stress. Even parents who experienced adequate nurturing in childhood become vulnerable to misperceptions and misresponses with their children when they are under stress. Stress can disconnect any of us from the rational, logical part of our minds leaving us vulnerable to functioning totally out of our emotions. Chapter Seven provides some tools to help parents cope with stress and distress.

1. PLAYING "KEEP AWAY!"

If a parent's needs for closeness in childhood were too often ignored she may have learned to cope with feelings of rejection by pushing away her feelings and denying her needs. She will naturally try to avoid remembering her painful childhood feelings. Unfortunately, the sound of her *own* child crying out for *her* may trigger these painful feeling memories. Her automatic response to the emotions inside herself will be to shut down and close herself off emotionally, once again, to stay safe. The walls which automatically go up to protect her subsequently prevent her from empathically tuning into what her child is feeling. It may be as difficult for the parent with internal walls to have good attunement with her child as it is for someone to get a good T.V. reception in a bomb shelter. With the internal walls around her own emotions, her child's signals cannot penetrate. When her child tries to get past her walls and get the closeness he needs, she may *perceive* him as uncomfortably *invading* her personal and emotional space. Her natural response, without her consciously being aware of it, may be to distance from him until she can find her comfort zone.

The child who is unable to achieve the closeness he naturally desires is at risk of developing his own core beliefs that his needs for closeness are bad, or just plain futile. Rather than continuing to set himself up for rejection, he, too, may learn to shut down his attachment needs and put up walls, although inside those walls the hurt and anger remain.

Emily brought Tim in for assessment because, she stated, he was just "too clingy!" Tim was two, and Emily stated she felt like he was trying to suffocate her with his constant need to be on her lap or be close to her. In taking down the family history it became apparent that Emily had suffered severe rejection as a child. She agreed to do some work of her own, and as she began to find her own recovery she began to enjoy Tim's hugs for the very first time. Tim, luckily, had never given up trying to get his needs met.

2. BUT HE'S TOO NEEDY!

Some parents who grew up feeling rejected may have come to feel ashamed of their normal needs for affection and attention. In this situation, a parent may be left with a core belief that these needs are shameful, bad, or weak. Due to logic based on her distorted beliefs she may perceive her *child's* needs for attention and affection to be shameful.

The truth is *all children need attention.* What does that mean? It means they need to be "attended to," to be noticed, acknowledged, and even further, to be acknowledged with attunement and affection. All children seek to obtain this kind of attention in many different ways. If a child is seeking the attention he needs primarily through misbehavior, it may be that more direct methods tried in the past didn't work. In attachment terms, if a child feels physical or emotional distance from his parent, his attachment system will become activated. He will attempt to get reassurance or attention from his parent through any number of methods such as engaging the parent in a positive emotional exchange, asking for what he needs, or whining, clinging, or acting out in "attention-seeking" ways. Seeking attention is a biologically programmed behavior to help children achieve the parental closeness they need for their physical and emotional survival. If your child uses primarily negative methods to seek attention, Part Three will help you change these negative signals into more positive ones.

3. TOUGHENING UP BABY

Another common misperception related to children's needs for attention and affection is the parental belief that if the parent gives her child too much attention or affection she will spoil him or cause him to become babyish or overly dependent upon her. Although failure to set limits with a child may "spoil" him, affection will not. Overprotectiveness and smothering control may thwart a child's sense of self-confidence and create more dependency, but *affection will not stifle independence.* Affection creates a secure attachment and therefore a sense of a secure base so that the child has *more* self-confidence as he gets older and goes out into the world. All children are born with both a desire for a close secure attachment *and* a desire to be independent and autonomous. By giving our children the love and affection they need we are fostering their sense of self-worth and self-confidence so they will be able to become as independent as they need to be at each stage of their growth.

4. MY CHILD DOES NOT LOVE ME!

A parent who was abused or rejected as a child may interpret her infant's screams or her older child's misbehaviors as evidence that her child does not love her. During those moments when her infant is raging she may *perceive* the howls as rage directed "at her"—as hatred and rejection. She may take the older child's misbehaviors very personally. In the face of this kind of interpretation, she may experience feelings of hurt, despair, and shame. She may conclude that she is simply inadequate as a parent, and therefore no child could love her! It is obvious that this misperception of her child's feelings and actions interferes with her attunement and her ability to effectively respond to him. She may find it very difficult to soothe or comfort her crying child because her feelings are so overwhelming that she needs comforting and reassurance herself. She may overreact to the acting out of the older child because of her hurt feelings, or she may try to pacify the child to make the child love her more. Unfortunately, these responses may cause her child's behavior to intensify, snowballing the whole situation!

Janet was a new mother who came in with her new baby, obviously feeling quite anxious and upset. She stated, as if it was an unmistakable fact, that she was a rotten mother and she should just do everyone a big favor and leave. "I'm a good lawyer," she said. "But I'm absolutely worthless as a mother. I love Shannon, but I think she is really disappointed in me." I could hear Janet's oversized critical parent voice speaking, and I could sense the overwhelming feelings of the inner hurt child. I began talking to Janet about these internal ego states when a look of relief crossed her face and she exclaimed, "I get it!" She looked down at the baby in her arms, sleeping and looking peaceful now, and went on to say, "I know what's happening! When Shannon cries my internal critic starts in with, 'See there—You're not a good parent. You don't even know what your baby needs. You're worthless and she doesn't love you.' My hurt child believes it's all true!" Janet came to realize that each time her hurt child feelings were triggered and she became distressed, Shannon sensed her anxiety and grew even more upset. Her insight helped her stop the vicious cycle.

5. THE MONSTER-CHILD

The parent who experienced abuse, harsh treatment, or rejection as a child may consciously or unconsciously fear her baby *is* her abuser in her life all over again. She may imagine her child has inherited the abusive or rejecting characteristics of her parent, sibling, ex-spouse, or other relative. Whether or not it is a conscious thought, the fear is, *My baby is bad!* or *My child is a monster!* In her imagination her child *becomes* the hurtful other, and thus, normal childlike behaviors become symbolic to her as signs of her child's innate badness. She may perceive her child's cry for comforting as a scream of hate, or as an attempt to "control" or "manipulate" her. She may perceive her infant playfully batting her arm as attempting to hurt her, or her baby squirming to get off of her lap to play as rejecting her. The cries of a tired infant, hair-pulling by a cranky toddler, or arguing by a teenager may all be perceived as malicious. She is vulnerable to misperceiving many of her child's normal acting-out behaviors as malevolent attempts to humiliate her in front of others, as evidence of lack of love, or as purposeful attempts to hurt her.

When a parent consciously or unconsciously views her child as an extension of a hurtful person from the past, many normal child behaviors can be perceived as personality characteristics resembling the other person, causing her to believe that she must endure a young version of the person who hurt her. Therefore, the child who leaves his toys lying around like most children do may be perceived as *sloppy, just like Dad.* The little girl with a loud voice may be perceived as a *yeller, just like my ex-wife.* Naturally, these misperceptions obstruct the parent's attunement with her child, and impede her ability to respond appropriately to his needs or to the situation. Even though most parents are able to identify *intellectually* that children are not born with malevolent motivations, many parents still carry that "gut level" fear that their children might be innately "bad."

6. THE FROZEN PARENT

If a parent perceives her child as an extension of the hurtful other she may find herself overwhelmed by feelings of anxiety and helplessness rooted in her past experiences of abuse. Triggered by what she perceives as abuser-like behaviors in her own child, the anxious and helpless feelings of her inner child may actually immobilize her when she is with her child. Thus, when her two-year-old begins showing the rather uncivilized behavior of the normal toddler, she may find herself frozen and unable to respond as he acts out. Remember the story of Nancy and Nate in Chapter One. Nancy secretly feared that her son, Nate, had inherited her older brother's sadistic tendencies. When she was a child, her older brother had terrorized her. As she watched her rambunctious son tear apart the house, the feelings of Nancy's inner child overwhelmed her and she felt power-less and incapable of responding, as if she were a child in the presence of her older brother. Unfortunately, the situation snowballed because with-out firm limits Nate's behavior had become increasingly out of control. The more out of control he had become, the more helpless Nancy had felt. Thus, perceiving her child as a monster had become somewhat of a self-fulfilling prophecy, as Nate did show some monster-like behavior. How-ever, Nate is not the abuser Nancy imagines him to be, but a normal child who desperately needs some limits!

7. I CAN SEE MYSELF!

Parents who were abused or rejected in childhood were usually blamed for this abuse or neglect by the older person. They may have been told, "It's all your fault," "You were asking for it," or "You're just such a disappointment." Ann Potter, psychologist and author of the workbook, *Inside Out: Rebuilding Self and Personality through Inner Child Therapy,* calls this the *feeling reality switch.* When a child is abused, he typically feels re-sponsible for the abuse. The child takes on the shame that really belongs to the abusive adult. Unfortunately, as the child becomes an adult he may continue to view the child within as shameful or disgusting. Potter writes, "Often people react to the feeling realty switch between themselves and real-life offenders by treating their own inner children as if they were the offenders rather than the victims. They may feel disgust or revulsion and dislike the Child intensely. The Inner Child then experiences rejection a second time and is blamed for being a victim."[2]

The parent who was shamed as a child for personal characteristics such as physical appearance, academic or athletic ability, or emotional sen-sitivity may also feel derision toward the child within. The parent who experienced generalized shaming or name calling such as, "You're worth-less," "You can't do anything right," or "You're a slob," is very likely to dislike her inner child.

The parent–child relationship was described as "a remembering con-text" in Chapter Two, a term used by Daniel Stern.[3] The parent with her child experiences herself as parent *and* empathically imagines what it is like to *be* her child. This imagining triggers memories of *herself* as a child, instantly connecting her to her shameful feelings about her younger self. The shame and disgust the parent feels toward herself as a child can easily get misdirected toward her real-life child, who becomes an external representation of herself. She may then perceive certain characteristics of her child as evidence that she has produced a dislikable reproduction of herself. If she was told she cried constantly as a baby, she may perceive her baby's cries as evidence that she has produced another "crybaby" like herself. A parent who had a weight problem as a child and was teased or shamed may perceive her child's normal healthy appetite as "gluttony," and may perceive normal "baby fat" as shameful. A parent who was told she was "bad" or "evil" as a child may perceive any normal child misbehaviors as evidence that she has produced a "bad" child like herself.

Barbara came to therapy asking for help because she had found herself losing her temper with her two-year-old daughter, Kelsey. "She reminds me of me," she explained. "Everything she does reminds me of me and I just hate her for it." Barbara began crying at that point in our first interview. "I have always hated myself! God must be punishing me for being so bad by giving me a child just like *me* to live with!" she sobbed. Barbara had a lot of work to do to develop a relationship with both her own inner child and with Kelsey. Her critical-parent ego state was very strong, as she had internalized many of the critical messages she had heard from her drug-addicted parents.

Obviously, these overreactions and misperceptions regarding a child's behaviors or characteristics will interfere with a parent's ability to be attuned to her child the same way that static in the atmosphere interferes with T.V. reception. As the parent focuses on the characteristics of the child that resemble the "hated self," she is not able to perceive the "real child"— his emotions, his needs, and his positive qualities. The confusion of one's child with one's hated *inner* child interferes with a parent's ability to appreciate and have fun with her youngster.

8. THE SIMMERING POT

The parent who felt rejected or who suffered abuse as a child may have built up a tremendous rage that had no safe way to get released during childhood. It certainly could not be directed toward an abusive or rejecting parent, as that would have meant risking retribution or further rejection. It may have spewed out sideways onto brothers, sisters, schoolmates, or even pets. But the bulk of that anger may have remained simmering inside and may still remain there in adulthood. The last thing most parents who experienced their own parents' rage wish to do is to repeat the cycle with their own children. The problem is, when the parent misperceives that her child is trying to hurt her, control her, or reject her, her unconscious mind *confuses her child with the significant others of her past.* It is all too easy, unfortunately, for that pent-up childhood rage to come exploding outward onto the *child-who-represents-someone-else.* And it may unfortunately get expressed in ways that were learned through the role modeling of the parent's parents.

On the other hand, a parent may feel like directing the rage she holds inside toward *herself,* especially toward the little one she once was when she first came to believe that she was bad, worthless, or shameful. If this is the case, and if she perceives her child as an *extension of herself,* the rage she feels may explode without warning outward onto the *child-who-represents-herself.* When this happens, parents sometimes report that they actually felt like they had *become* their own parent, lashing out at the child that they once were.

If your rage has exploded onto your own child in ways you experienced in your own childhood, it may be very painful to confront actions in yourself that resemble behavior you never wanted to imitate. However, getting honest with yourself is the first step to overcoming the problem and is the only route toward making real changes. Pain really does, sometimes, mean gain. If you feel guilty about past actions, this is evidence that you are growing and changing, that you are getting past your own defenses of denial and rationalization, and that you are beginning to look at things very differently than you used to.

9. I HAVE NO FEELINGS: A BOWL FULL OF FISHHOOKS

In the 1996 movie, *Marvin's Room,* Meryl Streep plays a character named Lee who, by all appearances, has very little feeling for her 15-year-old son, Hank. As the movie unfolds the viewer learns of Lee's painful past, including an abusive relationship with Hank's father. At one point she states to her son, "My feelings for you are like a big bowl of fishhooks. I can't just pick up one at a time—I pick one up and they all come, so I just had to leave them alone."[4]

Like Lee, some adults have learned to cope with their painful feelings by blocking them completely from their conscious minds. Their feelings are like fishhooks, and they dare not touch them. Unfortunately, neither children nor adults can keep negative feelings suppressed without suppressing positive feelings as well. Second, in order to avoid having feelings, a parent must stay detached from her feelings for her child and avoid empathizing with the child's feelings. Obviously, when a parent avoids her own feelings as well as her child's feelings she allows her child to form only the most insecure type of attachment with her.

10. MY CHILD HAS NO FEELINGS

In order for a parent to successfully block her child's feelings from her awareness, she may have to convince herself that her child has no feelings. A parent who grew up in an environment that devalued the feelings of children will adopt this belief more easily than a parent who grew up in an environment that validated the feelings of children. A parent who learned while growing up that children are to be seen and not heard may have adopted a core belief that her feelings and thoughts are unimportant, and additionally, that the feelings of *all* children are unimportant.

11. TWO WAYS TO EXIST: ABUSER OR VICTIM

Some parents who were abused as children came to believe early in childhood that there were only two ways to exist in this world: as the abuser or as the victim. This makes sense to the child whose thinking is still very black and white, and who perceives each member of the family as either an abuser or as another victim like herself. Considering the two choices that children in these circumstances perceive, it is no wonder that some children choose to identify themselves with their abusers. When this is the only choice that feels powerful and safe, the child may grow up trying out the abusive identity on siblings, peers, and pets. By proving to herself that she is not a victim, she becomes a victimizer. If she becomes a parent, she, too, must perceive her child as having no feelings in order to avoid her own underlying feelings of powerlessness and pain. Thus, due to her identification with the abuser and her perception that her child has no feelings, this parent is at extremely high risk for repeating the abuse with her own child. The good news is, this parent is capable of change. If she is willing to risk opening herself up to her own vulnerable childhood feelings, she can reevaluate the decisions she made about her role in life. This is not, however, an easy process. It takes tremendous courage.

12. THE HYPERVIGILANT PARENT

Adults who were abused as children learned that *if I am not in control of a situation I am leaving myself vulnerable to getting hurt.* As children they may have learned to maintain *hypervigilance* at all times—remaining aware of what was happening around them, their parents' moods, and keeping an eye on the escape routes "just in case." Children in these situations learn to remain in this type of "survival mode" out of necessity. They tend to remain in a chronic state of hyperarousal and hyperanxiety as a result.

As these children grow to adulthood they tend to maintain their hypervigilance in order to feel in control and safe in any situation they are in. When the hypervigilant adult becomes a parent, her need to feel in control is *really* challenged. Starting with the pregnancy and birth process, through colic and sleep problems, illnesses, tantrums, acting out, choices of peers, report cards, and dating, there is *so* much over which parents do not have control. We have *influence* over our children's lives in many ways, but we do not have absolute *control* over very much at all. Our children have their own feelings and their own minds. They have sicknesses and accidents. They have their own *worlds*, involving their own peers, teachers, music, and the culture of their own generation. The older they get, the more choices they make and *should* make for themselves. For parents who feel anxious when they don't feel in control, the experience of having and raising a child can be extremely anxiety provoking. Let's face it—we *all* experience anxiety about our children and all of the situations over which we do not have control! But for parents who developed chronic hypervigilance and hyperarousal in childhood, the anxiety and the *need to feel in control* in order to combat the anxiety can be much more extreme.

This hypervigilance does indeed affect parental *perceptions.* For instance, the hypervigilant parent may perceive that *something bad is going to happen* to her child. Often the hypervigilant parent believes herself to be so inadequate as a parent that she will surely make a mistake that will cause her child harm. Sometimes the parent's belief that something bad will happen to her child is triggered by feeling memories of her own childhood. Linda came to therapy due to incapacitating panic attacks when her daughter, Fran, was seven years old. Linda had been sexually abused at age seven. "I don't know what's wrong with me," she explained. "I can't get the idea out of my head that Fran is going to get sick and die, get run over by a car, or get kidnapped." At an unconscious level, Linda felt she needed to maintain her constant state of hyperarousal in order to be ready at all times to protect her child from impending danger. Unfortunately, Linda's chronic state of anxiety was not only uncomfortable for her—it was also negatively affecting her daughter. Previously outgoing, Fran had become fearful and withdrawn in response to her mother's panic.

Often the hypervigilant parent perceives that *she* is unsafe. This feeling becomes exacerbated when she is around her child, especially when she senses a lack of control. For example, when her child acts out in some way, even if the behavior is characteristic of most children, the parent's anxiety may skyrocket as she perceives that she is not in control.

Sandy, a secretary and divorced mother of three, grew up witnessing violent arguments between her parents. She never knew when her alcoholic father would begin hitting her mother, and she never knew when a blow would come her way. She was chronically anxious throughout her childhood. She explained to me that when her teenage son and daughter began to fight with one another she felt panicked. She did not understand why. "After all," she said, "they don't intend to hurt me. They are fighting with each other. I don't know why I feel so scared. So I find excuses to leave the house a lot. Sometimes I just drive around." When her children fought, Sandy's perception was, *I am not in control here. Therefore, I am in danger.*

I commonly hear parents who grew up hypervigilant tell me that their anxiety sometimes feels worse *when things seem to be going too well*. What does this mean? As a child, the hypervigilant parent learned not to trust when things seemed to be O.K. In childhood, she learned that the mood of the house could change in an instant. When things seemed O.K. it was only a matter of time before disaster would erupt. Therefore, when the hypervigilant parent looks around and finds that the children are healthy, the bills are caught up, and the atmosphere is calm, she may find herself extremely anxious—just *waiting* for the other shoe to fall. Often hypervigilant parents have an unconscious superstition that by worrying they are somehow *preventing* the bad things from happening. It is very difficult for a parent to give up worrying when she believes the worry itself is somehow keeping her world from crashing down around her!

13. KEEPING MY DUCKS IN A ROW

Once their children begin exhibiting self-will and the drive to be more independent, many parents attempt to maintain a feeling of being in control by adopting a strict, authoritarian approach. Sometimes this method of coping with the anxiety of not being in control means remaining hypervigilant to every infraction of the rules and enforcing every rule with strict punishments. Often authoritarian parents were raised in families where the issue was power and control, and only the adults had it. For the children in an authoritarian family, power and control become the Holy Grail. Power becomes coveted and yearned for, but is always out of reach. When a child from this family becomes a parent herself, without her consciously realizing it the natural response is, "At last, it's my turn now." In the new family, power and control again become the central issue, the big prize, as the new parent takes her turn in the authoritarian role. The parent believes that this is the way it is supposed to be because this is what she was taught. Often this role is taken on in other relationships as well—dictating to one's spouse, coworkers, or employees in the same authoritarian style. Sometimes the need to keep the feeling of having power and control extends to keeping one's environment in the home or office in perfect order. Sometimes the need to control extends to using verbal threats and commands with other drivers in traffic or with clerks in stores. Parents who use this method of coping are at high risk for crossing the line from authoritarian style into verbal or physical abuse.

Melissa had come to therapy due to symptoms of post-traumatic stress disorder related to sexual and physical abuse in childhood. As she worked to resolve her past trauma she began to gain more and more insight into her parental misperceptions. She said to me one day,

> "When my children ask me if they can do something—anything—even if it's just to go outside and play—my instinctual response is to scream, 'NO!' When they ask me if they can do something it feels like a violation! I automatically think, 'How dare they ask me if they can go outside!' This is exactly how my mom always responded to me. She always told me no. I was never allowed to do anything. She had complete and total power over me. Underneath my behavior is a little scared kid who feels helpless. When you feel that little and helpless as a kid and then you do get big, physically, you think, 'I sure as hell better have some power now.' My poor kids—I say no over the stupidest things! But now I am starting to ask myself, 'Why did I say no?' I'm catching myself. Then I go to my kids and I tell them, 'I changed my mind. Go ahead and play.'"

If you are a parent who adopted the myth passed down in your family that power and control are the Holy Grail, by now your children may have adopted the myth as well. In Part Three you will learn how to parent without making power and control the most valued commodity in your family, and how to instead make the spirit of cooperation the family goal.

14. PARADOXICAL METHODS OF CONTROL

Often hypervigilant parents attempt to maintain an illusory feeling of control through addictions. The immediate emotional gratification of the substance or behavior, an effect that can be reliably predicted and counted on, provides a temporary feeling of being in control. This feeling is an incredible relief for someone who otherwise lives constantly in a state of hypervigilance and anxiety. For the adult who feels disconnected from others and is unable to depend on the people in her life, her chosen substance or behavior becomes a relationship she can depend on. There are two catches, however. The first catch is that the feeling of control is *temporary*. The second catch is that the feeling of control *is only an illusion*. The hard reality is, the more an individual relies on her chosen substance or behavior, whether it is alcohol, drugs, gambling, food, or sex, the more *out of control* her life *really* becomes. This is the ultimate paradox. But until she gets help the only answer she knows to feeling more out of control is to use her substance or behavior of choice *again,* resulting in a life that continues to spiral even further out of control. Feelings of shame and panic are pervasive, and dealt with by the use of rationalization, denial, and more using. Unfortunately, in almost every case where a child is involved, the child takes this emotional roller coaster ride *with* his parent. The parent's reality becomes the child's reality—an out-of-control existence living crisis to crisis, with disaster around every corner. The addictive parent usually does not perceive the reality of how her addiction is affecting her child. This is a primary misperception of addicted parents, caused by the denial and clouded thinking of the addiction which allows the parent to continue using.

Another paradoxical method of maintaining an illusion of control for some parents is through some sort of self-abuse or self-sabotage. This can actually create an illusion of control. The logic is, *if I am hurting myself in some way, or keeping myself down, then at least I am in control of that.* In other words, the parent who harms herself feels consciously or unconsciously that she is beating anyone else to the punch. The belief is, *if I keep myself down, I don't have to worry about getting my hopes up for feeling good about myself, only to end up hurt and disappointed.*

Self-abuse can take many forms. Some adults simply play the critical-parent messages over and over in their heads, listening to a barrage of negative self-talk: *I'm so stupid, I'm ugly, I'll never succeed*, etc. Other adults actually physically harm themselves by cutting or burning themselves. Temporarily, it feels empowering because *I am in control of my own pain.* There is also some evidence that the endorphins released by the brain when our bodies become stressed or in pain can become another form of addiction.

Parents who harm themselves or use addictive substances or behaviors to find an illusory sense of control will obviously be at risk for experiencing extreme anxiety about the lack of control that accompanies the job of parenting. Due to the emotional roller coaster ride of addictions or self-harm, parents may have difficulty with the stresses that accompany their role such as crying babies, sick children, or behavioral problems. The intensity of the emotions related to the roller coaster ride naturally impairs a parent's ability to respond effectively with her child. As a result, she may feel even less control and consequently wind up turning once again to the illusory methods of gaining control upon which she depends.

15. DON'T TOUCH ME!

Parents of either sex who suffered sexual abuse will probably struggle with the hypervigilance caused by experiencing trauma. The parent who was sexually traumatized will often unconsciously avoid being vulnerable by remaining vigilant to any external cues that resemble any aspect of the traumatic experience. Because of this hypervigilance, parents who were sexually abused sometimes become anxious in response to their child's needs for physical closeness and touching.

To have a better understanding of how touch by a child could create anxiety in a parent who was sexually abused, it is helpful to understand that trauma memories are actually stored and retrieved differently in the brain than other memories. Bessel van der Kolk, M.D., a renowned trauma researcher, explained in a recent lecture that when trauma memories are recalled, the right side of the brain and the limbic area near the brain's base become activated. These are the areas of the brain where emotions are located. During recall of trauma memories the left side of the brain, which is the analytical, reasoning part of the brain, becomes deactivated. Van der Kolk presented slides of PET (positron emission tomography) scans of an adult brain during recall of a traumatic event. It was evident in each slide that the right side of the brain was lit up with activity, while the left side of the brain appeared completely dark. One of the biggest problems for trauma survivors is that anything that in *any way* reminds the individual—consciously or unconsciously—of the past trauma can cause this automatic activation of the emotional centers of the brain. Without access to the analytical side of the brain the trauma survivor is helpless to reason her way through the experience. In other words, a harmless event that merely *resembles* the trauma can trigger an emotional reaction because the individual loses touch with the logical part of her brain that knows there is no danger.[5]

Because of this hypervigilance, it is not unusual for a parent who was sexually abused to respond to her child's attachment needs with anxiety and confusion. Melissa, who tells her story in Chapter Sixteen, was sexually abused by her mother as a child. Melissa found she was able to cuddle and show affection to her three sons, but from infancy she had struggled with the feeling that there was something unsafe about cuddling her daughter. Sometimes her little daughter's hugs triggered "flashbacks" of the abuse. Melissa described feelings of extreme anger, shame, and fear—all triggered by the innocent, loving touch of her daughter. Intellectually, Melissa knew there was nothing wrong with her daughter's touch, but emotionally she was stuck in the feelings of her past trauma. Melissa's daughter, as a result, became more and more insecure in her relationship with her mother. Melissa was helpless to do anything about it until she accomplished the difficult work of resolving her own past trauma which allowed her to perceive her daughter's touch accurately.

The parent with a history of sexual abuse may also be uncomfortable with any expression of sexuality in her child. Most young children explore and touch their bodies, discovering sensations that feel good. It's common for very young same-age children to playfully explore one another's bodies out of curiosity as well. Parents who were sexually abused often *perceive* these kinds of behaviors in a child as reflections of what they believe to be their own shameful sexuality, or as evidence that their child has inherited a perversion of some kind from the parent's abuser. When this happens, the child is at risk for picking up the parent's feelings of shame about his or her sexuality.

16. CHILD AS SAVIOR

Many parental misperceptions are related to unrealistic expectations held by the parent. Often, as parents, we develop an image of "the perfect baby" before the baby is born. Bertrand Cramer, M.D., writes, "The real baby will never correspond to the imaginary baby. A gap opens up as soon as the cord is cut."[6] Unrealistic expectations can set a child up for certain failure, and can set a parent up for disappointment in the very "real" baby or child she has. Sometimes when a marriage is not going well, it can be tempting for a couple to imagine a perfect baby who will bring such joy to them that it will pull them together and solidify their relationship. The idea may sound pretty good in theory, but the expectations for the child are unrealistic and unfair. It is a sure-fire setup for failure in the first major job of the child's whole life. He naturally turns out to be a normal child, not a savior, bringing his parents not only the joy of new parenthood but the stresses as well—cranky and sleepless nights, illnesses, and messy diapers. Few marriages are saved by children. When the marriage falters despite the new child, one or both parents are at risk for perceiving the child as a disappointment because he was not the savior he was supposed to be. The child in this situation won't understand why, but he may well sense he is somehow not good enough.

A child is also set up to fail when a parent perceives that her child will somehow make her whole or make her a more worthwhile person. Mothers and fathers sometimes fantasize about the perfect child who will have the great looks they don't have or who will have superintelligence or superior athletic abilities. As her child is held in high esteem by others, her own worth will rise due to having produced this perfect child. The child is set up for certain failure, for if he is at all a typical child he will be gifted at some things and not so gifted at other things. He will usually be healthy, but sometimes cranky or sick, and well behaved sometimes, but not always. This parent is at risk for overreacting in disappointment when her child does not meet her expectations. The parent who imagines a perfect child who will make her worthwhile will likely perceive her imperfect child as living proof that she is not worthwhile after all. Her infant's cries may be perceived as evidence of her inadequacy as a mother. The toddler's misbehavior may be perceived as proof that she is in fact a parental failure. Her child is at high risk for feeling like a failure to his parent in response.

Anytime we perceive our children as responsible somehow for our well-being we are misperceiving them. When we are stressed or depressed and either looking to our children to make us feel better or blaming them for the way we feel we are putting an unfair burden on their shoulders. Even parents who were raised in nurturing environments may, due to human nature, tend to look to anyone available to either help them feel better or to blame when feeling overly stressed. For many parents this feels normal, however, because they felt responsible for *their* parents' well-being when *they* were children. Their parents may have had similar roles as they grew up. This misperception, like most misperceptions, is often passed down generationally right along with grandma's sugar cookie recipe.

17. FOURTEEN COMMON PARENTAL MISPERCEPTIONS:

The following list summarizes 14 common parental misperceptions:

1. *My child is invading me.* If, as a child, my needs for closeness were not adequately met, I may have coped by turning off my needs for closeness. I may have learned to maintain a certain distance from others to protect myself from feelings of rejection. As a result, I may perceive my child's needs for closeness as an invasion of my personal space. Closeness with my child may trigger feelings of discomfort or anxiety.

2. *My child is too needy.* I perceive my child's needs for attention and affection as shameful, babyish, or as motivated by the need to control me. I may fear that if I am too affectionate with my child I will spoil him or cause him to become babyish. I fail to recognize the universal need all children have to receive loving attention and affection from their parents at all ages and stages of their growing-up years.

3. *My child doesn't love me enough.* I tend to interpret my child's willfulness, tantrums, or tears as evidence that he doesn't care about me. I tend to perceive normal child behaviors as attempts to hurt me, humiliate me, or put me down. As a result, I may either overreact with anger or give him things to make him love me more.

4. *My child is abusive.* I perceive some of my child's behaviors or physical characteristics as evidence that he has inherited traits from someone who was hurtful to me such as a parent or spouse. This perceived inherent "badness" in my child triggers overwhelming feelings of anxiety or anger in me, preventing me from being able to respond to my child in a rational way.

5. *My child is shameful.* I perceive either physical or behavioral characteristics in my child that I was once made to feel ashamed of in myself. As a result, I tend to feel ashamed of these characteristics in my child and I may find myself shaming my child the same way I was shamed.

6. *My child doesn't have real feelings.* I need to feel powerful and in control in order to avoid feeling vulnerable in this world. I have cut off my own vulnerable feelings from childhood in order to feel safe and in control. I cannot risk empathizing with my child's feelings, as that would tap into feelings of my own.

7. *I am not safe with my child.* I need to feel in control at all times, or I feel unsafe. My child is not always in my control, and as a result I often feel unsafe with my child.

8. *My child is not safe.* I was not safe as a child. I never knew when something bad was going to happen. Even though things are different for my child, I fear that something bad will happen to him too. I have a hard time believing he is really safe. I often feel anxious and afraid.

9. *The parent should have absolute authority over the child.* I was raised in a family where the important issue was who had the power, and the power rested with the adults. As a result, I believe that it is my turn to have the power now, and my child should have none of it.

10. *My child is not affected by my addictions.* I have formed an addictive relationship with either a substance, a behavior, or another person and my relationship with my child has taken a backseat. My child is affected by my highs and lows as I ride the addictive roller coaster, but my thinking is clouded by the denial of addiction and therefore I easily misperceive the reality of how the situation is affecting him.

11. *Closeness with my child is shameful and unsafe.* I was sexually abused as a child either covertly or overtly, and I am troubled by the misperception that affectionate touch with my child is dirty or shameful. Touch or closeness may even make me feel I am somehow not safe with my child.

12. *Our child will fix our marriage.* I perceive my child as a savior. I believe he will bring so much joy and happiness that my marriage will be saved by his presence. When the marriage is not saved, I may feel resentful toward my child for failing me.

13. *My child will make me a worthwhile person.* I tend to perceive others' good opinions of my child as vital to my worthiness as a person. I therefore often have unrealistic expectations of my child which set him up for failure. And because my child's achievements make me feel worthwhile, my child's imperfections tend to make me feel worthless.

14. *My child will make me feel better.* When I am stressed or distressed I tend to perceive my child as responsible for my emotional well-being, instead of the other way around. I may turn to him to make me feel better, or

blame him for the way I feel. I may perceive this to be natural because of feelings of responsibility I had for my parents' well-being, or I may fall into this misperception only at times of extreme stress.

18. THE CASE OF THE UNATTACHED CHILD

If you are the parent of an unattached child at least three of the misperceptions in the list may not apply until your child's defensive walls have been broken through. *My child is abusive* may actually be a true statement in the case of an unattached child. *My child doesn't love me enough* may be true in the sense that your child may be incapable of feeling genuine love for you as yet. *My child doesn't have real feelings* may be the case for the unattached child, as his more vulnerable feelings may be shut down and hidden behind protective walls of rage. If you are parenting a child with severe attachment problems, addressing your own issues and taking care of yourself both physically and emotionally is vital to maintaining the objective approach that is most effective with this challenging problem. More about this issue can be found in Part Three.

19. IN CONCLUSION: THE GHOSTS EXPOSED

Luckily, as you have most likely discovered by now, the ghosts that may have crept into your relationship with your child no longer have to be invisible. The ghosts of the past enter our present-day families by way of misperceptions and triggered emotions. Misperceptions may be created by negative core beliefs about self-worth, safety, or trust. They may be the result of the hurt feelings of the inner child, the negative messages of a powerful inner critic, or the hypervigilance caused by past trauma. As a result of these misperceptions our emotional responses can become out of proportion to the situation, interfering with our effectiveness as parents and creating obstacles in the formation of secure attachments with our children. As you solve the mystery of your own ghosts and expose them for who or what they are, you take an important step in eradicating them from your family.

Part One provided the foundation: a better *understanding* of your "broken instincts." In Part Two you will learn what you can do to begin healing from the effects of the past and *mending* your broken instincts.

Part Two

The Second Key

Mending Your Broken Instincts

Now that you have an understanding of attachment and how your earlier experiences may be influencing your responses as a parent you are ready to begin Part Two. In this part you will begin actually mending your broken instincts. You will learn to change your parental misperceptions and better manage your emotions. You will begin to heal your inner child and strengthen your internal nurturing parent through imagery. You will be guided in making healthy connections with others and a new life story.

Chapter Six

"I Can See More Clearly Now"

Challenging Your Misperceptions

The second important method of changing parental misperceptions is to tackle them directly. The first step is to be able to recognize them! Initially, you will catch yourself only *after* your misperceptions have created problems. The situation may be all over and done with before you think, "Hey, I was more upset than that situation warranted. I was perceiving my child as abusive instead of recognizing normal kid misbehavior!" As you continue to observe and identify your perceptions, however, it will begin to get easier to catch them *as* you respond to your child or, better yet, *before* you respond to your child!

Consciously changing one's thoughts to change the resulting feelings and behaviors is the approach taken by cognitive therapists such as Albert Ellis, psychologist and founder of the Institute for Advanced Study in Rational Psychotherapy, who advocates changing irrational thoughts in his book, *A New Guide to Rational Living.*[1] Dr. Aaron Beck, President of the Beck Institute and author of *Cognitive Therapy and the Emotional Disorders,* developed techniques to change errors in thinking.[2] Dr. David Burns, psychiatrist and teacher at the University of Pennsylvania, wrote about changing automatic thought distortions in a popular guide called *Feeling Good: The New Mood Therapy.*[3] I have used a cognitive type of approach in designing the following two exercises specifically to help parents catch and directly challenge their parental misperceptions. The exercises are designed to help you catch more easily your parental misperceptions so that you can begin to get a clearer view of the *actual* situation at hand—before you respond to your child! Many parents find this direct approach to catching and changing misperceptions to be extremely helpful in the day-to-day interactions with their children. With practice and more accurate perceptions, you will become more attuned to what your child is really feeling or needing and you will be able to respond much more effectively as a result.

As you work the following exercises, practice observing yourself objectively and nonjudgmentally. Remember, you are working hard because you have a desire to grow and improve yourself as a parent, and you are just beginning. Don't put yourself down because you're not there yet. Like changing any habit, changing your patterns of thinking will take time!

1. CATCHING AND CHALLENGING YOUR MISPERCEPTIONS

The first two exercises are designed to challenge directly your parental misperceptions.

Exercise: Each time you are uncomfortable with a response you have had in an interaction with your child, open your notebook. Down the left side of the page write the following:

Situation:

Automatic Reactions:

Misperceptions:

Rational Responses:

Then go back and briefly note the "Situation" that preceded your reactions. After "Automatic Reactions," list your feelings and behaviors. To list possible "Misperceptions," refer to your list of the "Fourteen Most Common Parental Misperceptions." Finally, write down as many "Rational Responses" to your misperceptions as you can think of. Try imagining what your therapist or a trusted friend might say. You may want to ask your therapist to help you in writing some of your rational responses. Sometimes it's difficult to see the forest for the trees, and he or she may be able to help you spot misperceptions that you can't see.

Following are three examples of this exercise:

Maggie wrote the following in her notebook after receiving a phone call from four year old Danny's nursery school teacher:

Situation: Mrs. Brown called to tell me that Danny threw a rock at another child today.

Automatic Reactions: Embarrassment, humiliation. I feel like screaming at Danny when he gets home.

Misperceptions: "My child will make me a worthwhile person," because when Danny misbehaves like this I feel worthless—like everyone knows what a bad parent I am!

Rational Responses: I am not worthless because Danny misbehaved. It was Danny's choice to throw the rock, not mine. Mrs. Brown is not angry with me, she is unhappy with Danny's behavior. She has had to call parents before, and she will again. That's her job. We can expect things like this to happen when we raise kids. I need to talk to Danny calmly today. This will set a good example for how to talk about problems instead of yelling or hitting.

Frank wrote this entry in his notebook after his teenage stepdaughter, Lisa, commented that she wanted to spend Christmas at her "real" dad's house.

Situation: Lisa wants to spend Christmas at Harold's house.

Automatic Reactions: After all I've done for her all these years it makes me mad that she doesn't want to spend Christmas with her mother and I! We've always had a nice celebration here. Harold has never gone out of his way to do anything for her! Why should he get to spend the holiday with her? I feel hurt and used. I asked her why she would want to spend Christmas at that cheapskate's house.

Misperceptions: "My child does not love me enough." It DOES seem to me that she must not care about me very much if she can hurt me this way, and that if she loved me she would want to be with me!

Rational Responses: O.K., her father doesn't do anything for her—but he IS still her father, so of course she wants a relationship with him, and of course she *wants to spend time with him. It doesn't mean she doesn't care about me. She knows she can always count on our relationship. And she can always count on her relationship with her mother. She has to work harder to keep a relationship going with her dad. It's really not fair of me to make her feel guilty. She shouldn't feel she has to choose one of us over the other. I need to tell her that it's O.K.*

Bridgett, who had survived two years of childhood sexual abuse by an uncle, wrote this entry after her four-year-old twin boys began playfully grabbing at one another's penises in the tub.

Situation: *The boys were grabbing for one another's private parts this morning.*

Automatic Reactions: *I wanted to scream at them and hit them. I thought I would explode!*

Misperceptions: *"My child is abusive," and "My child is shameful." I felt like the boys were being perpetrators to each other—like they were acting like Uncle Don. And at the same time, I have this feeling that they have MY badness inside them. I'm so ashamed of my own sexuality—I don't want them to have any sexuality at all!*

Rational Responses: *According to my therapist, it's normal for little kids to play around like that. They were just acting like normal kids. They don't have anybody's "badness" inside of them. I need to talk to them matter-of-factly about it, and just let them know it's not O.K. to touch other people's private parts—not because private parts are bad, but because our private parts are SPECIAL.*

2. REMINDER CARDS

For those misperceptions that seem to cause you the most problems, a regular reminder of the more rational viewpoint can help keep you from falling into the misperceptions trap.

Exercise: On small note cards, list the parental misperceptions that interfere with your parenting most often, and write down a rational response to each misperception. Carry the cards with you in your purse or wallet and read them through each day.

Figure 1 gives examples of reminder cards made by Pam, a mother of two. Pam had to shut down her needs for closeness and affection as a child, and she wanted to work on perceiving her children's needs for affection and attention more accurately. She also identified that she tended to look to her children to make her feel better, especially when she was stressed.

Figure 2 gives examples of cards Jim carries in his billfold. Jim experienced feelings of shame and powerlessness as a child that distorted his perceptions and interfered with his relationships with his children.

Figure 3 shows cards carried by Gloria. Gloria had trouble setting limits with her son, Danny. Her inner child responded to Danny as if he were her abusive father instead of a normal, active, mischievous little boy.

My child is invading me:
Shannon and Ben are innocent children who need touch and affection every day. Their needs for closeness are normal and healthy, and part of the mother-child bond. My touch nurtures their souls and their touch is safe and loving.

My child is too needy:
Shannon and Ben need to see themselves reflected in my eyes in order to become whole and feel worthwhile. I am the center of their universe right now. There is no one more important to them than me. They need my attention and affection like they need air to breathe.

My child will make me feel better:
It is my job to take care of myself emotionally and to get my needs met through my relationships with other adults and my Higher Power. It is my job to nurture Shannon and Ben emotionally. It is not their job to take care of *my* feelings or *my* stress. I need to ask myself, have I done anything for myself today to replenish my energy level?

My child will make me a worthwhile person:
I know what it is like to have parents who demand that you be perfect in every way so they can feel better about themselves. I don't want to put those kinds of expectations on Shannon and Ben. I don't want them to be afraid to try different things for fear that they might not be good enough. My self-worth is not dependent on the achievements of my children. I can take responsibility for taking care of my self-esteem in other ways.

Figure 1. Pam's reminder cards.

The parent should have absolute authority over the child:
My dad needed to feel in control at all times and left me feeling worthless, powerless, and resentful. I also wound up with an excessive need to be in control myself. I will have a stronger relationship with my kids and will help them feel better about themselves as I learn to listen to what they have to say and show them that their feelings and opinions do count.

My child is shameful:
I was always told I was lazy, stupid, and fat, and so deep down inside I fear my own kids have inherited some kind of defectiveness from me. But I wasn't defective and neither are they. In fact, my kids are very special and unique and they need to hear that from me so they can grow up feeling good about themselves.

Figure 2. Jim's reminder cards.

My child is abusive:
I have been responding to Danny as if he could hurt me—and yet he's only four years old! I need to remember I am an adult. Danny is a normal, active, spirited child. He is not my father. He will never be my father. I can give him both the limits and the love that he needs.

My child does not love me enough:
All children have tantrums, get angry with their parents, and try to manipulate to get their way. It has nothing to do with not loving their parents. Danny needs me to be firm and set limits for him as he goes through these normal stages of development.

I am not safe with my child:
I am a strong and competent adult and Danny is only a child. Even though the child part of me may feel anxious, I can stay adult and parent Danny effectively.

Figure 3. Gloria's reminder cards.

3. CHALLENGING YOUR MISPERCEPTIONS
RELATED TO SHAME

Exercise: a. Finish the sentence, identifying any characteristics you were shamed for as a child and list them in your notebook.

I was told I was ——.

   too weak
   too fat
   too thin
   too small
   too slow
   selfish
   conceited
   a crybaby
   not smart enough
   not good-looking enough
   bad
   other _ _ _

b. Write down any specific memories you have of being shamed as a child for any of these characteristics.

   As a parent you may be at risk for misperceiving these characteristics in your own child, thus triggering feelings you may have toward your own inner child.

c. List any of the above characteristics for which you remember feeling shame toward your child.

d. Write down any memories you have of expressing shame toward your child for any of these same characteristics.

e. Continue noting any shame responses you have with your child on an ongoing basis, and write your feelings down in your notebook.

   If you continue these exercises on an ongoing basis, your awareness and insight will steadily improve. As you make the unconscious conscious, you will gain more and more control over the influences of the ghosts of your past. These unconscious forces will have much less influence in your relationship with your child as you identify the misperceptions and tackle them head on.

As you gain power over these troublesome misperceptions you will begin to find greater enjoyment in your relationship with your child because you will begin to view situations that arise from a different perspective. You may find yourself seeing things a little more objectively as you take your child's behaviors less personally. You may even find yourself chuckling at times over situations that used to upset you! You will very definitely find yourself more capable of thinking through your responses and acting in a more effective manner with your child.

Again, be patient with yourself. Old habits are hard to break. Change takes time and plenty of concerted effort. Remember, as long as you keep trying you will keep making progress.

And don't stop here! The next chapter deals with another port of entry for those troublesome ghosts—*emotions!* Although changing your misperceptions will alleviate many unnecessary overreactions with your children, emotions are part of all of our lives and all of our relationships every day. Enjoyable emotions and painful emotions are all part of being human. Some of our emotional responses with our children are tied to our misperceptions, some emotional responses are tied to feeling memories, and other emotional responses are tied to the ordinary demands of day-to-day living and parenting as we cope with stress and frustration. The next chapter will be a very important component of your personal recovery program.

Chapter Seven

Riding the Stormy Sea

Learning to Manage Your Tough Emotions

Emotions make us human and can give us the ability to enjoy life; yet emotions can be incredibly uncomfortable. A high level of emotions can cause us to do things we would normally never do. Intense emotions have incited normally rational people to kill or maim themselves or others, abuse their children, run away, take drugs, and get drunk. Intense emotions can cause any one of us to to say things we don't mean, scream and yell, make poor decisions, forget things, forget where we are going, and crash our cars. Wow!

Bessel van der Kolk, an internationally renowned trauma researcher, in a recent lecture explained how children who grow up in families where they are given adequate emotional nurturing and support are able to internalize skills they can use to manage their emotions. As a result, when they are adults they tend to respond to distress with what he refers to as "problem-focused coping." Problem-focused coping simply means responding to the situation at hand in a way that helps to solve the problem that is causing the distress. Such individuals have the ability to use problem-focused coping because they have the ability to manage their feelings.

Van der Kolk went on to describe how children growing up in environments that do not provide adequate emotional nurturing lack adequate resources for coping with their emotions. Instead of using problem-focused coping, the only means they have for getting through distressful situations is by using what van der Kolk calls "emotion-focused coping."

This means that all of the child's energy is focused on *getting rid of the emotion* through any means possible. If emotion-focused coping was the primary method of handling feelings in childhood, the individual will likely continue this method of coping into adulthood, because he or she knows no other way to handle distress. Adults who use emotion-focused coping frequently use addictive chemicals or behaviors to escape from overwhelming emotions.[1]

Parents who just happen to be lucky enough to grow up in environments that provided reassurance and appropriate skills for managing feelings naturally have more of an instinctive ability to provide the secure holding environment their children need to learn to soothe, comfort, and cope. However, no matter how secure their upbringing, everyone gets overwhelmed at times and can benefit from additional skills to cope with the array of emotions that accompany ordinary living.

1. THE ZEN APPROACH

Marsha Linehan, a psychologist at the University of Washington, for years researched how to best help people who chronically feel miserable, empty, and worthless, and who intermittently become so overwhelmed by their emotions that they attempt to either kill or injure themselves. This condition is called "borderline personality disorder."

As she worked closely with people who had severe difficulty managing their emotions, Linehan came to recognize that an "invalidating environment" in childhood is a major factor leading to severe coping problems in adulthood. An invalidating environment discounts a child's feelings and fails to supply adequate reassurance and comforting. Linehan explains that the invalidating environment "generally emphasizes controlling emotional expressiveness, especially the expression of negative affect."[2] For example, if a child appears to be sad, instead of inquiring about the child's feelings and offering comfort, an invalidating parent might respond, "Stop frowning and put a smile on your face. You have nothing to feel sad about!"

Because adults who grew up in invalidating environments did not have the opportunity to learn skills to manage their emotions through their early experiences, Linehan recognized that she needed to find a way to help people compensate for their lack of skills. Linehan thought about where she might go for help in identifying skills that could aid people in learning to manage their emotions and she came up with a surprising idea. Instead of studying Western psychological theories, Linehan went to live and study with a Zen master. Her study of Zen became a very important component of the treatment program Linehan developed. Despite the vast difference between Western thought and the philosophy of Zen, Linehan was able to break down the Eastern philosophy into steps or skills. In addition, Linehan developed a set of skills to cope short term with peaks of severe stress or overwhelming emotions. She calls her therapy program Dialectical Behavioral Therapy (DBT). The skills component of the program is in a workbook format and is intended to be used with a therapist. The DBT skills can be practiced by anyone on a daily basis to help stay more centered and serene. Linehan's approach to emotions is helpful not only for suicidal individuals or people with the borderline diagnosis, but for *any* individual trying to cope with the normal stresses and strains of living. I have found the skills to be very helpful personally whether I am coping with ordinary day-to-day stress or dealing with one of life's major curveballs. The skills are the best I have found for helping adults learn to manage emotions and can help *any* parent become more capable of providing a secure holding environment, even when life becomes rocky! For this reason I am indebted to the work that Marsha Linehan has done in the area of emotion management, as I have adapted her skills for mindfulness, emotion regulation, and distress tolerance throughout this chapter.[3]

1.1. The States of Mind

Figure 1 is Marsha Linehan's model of the three states of mind: emotional mind, reasonable mind, and wise mind. Notice how wise mind overlaps both emotional mind and reasonable mind.[4]

1.1.1. "Emotional Mind"[5] Remember a time when you were so emotional that you were unable to think rationally. In this state of mind, called "emotional mind," thoughts, perceptions, and actions are dictated by emotions. Emotional mind can be a wonderful place to be when the overwhelming feelings are of love or passion for a mate, a child, a piece of beautiful music, a gorgeous sunset, or a wonderful idea. But emotional mind can be a precarious place to be when you are overwhelmed with feelings of despair, frustration, anxiety, or anger. When overwhelmed and without skills to manage intense feelings, emotion-focused coping may be

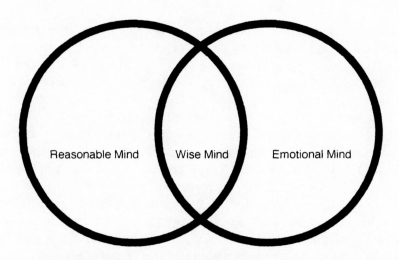

Figure 1. Marsha Linehan's model of the states of mind. From *Skills Training Manual for Treating Borderline Personality Disorder* by Marsha Linehan. © 1993 by The Guilford Press. Reprinted with permission of the publisher.

employed by either blocking feelings and escaping to reasonable mind, or finding a "high" like alcohol, drugs, or spending to change the mood as quickly as possible. When emotional mind is dominant, acting impulsively out of intense emotions is likely. Many harmful and even tragic mistakes have been made in emotional mind. There is surely no one on earth who has not said or done something impulsively (and deeply regretted it later) while in the state of emotional mind. Every parent at one time or another has responded to his child irrationally when emotional mind was in control. Emotional mind can be both the result of parental misperceptions and the cause. When we are overwhelmed by the hurt feelings of our inner child, emotional mind rules. When we feel defeated by an onslaught of negative messages from an "inner critic," emotional mind is in control. We are all more vulnerable to emotional mind when financial problems, job problems, relationship problems, or lack of respite are creating overwhelming stress in our lives.

1.1.2. "Reasonable Mind"[6] "Reasonable mind" is the state of mind you are in when you are disconnected from your feelings and functioning solely out of logic and rational thought. Disconnecting from emotions can be very helpful to balance a checkbook, make a grocery list, study for an exam, or complete a task at work. On the other hand, you may discover that you habitually disconnect from your emotions and move into reasonable mind in situations when it would be appropriate to have feelings because it is the best way you know how to cope. There are several problems with this type of "emotion-focused coping," however. For instance, blocking feelings or repressing them interferes with the ability to empathize with children and others, and hinders the capacity to form emotional bonds. A lack of sensitivity in responding to the feelings and needs of others is more likely if you tend to cope by moving into reasonable mind. Reasonable mind can leave you more vulnerable to the misperception, *My child doesn't have real feelings,* because you aren't in touch with your own. Additionally, emotions are an important source of information when thinking about a problem and deciding what to do. Habitually remaining in reasonable mind deprives you of the intuitive part of yourself as you make decisions and solve problems. The habit of mentally disconnecting from feelings instead of expressing and working through them can also leave your body holding the emotional baggage. You may wind up paying a price physically with headaches, ulcers, or other stress-related illnesses.

1.1.3. "Wise Mind"[7]   Remember a time when you felt centered and serene and you were able to calmly reflect on a situation, think about your feelings, and act effectively. Wise mind is that wonderful state of mind when reasonable mind and emotional mind are integrated. It is much easier to get in touch with both reasonable mind and emotional mind when you can find a calm place inside from where you can observe your feelings objectively, even while you are experiencing them. This makes it possible to draw upon both rational thought and emotions in deciding what to do in any situation. In wise mind you are intuitive, clear-headed, and less vulnerable to misperceptions or impulsive actions. In wise mind, you have the ability to use problem-focused coping, allowing your emotions to help you understand the problem while your reasonable mind thinks about what needs to be done.

Figure 2 illustrates a Zen analogy for wise mind: a still pool of clear water. The surface of the calm, clear water reflects the tree at the water's edge with the clarity of a smooth mirror. In the same way, when you find that centered place inside called wise mind, you can reflect on the situation around you with intuition, accurate perceptions, and clear thinking. By contrast, throw a stone into the middle of a pool and notice how distorted the reflection of the surroundings becomes on the surface of the rip-

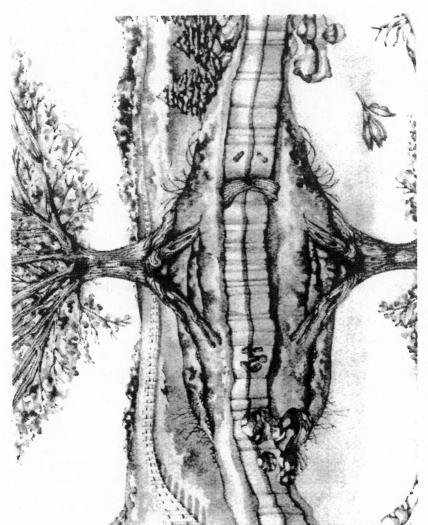

Figure 2. The wise mind: the still pool of water clearly reflecting its surroundings.

pling water. In emotional mind, perceptions become distorted like the reflections on the surface of the rippling pool.

1.2. "Mindfulness"[8]

By practicing the DBT Zen skills to achieve mindfulness, any individual can calm the waters and stay more in wise mind. Mindfulness is a conscious, focused awareness. To practice mindfulness, practice focusing your attention on and observing whatever you are experiencing at any particular moment in time. Become conscious. Practice observing. Observe what you are noticing through your senses. Notice the colors and images around you. Notice what you can hear and smell. Observe the taste of your food or drink. Notice what you can touch and feel.

Stop occasionally and tune in to your breathing. Notice your breath moving in and out. Observing your breathing is very centering. Breathe all the way into your abdomen. Inhale and exhale, following your breath in and out. Do this several times a day.

Tune in to your emotions. Imagine yourself standing outside looking inward, objectively observing your internal experience. Put words to your emotions if you can. Acknowledge your emotions without judgment. Feelings are not good or bad, right or wrong—they just are. Although one can choose to *act* on a feeling in a manner that might be harmful, no feeling has ever actually harmed anyone. Practice observing your thoughts as well. Just notice the thoughts and the feelings nonjudgmentally. Practice accepting all thoughts and feelings equally. Don't try to repress or avoid them. Linehan states, "Accept each moment, each event, as a blanket spread out on the lawn accepts both the rain and the sun, each leaf that falls upon it."[9]

Try applying mindfulness to actions as well. Practice becoming mindful of whatever activity you might be participating in at the moment. Let go of self-conciousness, whether it makes you feel grandiose or self-critical. Focus your attention instead on the activity. If you are washing dishes, focus solely on washing dishes. If you are in a conversation, focus only on the conversation. If you are dancing, playing a sport, or working, participate mindfully in the activity without self-consciousness. Instead of judging your actions or the actions of others as good or bad, try thinking only in terms of whether behavior is helpful or unhelpful, effective or ineffective. As a parent, instead of judging your responses as good or bad, think in terms of increasing those responses that are effective and eliminating responses that are ineffective with your child.

In summary, the basic strategies for developing Zen mindfulness in your daily life are as follows:

1. Focus your attention on the present moment and observe whatever you are experiencing.
2. Let go of self-consciousness (concern for how others perceive you.)
3. Observe and put words to your feelings and thoughts, and to your experiencing of sight, smell, sound, touch, or taste.
4. Quiet your mind and notice your breathing several times a day.
5. Practice the art of being nonjudgmental.

1.3. Becoming Mindful of Negative Emotions

When experiencing negative emotions Linehan's Zen mindfulness skills will help you ride out the experience without allowing emotion mind to rule. In Linehan's words, "By exposing yourself to emotions, but not necessarily acting on them, you will find that they are not so catastrophic."[10] As you become more at home with even your uncomfortable or painful emotions, you will gradually become more capable of problem-focused coping instead of focusing on escaping from the emotions.

The following five steps for becoming mindful of negative emotions are adapted from the DBT program.[11] The first step is identifying and acknowledging the negative emotion. Step back from it and observe it without reacting to it. Ask yourself, "What is this emotion?" Describe it with words.

Looking over a basic list of negative feeling words may help:

sadness	fear	shame	despair	anxiety
grief	hurt	resentment	guilt	loneliness
devastation	rage	annoyance	frustration	rejection
anger	inadequacy	disgust	uncertainty	abandonment
confusion	loss	boredom	worthlessness	hopelessness

You may wish to copy these words down on the back page of your notebook for easy reference.

Second, remove any judgment about your emotion. It is common for all of us to judge our negative emotions with such thoughts as, *I shouldn't feel this way, I'm weak for feeling this way,* or *I'm stupid for feeling this way.* Rebut such thoughts by reminding yourself that a feeling is not good or bad, right or wrong. The feeling itself won't harm you or anyone else.

Third, remind yourself that you are not your emotion. Your emotion is not you, and it won't be around forever. You are experiencing a feeling just for *now.* Remember a time when you did not have this feeling. Remember that there will be many more times when you do not have this feeling.

Fourth, remind yourself that you do not have to act on your emotion. Actions taken in the height of negative emotions are usually dictated by emotion mind, and are often harmful, not helpful. You are not your emotion. It is temporary. If there is some kind of action that needs to be taken and it cannot wait, ask yourself what wise mind would do.

Fifth, practice being willing to experience your emotion. Ride it out like you would a raft during a storm at sea. You can ride it out, knowing that no matter how rough it is, the waters will calm down in time. Observe how the emotion ebbs and flows. It's fluid, not static, even when the emotions are at their peak intensity.

In summary, the basic steps to practice for using Zen mindfulness to manage negative emotions are as follows:

1. Acknowledge and describe your emotion.
2. Try to remove any judgment of your emotion.
3. Remind yourself that your emotion is temporary.
4. Remind yourself that you do not have to act on your emotion.
5. Practice riding the emotion out the way you might ride out rough waves in a storm.

1.4. Becoming Mindful of Positive Emotions

Practice staying "mindful of positive events that occur."[12] So often we notice all our negative experiences and emotions and yet fail to notice the pleasurable ones. We dismiss from consciousness the people who care about us, the accomplishments, and the positive opportunities that come our way. You will increase your positive emotions by focusing your attention on each pleasurable experience that comes along. Make a list of the things in your life for which you are grateful. Take note of each small step you take toward a goal. Acknowledge your feelings of love, caring, or appreciation toward the children and the adults in your life. Take time out to enjoy the pleasure of a sunset, flower, or other experience of natural beauty. Notice and enjoy watching your growing child accomplish each new feat. Don't allow yourself to miss out on the pleasurable feelings of life by letting those experiences pass unnoticed.

To help you identify your positive feelings you can refer to this list of basic positive feeling words:

happiness	love	pleasure	calm
fondnesss	satisfaction	relaxation	enjoyment
pride	peace	curiosity	caring
comfort	admiration	joy	accomplishment
	interest		liking

Copy the words onto the back page of your notebook for easy reference.

If your life is truly lacking in pleasurable experiences, mindfully and consciously create a life that is more enjoyable. Make it a point each day to do something for yourself. If you don't have time, make time, even if it is just 15 minutes a day. Find a passion, whether it is reading, gardening, sewing, hiking, exercising, socializing, or something else that draws you. Create some pleasurable experiences that involve the whole family such as picnicking, fishing, camping, going to the zoo, or other activities offered in the community.

2. COPING WHEN THE SEA BECOMES TOO ROUGH TO RIDE

In the past, when sailors were at sea and hit a raging storm that was too rough to ride out safely, they would tie themselves to the mast of the boat to keep from being thrown overboard. When stress gets too high, it can be very difficult to stay on board the boat and not get sucked into the churning sea of emotional mind. Additional healthy strategies to self-soothe can help ensure that you keep afloat in a crisis situation. Even adults who grew up in healthy homes can easily get knocked overboard without the right skills during times of extreme stress. A time of crisis can be created by any number of situations:

You may have too many tasks to accomplish in too little time.

Past overwhelming feelings may have been triggered by something in the present.

A relationship may be ending or going through a rocky time.

Your child may be going through an especially difficult phase.

You may have suffered some recent losses.

You may be worried about finances.

The following skills for self-calming are adapted from DBT.[13] If you were not able to learn methods for soothing, comforting, and reassuring yourself as you were growing up, it will be very important to consciously practice these skills on a regular basis even when you are not in crisis. The more adept you are at using these healthy coping skills when the sea is relatively calm, the easier it will be to put them in place when you are feeling overwhelmed.

2.1. Soothe Yourself with Your Senses[13]

Allow your five senses to be pleasure detectors for self-soothing. Stay aware of any opportunity for soothing yourself mindfully with any of your senses. Practice focusing your attention with mindfulness on a sense-based pleasure. If distracting thoughts or worries enter your mind, just notice them and then gently bring your attention back to the sense-based pleasure. Remind yourself, *All I have to do right this moment is enjoy this.*

Look for images you can absorb visually such as a pretty sky, a beautiful flower, an interesting work of art, or your favorite room in your house. Be mindfully observant of all the details, the colors, the shapes, and the designs.

Use your hearing and mindfully listen to a beautiful piece of music, a bird, or the leaves rustling in the wind. Consciously focus your attention and allow your mind to absorb the sounds.

Enjoy the fragrance of a candle, incense, or potpourri. Mindfully take delight in the scent of a flower, your favorite perfume, or the air following a rain.

Sit down at the table and relax as you enjoy your food slowly and with mindfulness, without the distraction of reading or watching T.V. Use your sense of taste and slowly savor each sip of tea, each bite of strawberry. How many times have you eaten a meal without really tasting it? If binge eating is a problem for you, staying mindful as you eat and savoring each bite slowly will be helpful for you.

Soothe yourself with your sense of touch as you soak in a hot tub, relax between clean sheets, or stroke your dog's fur. Revel in the comfort of your favorite chair, enjoy a hug, or receive a massage.

Soothing yourself through your senses when the going gets rough will help you stay afloat until the storm dies down. When you are not in crisis, practicing self-soothing with your senses is a healthy way to take care of yourself.

2.2. Words of Encouragement

Adults who grew up without hearing many words of encouragement generally have a difficult time giving themselves the encouraging words they need because they did not get a chance to internalize a nurturing voice. Because it may feel awkward and foreign to you, it will take practice. Again, the more you practice when your distress is low, the more natural it will feel to use the skill when your distress is high.

Linehan explains, "The idea is to talk to yourself as you would talk to someone you care about who is in a crisis. Or talk to yourself as you would like someone else to talk to you."[15] Practice encouraging self-talk such as: "I can handle this." "This too shall pass." "It will be O.K." "I'll be all right." "I can think about what to do." "I can let others help me with this." "I don't have to handle this alone." "Everything will work out eventually." "I can turn this over to God." "God will guide me." "All I have to do is take one step at a time." "All I have to do is what's in front of me at this very moment."

When you hear the negative messages of the inner critic, try to notice the critical thoughts without judging them and respond to them with rational, encouraging self-talk.

2.3. Prayer

Prayer as a way of coping is as old as civilization. Human beings of every ethnic background and religion have found prayer an important way to transcend our earthly problems. Through prayer any one of us can draw upon our faith for strength and guidance, and become more connected with a Higher Power. Prayer can bring inner calm when chaos reigns, and help us find our wise mind. The following prayer is called the Serenity Prayer, and it is a tradition in all Twelve Step programs. It is a very helpful prayer, as it helps us separate what we can control from what we cannot control. When we can let go of the things that are beyond our control and turn them over to a Higher Power, we can find our wise mind and change the things we can change with more effectiveness:

"God, grant me the serenity to accept the things I cannot change, the courage to change the things I can, and the wisdom to know the difference."

Following is another wonderful Twelve Step prayer, called the Third Step Prayer. It is a short prayer, and it is simple. But millions have found this prayer helpful for letting go of control and tuning into that centered, wise, spiritual place inside.

"God, please guide me in your will for my life and give me the strength to follow your will."

There are as many ways to pray as there are people. There is no way you can make a mistake! Many have found inner peace, strength, healing, acceptance, positive attitude, gratitude, and guidance through the power of prayer.

2.4. Activity

Remember the skill of mindfulness: a conscious focusing of one's attention on one's present experience. An important skill for self-calming when you are feeling overwhelmed is distracting yourself from your distress by mindfully becoming involved in an activity. By focusing on the activity you can give yourself a minivacation from your distress and free yourself from emotion mind. You may be able to come back to your problems later on with a rested mind, and perhaps a little bit different perspective on your situation.

There is an endless number of possible activities that can be helpful. Everyone is different, so develop your own list of activities that are helpful to you.

You may find that mowing the grass, pulling weeds, or cleaning the house distracts you from distressing emotions and gives you a sense of accomplishment at the same time. Riding your bike or jogging may improve the way you feel. Physical activities not only distract you from distress, but they also give you a sense of mastery, release physical tension from the body, and lessen depressive symptoms.

It is important also to have some comforting kinds of activities on your list. For example, you may find you can both distract and soothe yourself with a cup of tea and a mystery novel, a crossword puzzle, or a favorite magazine.

Other distracting activities can make you laugh, such as watching a sitcom or a funny movie, or reading a humorous book. Humor is a great coping skill and can often bring a new perspective to your situation.

Many people refocus their minds by immersing themselves in a creative endeavor, such as playing a musical instrument or singing in a chorus or choir. You may be able to express yourself through poetry, painting, or crafts. You may find a creative outlet in home decorating or landscaping. Tapping into your creative resources will help you get centered and find your wise mind.

It can sometimes be very difficult to refocus your mind when you are all alone. Isolation from other adults can allow emotion mind to go unchecked. Connections with supportive others can bring a reality check to the situation and put things back in perspective. Through activities that connect you with others you can distract yourself from your distress and gain strength from the connection. Phoning a friend, chatting with your neighbor, getting together with a friend for coffee, attending a regular support group, going to church, joining a committee, or going to see a counselor can help you get outside of yourself and find a fresh outlook on things.

2.5. Staying "One-Mindful"[16]

To practice one-mindfulness, try to narrow the focus of your attention to just *one thing* at a time. For example, if you are digging in the garden, remind yourself that all you have to do right now is dig in the garden. Focus on the action of digging. As distracting thoughts enter your mind, acknowledge your thoughts without judging them, and then bring your attention back to the digging. If you are taking a walk, focus one-mindfully on the sensation of walking, and on the sights, the smells, and the sounds. If you are in a conversation, focus your attention solely on the conversation. Practice one-mindfulness often. When your mind is cluttered and you are worried or distressed you will find there is great relief in centering your mind as you focus on just what is in front of you at that moment.

2.6. Meditation

Meditation is a very important part of the practice of Zen. Any form of meditation helps to calm, center, and focus the mind. Making meditation a daily ritual and a part of your regular routine will help you stay in touch with your wise mind. Some people like to meditate before getting out of bed each morning. Others meditate at night before going to bed, because it is also a nice way to fall asleep. When you are under duress, the meditative state is similar to the deeply relaxed states you experience every day when you are engrossed in a movie or a book, when you are relaxing on your patio, or just before you fall asleep at night. Like the other skills, the more regularly you practice meditation when you are not in crisis, the easier it will become to focus your mind and calm your body when you are distressed.

There are many ways to meditate. A very basic meditation starts by your getting into a comfortable position and closing your eyes. Observe your breath as it moves in and out of your body. Continue focusing on your breath one-mindfully. As other thoughts enter your mind, such as what you're going to make for dinner or thoughts of a problem at work, just notice the thoughts and then gently let them go, returning your attention to your breath. Don't get upset when outside thoughts enter your mind. Just redirect your attention back to your breath. Think of how you handle a weather report running across the bottom of the screen when you're watching a T.V. show. You just notice the words and then refocus your attention back on the show!

Some people prefer to use a mantra of some kind. For instance, instead of focusing on your breath, you can focus your mind on the sound of the word "one." You don't need to repeat the word with any special rhythm. You may just think of the sound of the word "one," holding the sound of it in your mind. Or, repeat the sound of the word "one" softly to yourself either in your mind or aloud, whichever is easier for you. Again, just bring your attention gently back to the word "one" as other thoughts enter and leave your mind.

Another simple method for meditation is to focus visually on something such as a candle flame. If you focus on a candle flame, be careful not to fall asleep and leave the candle burning!

Another method I especially like is to touch the thumb and forefinger together and focus on the feeling of their touching. This is especially useful because as your mind and body learn to associate the feeling of your thumb and forefinger touching with the relaxation response, you can use it anywhere to help you get more centered and relaxed—even standing in line at the supermarket or just before speaking at a big business meeting! Each method of meditation shares the same goal; focusing and calming the mind and helping you to stay in wise mind. You may have learned other methods of meditation that work for you. That's fine, use whatever works to help you get centered and then practice it daily.

2.7. Visualization

Visualization is another useful method of focusing and calming the mind and body. The following safe-place visualization exercise has a dual purpose. The visualization will help you focus your mind and relax you. In addition, if your early life experiences created a general feeling that you were not safe, the inner safe place can create a sense of safety inside that you may not have developed growing up. Creating a safe place inside can help to create a secure holding environment internally. In fact, the safe place is a metaphor for the secure holding environment.

You can just read the visualization, get the gist of it, and then try to do it on your own after getting yourself into a meditative state. But it's probably much easier, especially at first, to put the meditation on tape or have your therapist read it aloud to you. You will notice there are many places for pauses within the meditation. These pauses create a rhythm similar to the rhythm of breathing and the beating of the heart, which adds to the relaxation effect. It should be read slowly in a quiet tone of voice. DO NOT listen to the meditation on a tape while driving, as this would be unsafe.

If you lack an internal sense of safety as an adult because you were not given a sense of safety and security as a child, an image of a safe place you can use for yourself may not come to you immediately. You may need to work with the visualization awhile. You can use a place to which you have traveled some time in your life that was safe and comfortable. Or you can create a place totally out of your imagination. It could be a beach, a cabin in the woods, or a tropical island. It could be a place you have seen in a magazine or in the movies. But the place you choose needs to be both safe and comfortable for you.

Some people can't visualize pictures. Don't worry about it. You might experience the visualization more in terms of textures, sensations, and feelings.

Safe-Place Visualization   *As you relax there . . . you may wish to close your eyes . . . and notice, just notice . . . the feel of the cushions beneath you . . . that's right, just notice . . . the feeling of gravity, pulling you . . . yes, pulling you, toward the earth . . . comfortably, safely, you are held . . . here, where you are . . . safely held, by the gravity of the earth . . . and you can really enjoy . . . this safe, comfortable, enjoyable . . . feeling of calm, and comfort . . . that's right. And you are invited, to go inside . . . and you are invited, to picture there . . . to visualize, a wonderful place . . . this place, is a special place . . . it's all yours, it's just for you . . . it's a safe place, and a comfortable place . . . no one else can enter this place . . . unless you would invite them. That's right . . . this place is just for you . . . and look around you there . . . notice, what you can see . . . the colors . . . the images . . . around you there, and you can enjoy . . . the beauty there, and notice now, the sounds . . . any sounds, that you can hear there . . . enjoy the peaceful sounds . . . and you can notice now . . . what you can touch and feel . . . around you there, and you can relax and enjoy . . . knowing that this place, is all yours . . . very special, very safe . . . very comfortable, where you can go . . . anytime that you need to . . . anytime that you want to . . . you can return here, to this place . . . it will always be here, just for you . . . that's right, and enjoy being here, now . . . for as long as you want to, or need to . . . and take all the time you need . . . and then, when you're ready . . . you will be able to keep this place . . . tucked snugly within your heart . . . and you will be able to wake up your arms, and your legs, and open your eyes . . . feeling refreshed, and relaxed.*

As you continue to practice the safe-place meditation, your connection to your internal resources for safety, your internal holding environment, will strengthen. You will soon be able to go to your safe place internally without your tape. Even if you have only half a minute at work or at home with the kids, you will be able to close your eyes and make a quick connection to your safe place to get centered and relaxed.

2.8. Directly Counteracting Negative Emotions

Linehan suggests mindfully and consciously counteracting negative emotions such as fear, guilt, anger, or sadness with opposite actions whenever you can.[17] If the emotion is fear and you have a specific fear, the best antidote is to directly approach the people, places, or activities you fear . . . again, and again, and again. If the fear is too strong to work through on your own, you may need to enlist the help of a professional. As long as you avoid what you fear, the fear will not lessen.

If the feeling is guilt and shame and you have done something inconsistent with your own values, use the sixth step of Alcoholics Anonymous, which tells us to make amends to others whom we have harmed, except when to do so would injure them or others.[18] Keeping the sixth step in mind is helpful because each of us feels better without a load of guilt to carry. Sometimes it is helpful to simply say, "I'm sorry, I was wrong." Sometimes it be helpful to make up for the wrongdoing in some way, even if it is done anonymously. Sometimes the best amend is how one lives life from here on out.

If the feeling is sadness or depression, avoid inactivity and isolation, no matter how strong the urge! Search for activities that are pleasurable and help you feel competent. Seek out activities you found in the past to be enjoyable or fun. Avoid people who are unhealthy for you. Seek out people who can be supportive to you. Individuals who feel depressed naturally want to hibernate, but isolation only worsens a depression.

Another important antidote to negative emotions is staying physically well! Feeling physically unwell leaves us more vulnerable to emotional mind. Many people have a difficult time even distinguishing between the way they feel when depressed and the way they feel when they are tired, hungry, or sick. Don't feed your negative emotions by letting yourself get run down, tired, or ill. Counteract emotional mind by getting adequate sleep, exercise, nutrition, and health care. The stronger and healthier you feel, the easier it will be to stay in your wise mind.

3. SUMMARY OF SKILLS FOR COPING IN CRISIS

As you mindfully and purposefully set out to practice the skills outlined in this chapter to stay centered, increase your positive emotions, and cope with crisis, you will be more able to supply the steady emotional environment your child needs to feel secure. As you spend more time in wise mind, you will be able to stay more attuned to your child and you will become less vulnerable to misperceptions. But these skills do take practice—mindful and purposeful practice.

In summary, to learn to cope with distress, practice the following skills:

1. Soothe yourself with your senses.
2. Use encouraging self-talk.
3. Pray.
4. Immerse yourself in a pleasurable, physical, or creative activity.
5. Practice one-mindfulness.
6. Meditate.
7. Visualize your safe place.
8. Counteract negative emotions with opposite actions.
9. Take care of your physical health.

4. I DON'T DESERVE . . .

Many adults deprived of adequate emotional nurturing in childhood initially feel uncomfortable with self-soothing and self-calming techniques. It doesn't feel natural to them or they believe they don't deserve to feel better. To help you get past your own personal roadblocks, try completing the following exercise.

Exercise: List your objections to practicing self-calming techniques. Next, list the risks to yourself and your children if you don't use self-calming techniques.

Lisa completed this exercise and wrote the following:

Objections: When I think of using self-soothing, encouraging self-talk, or pleasurable activities to improve the way I feel, I hear my inner critic say, "That's silly! You don't have time for that! Get busy! You have things to do! Why would you think you deserved to make yourself feel good like that anyway?"

Risks If I Don't: If I don't start learning how to soothe and calm myself I will continue to deal with my feelings by raging at my kids, binge-eating, and snapping at my co-workers. I'll continue to gain weight, I'll get in trouble at work, and my kids will grow up doing the same kinds of dysfunctional stuff I do!

To my inner critic I say, "You may be trying to keep me from shirking my responsibilities, but you are sadly misinformed about this. If I take good care of myself emotionally I will actually be better able to meet my responsibilities at work and at home!"

5. GET TUNED INTO YOURSELF

It is difficult for most of us to use these skills when very strong emotions overwhelm us suddenly and unexpectedly. Most of us have experienced feelings so sudden and intense that our perceptions and actions are affected before we know what has hit us. Often when we find ourselves lashing out toward our children, we are just as surprised as they are. Usually, however, we have had some early warning signs that we were becoming distressed. The problem is that we haven't learned to identify them!

Become an observer of yourself. Ask family members what they have noticed about you when you have been stressed. Learn to look for red flags that say, "Use the skills before things get out of hand!"

The following exercise can help you get a handle on your distress before it gets a handle on you

Exercise: Make a distress cue card to carry with you in your purse or wallet. Look at it frequently as a reminder. On the front of your card, list your distress cues. These cues can help you stay mindful of your level of distress. On the back, list specific strategies that you can choose to help you cope.

Example: The front of Pam's card looked like this:

Cues: Trouble swallowing.
            Tense feeling in my chest.
            Nerves feel raw.
            Begin nitpicking at Ed and the kids.
            Stop listening to what they have to say.
            Start raising my voice.
            Start reaching for cookies.
            Begin feeling overly sensitive.
            Begin taking everything personally.
            Begin obsessing on little things that aren't even important.

The back of her card read as follows:

Strategies: Acknowledge my feelings. Put a name to them.
            Remind myself, "I'll be O.K. Feelings are not good or
              bad. All feelings are temporary."
            Long hot bath with a candle.

Extra sleep.

Rent a movie and take the evening off.

Go for a walk, garden, cross-stitch, or read.

Call someone from my support group.

Practice one-mindfulness: focus on just what's in front of me.

Say the Serenity Prayer.

List the things for which I am grateful.

Pam carried her "stress cue card" in her purse along with her reminder cards for disputing her parental misperceptions. The cards are always handy and she reads them quickly to "check in with herself" each time she has a few moments while she waits in the car to pick up a child or waits in a line of traffic. As a result, Pam has become much more self-aware and now is better able to use her skills before she becomes so overwhelmed she loses control.

6. PROBLEM-FOCUSED COPING FOR LIFE

Coping with uncomfortable emotions is a challenge for all of us. If you had to use emotion-focused coping to get through childhood, the prospect of actually experiencing feelings instead of getting rid of them—in any way possible—can be a startling idea! However, just imagine how much more effective you could be as a parent and in every other facet of your life if you could become more accepting of your emotions than you are right now. Imagine if you could use your emotions as a signal that there is a problem and the focus of your energy could be directed toward finding the best solution! A therapist can help you stay on track and apply these skills to situations that arise in your own life. However, a slogan often heard in Alcoholics Anonymous will be very useful to keep in mind as you practice these skills: Strive for progress, not perfection! Remember: Lifelong habits take time and a great deal of effort to change. As long as you keep trying, you *will* keep progressing.

Chapter Eight

Creating a New Wellspring of Nurturing Experiences for Both You and Your Child

If you had adequate emotional nurturing as a child, you will have an abundance of memories of feeling loved and nurtured. When you interact closely with your child your mind will automatically tap into this internal wellspring of warm, loving feeling memories. Your instinctive nurturing responses as you attend to your child will come as naturally to you as the instinct to breathe. But unlike the instinct to breathe, your nurturing instincts were not born with you. If your parents had problems that caused them to be unable to provide adequate nurturing, your internal wellspring of loving feeling memories may be running on empty.

Through meditation and visualizations you can create a new wellspring of loving, nurturing experiences to help you tap into compassion and love for your own inner child. As you work to fill your wellspring, the internal experiences you create will strengthen your capacity for nurturing yourself and your child. As you draw upon your wellspring of nurturing experiences to respond more instinctively to your child's needs for nurturing, you will be providing your child with a wellspring of nurturing experiences that will allow him to become more caring and compassionate toward others and toward himself.

Meditation is an ideal tool, because in the meditative state you will be less likely to hang on to your conscious defenses. You can tap into the power of your unconscious mind to help you alter your thoughts, feelings, and attitudes in a positive way.

The purpose of the following three meditations is to create internal nurturing experiences that can then become a part of your internal wellspring of positive feeling memories. By giving your younger ego states experiences of safety and care you are helping to heal early negative experiences and strengthen your internalized nurturing-parent part. The more you practice these meditations, the stronger your capacity for nurturing will become—allowing you to better nurture yourself in healthy ways and to be a more instinctive nurturer for your children. There is a special meditation for your infant self, your toddler self, and your school-age self. If there was a certain age at which you feel you were especially hurt or lonely as a child, you may want to repeat one of these meditations with that particular age in mind. For example, the school-age meditation can easily be repeated with the image of a 15-year-old self. Feel free to be as creative as you wish to be. Alter the visualizations or add to them in any way that is useful for you. If you have any difficulty with any part of these visualizations enlist the help of a therapist who is skilled in the use of imagery and meditation.

You may want to record these meditations yourself, or you may have a therapist who can read them aloud to you. Either way, a tape recording will be helpful, as it will allow you to repeat them as often as you like.

1. VISUALIZATION FOR NURTURING THE INFANT SELF

In this meditation you will be guided in finding a safe and comfortable place for your infant self. Working with your infant self is especially important if you believe you may not have developed a solid, secure attachment with your primary caregiver as a baby. Your infant's safe place may be part of your adult safe place—or it may be completely separate. It is important to find a safe place that provides your inner infant self with the "holding environment" you may not have had when you were small, so it should be comforting, cozy, and secure. You will also be asked to find a nurturing caregiver for your infant self. This caregiver can be any kind of a figure or being that represents safety, comfort, love, and protection. Some people create their own ideal parent or grandparent figure. Other people choose a favorite aunt, teacher, or neighbor from their own lives. Some people choose a favorite movie star or singer. Others choose an angel or other spiritual figure, or even a special animal as their caregiver. You can choose whatever feels right for you.

As you relax there, and you breathe . . . following your breath, in, and out . . . you can enjoy the comfortable feeling . . . of following your breath, deeply . . . Moving down, inside yourself . . . down, inside, that's right . . . toward that inner spark, within . . . that spark inside that was you . . . before you were even born . . . that spark that was you, even . . . when you were just an infant . . . so small, you couldn't speak, or walk . . . that's right. And you are invited to visualize . . . the perfect place, the holding place . . . for that infant self, so small and trusting . . . the infant self that is still within you . . . a place, that is cozy and warm, snugly and safe . . . just right, for an infant who needs to feel secure . . . And you can look around . . . and see this place, and how it looks . . . See the images, the colors, the lighting . . . You can touch and feel this cozy place . . . You can listen to the sounds . . . Smell the pleasant smells . . . And you can change . . . anything you want to change about this place . . . to make it even more safe, secure, and cozy . . . And you can see within this beautiful place now . . . that little infant, so small and hopeful . . . See her there, safe, secure, and comfortable. Notice . . . how she looks, her hands, her face . . . and the feel of her soft skin, that baby smell. And if you can . . . you can hold her, gently, and tenderly . . . Cradle her there, warmly . . . Let her know she is lovable and precious . . . Explain to her that she is completely safe and protected there, in the safe place . . . And you can create for her there . . . a loving, nurturing, caregiver . . . who will watch over her and protect her . . . to comfort her and nurture her . . . And you can visualize this loving caregiver now . . . You are free, to give this infant . . . the perfect loving protector . . . to hold her and comfort her . . . She will never be alone . . . She will never be left to cry . . . She will be safe, and loved, and held . . . forever and always in this beautiful and loving place . . . cared for by this loving, nurturing caregiver within . . . Hold your infant self again . . . Tell her anything else you wish to tell her . . . Linger there, for as long as you want to . . . Know that you can return here and be with your infant self . . . any time you need to, or want to . . . And when you are ready, you can enfold the infant . . . and her caregiver in the safe place . . . Safely enfold them inside your heart . . . Feel the energy returning to your body. When you are ready you will be able to open your eyes, feeling serene and calm, rested and relaxed.

Through meditation and imagery we can help heal negative experiences from our earliest moments in life. I have found this meditation to be helpful not only for adults whose parents were unable to nurture them adequately, but also for adults who, as infants, suffered from a painful illness or who endured a lengthy separation from a parent.

2. MEDITATION FOR NURTURING THE TODDLER SELF

You may choose to visualize your inner toddler sharing the safe place and the caregiver with your inner infant. Or you may choose to give the toddler a safe place and a caregiver all her own. Again, do what feels right for you. Remember that you can be flexible as you go along, and make any changes you want to when something doesn't feel right for you.

And now, as you enjoy this peaceful moment . . . know there is nowhere else you have to be . . . This moment is all yours, as you follow your breath . . . Count each breath silently to yourself . . . One, two, three, that's right . . . and you can really enjoy each breath . . . allowing any stress or tension to fall away . . . as feelings of calm and peace flow throughout . . . Sinking down into the cushions beneath you . . . moving down inside you can see . . . that safe and nurturing place that is just right . . . where your toddler can feel safe and protected . . . comfortable and secure . . . free to play and have fun and just be . . . safe and warm and free to be . . . See this warm and cozy place where a toddler can play . . . See the images there, and the colors . . . See the comfortable and safe surroundings . . . Touch and feel whatever you can touch and feel . . . Hear the sounds . . . and smell the smells . . . See your little toddler self cozy and safe . . . See what this child looks like, playing there . . . Notice the toddler's size . . . hair, eyes, clothes . . . Approach your toddler there, and reach out if you can . . . You may want to hug her . . . or hold her on your lap . . . Let her know she is safe here . . . Let her know that she is lovable and beautiful . . . Visualize a very special caregiver . . . a nurturing caregiver, whose job it is . . . to watch over your toddler and keep her safe . . . to love her and hold her and nurture her . . . See there the loving caregiver protecting her . . . See her tenderly nurturing your toddler self . . . She will never be alone . . . She will never be scared . . . The caregiver will always be there . . . giving her the loving care a toddler needs . . . Hug or hold your toddler once again . . . Tell her anything else you wish to tell her . . . Remind her that she can stay here and be safe and protected . . . comforted and nurtured forever and always . . . Tell her she can play and have fun . . . See her enjoy the safety and the warmth . . . See the caregiver there, looking down on the little toddler with tender care . . . appreciating her specialness . . . Know that you can return anytime . . . Kow that your toddler will be safe here . . . And whenever you are ready, you can . . . enfold your toddler and her caregiver within your heart . . . and bring these feelings of peace along with you . . . as you bring the energy back to your body and open up your eyes.

Most of us begin recording episodic memories (actual pictures and words) shortly after we develop language skills, which leaves memories of toddlerhood quite sketchy or completely nonexistent. The visualizations, however, can help you to heal even what you cannot remember, and create warm, loving experiences for the child within.

3. MEDITATION FOR NURTURING THE SCHOOL-AGE SELF

When we reach school age our world rapidly expands from the very small environment of the family to a much larger world which includes peers, teachers, and neighbors. The world of school and neighborhood can be a harsh one, and many of us received significant emotional wounds there. The school-age meditation can help to heal the inner child's wounds from rejection or hurt at home or in the larger world of school and community. It will increase the experiences of loving, nurturing care and protection for the school age self.

As you close your eyes, you may notice . . . the patterns and colors behind your eyelids . . . And isn't it interesting how these patterns . . . can change, in subtle ways . . . And you can just enjoy, relaxing there . . . breathing out the tension in your body . . . focusing on how the patterns change and move . . . as your arms and legs relax comfortably there . . . Breathing in, breathing out . . . while feelings of calm, and peace . . . move gently through your body, that's right . . . And you can go inside, and find a safe place . . . that a school age child could enjoy . . . safe, comfortable, a place to play . . . And you can see this place now . . . Look around, and see the comfortable safety . . . Feel the warmth, the gentleness, of the air . . . And see your child there now, playing . . . so safe and comfortable she can play . . . free to just be, in this gentle place . . . Feel free to reach out and hold her hand . . . or hug her, or hold her on your lap . . . Let her know she is lovable and special . . . Let her know there is nothing she needs to change . . . that you love her just the way she is right now . . . And visualize there now, her loving caregiver . . . there to protect her, to nurture her . . . to watch out for her and give her all the love . . . all the care and tenderness she needs . . . See the loving caregiver holding her . . . giving her what she needs, that's right . . . She will always be loved, and protected . . . She will always feel safe, loved, and warm . . . Reach out to your inner child once again . . .

Hold her tenderly . . . Comfort her and nurture her . . . Tell her anything else you wish to tell her . . . Know that you can return here anytime . . . And whenever you are ready, gently enfold . . . your younger self and her caregiver within your heart . . . And let the energy return to your body, and open up your eyes, feeling calm and rested, peaceful, and serene.

Dan described his experience creating a new internal wellspring.

"The first time I tried to visualize a safe place I couldn't do it. I just couldn't think of anything that felt safe. I was able to find holes in everything I came up with. Finally, about the fourth time I tried this meditation I remembered this closet I loved as a kid. It was a huge walk-in closet and I always loved to play there. Nobody ever knew where I was when I was in there and I really felt safe. Now that closet is my safe place, only it's expanded. There's a big corner with an easy chair and a big-screen T.V. I have another area there that has a race track for the ten-year old part of myself. Then there is this other area with a huge teddy bear for the toddler. There was this really neat old guy who used to live down the street from us when I was a kid. He used to sit on his front porch every evening in the summer and I'd hang out there with him. He's the caregiver. He guards the closet door and takes care of the kids. I can see him there, playing with them and reading to them.

"I usually reset my alarm in the morning, and that's when I switch on my tape player and listen to my meditations. When I'm finished I feel centered—like everything's settled down and peaceful inside."

Pam described her experience with inner child visualizations.

"The first time I visualized myself as a little girl I just couldn't connect with her. I had an old photo of myself at home. I was this smiling, dimpled, cute little brunette. Yet when I tried to visualize myself as an adult approaching her and reaching out to her I had this strong feeling of repulsion toward her! I did not like this little girl at all. But then the third or fourth time I tried, I looked into her eyes. Suddenly I felt for her. I recognized how vulnerable and sad she was, and how I was buying into all of the critical messages I had heard all my life. I became very emotional as I felt her pain—which was *my* pain.as a child—and I realized that none of it had been my fault! After that I was able to visualize holding her and telling her that she should never have been treated like that and that she was safe now. I let her know that I would handle things from here on out. Now, whenever I feel fearful, childlike feelings creeping up on me I repeat this meditation right away. It really helps me get my child self tucked safely back inside the safe place and my adult self back in charge. This has especially helped me respond like an adult when I'm with my kids! I used to feel like a scared little kid raising kids, and that's how I acted! It seems like the more I practice nurturing my inner child, the more loving and nurturing I feel toward my children. I feel like a more loving person. I think I've always been a loving person, but I felt little and too scared and ashamed to be able to act on the loving feelings."

4. MEDITATION TO SEPARATE YOUR CHILD PART FROM THE PARENTING ROLE

By now you are probably fully aware that many of your automatic emotional responses as a parent and the misperceptions that accompany them are connected to your child ego state—your childhood memories, emotions, and beliefs. As a parent, when your child ego state is triggered your inner child takes charge of parenting! The purpose of the following meditation is to help you keep your present-day adult self in charge as you parent. This is accomplished by separating out the child part of yourself from the adult part and clarifying present-day roles. You can add this meditation to your other taped meditations and listen to it as often as you would like during your daily meditation time.

As you close your eyes, pay attention . . . to your breath, moving in and out . . . of your lungs, bringing oxygen into . . . your body, and releasing, the carbon dioxide . . . that your body does not need . . . You can continue to follow your breath . . . and enjoy the pleasant waves . . . of calm, peaceful comfort . . . washing gently throughout your body . . . like waves, lapping gently on a sandy beach . . . As you enjoy, the peaceful calm . . . you may go inside yourself today . . . and see your child self inside . . . nestled safely inside her special place . . . See the beautiful images there . . . the colors, the light, and hear . . . any sounds there, that you can hear . . . Touch and feel, what you can touch and feel . . . and let her know, that you are there . . . to tell her something very important . . . Let her know that it will be O.K. for her

. . . to just be a child, and play, and have fun . . . that you, the adult . . . will be the parent to [your child's name, for example, John]. Tell her "You can stay here in the safe place . . . Let me handle being in charge of [John]. It's not your job anymore . . . Being a parent to [John] is my job . . . You can trust me to take care of things . . . You don't have to be scared . . . that something will go wrong . . . I will keep you safe, and take care of things . . . [John] will not hurt you . . . . [John] is just a child, and so are you . . . I will keep you safe, and I will keep [John] safe too . . . You don't have to take care of [John], and [John] doesn't have to take care of you . . . Stay here, and be safe . . . Play and have fun, and just be a child . . . and [John] will play and have fun and be a child too," . . . Gently embrace your younger self . . . See her caregiver nurturing her, and protecting her . . . as you enfold her, lovingly . . . inside your heart, and feel the energy returning to your body, and open your eyes, feeling relaxed, and comfortable.

As you interact with your son or daughter on a day-to-day basis, keep these images in the back of your mind. Practice reminding your child part to stay in his or her safe place, letting you, the adult, be the parent. Identify those feelings and reactions that don't feel adult. When you notice childlike feelings and responses in yourself do a quick visualization and remind your inner child that she is safe, and that this is your job, not hers. For example, Joe, who tells his story in Chapter Sixteen, notices the fearful feelings of his inner child whenever one of his sons or daughters becomes angry or upset. Joe has learned to identify the feelings of his hurt child and reassure his younger part that he, adult Joe, can handle the present-day problems. He then visualizes his inner child back in his safe place with his caregiver. As you continue to practice this technique it will become easier and easier to tuck that child safely back inside, keeping your adult self in charge.

5. ENMESHMENT OF THE CHILD AND ADULT EGO STATES

Many people have an "enmeshment" of their child and adult ego states, which happens when they are used to being in the child ego state so often that they lose touch with what it is really supposed to feel like to be in the adult state. If this is true for you, sit back, relax, and remember a specific experience when you felt completely adult, competent, and self-confident. It may be a memory, for example, of accomplishing a task at work, or solving a problem at home. Run through the whole experience in your mind. Meditate upon that experience, remembering fully what it felt like—in your body and in your mind. Imagine, then, that you are bringing those same mind and body feelings with you into the present. Visualize yourself bringing those feelings and resources with you into an interaction with your child. In your visualization pay attention to how you feel, how you move your body, and how you talk as you interact. This exercise will help you separate out your adult self from your child self. Continue to practice this exercise during your daily meditation time.

6. ADOPTING A HEALTHY, SELF-NURTURING LIFESTYLE

As you begin practicing these meditations it will be important to also begin incorporating safety and healthy self-nurturing into your present-day lifestyle. Many people have scrambled all their lives to find some way to feel safe and secure. But without an internal wellspring of healthy, nurturing experiences to draw upon it can be like Mother Hubbard trying to satisfy her dog's hunger pangs when her cupboards are bare. Without the internal wellspring, adults often grasp for an illusory feeling of safety or nurturing through alcohol or drugs, loveless sexual encounters, food, withdrawal and isolation, or by looking to their children to provide them with comfort and safety.

There are many healthy ways to incorporate self-nurturing and safety into your life. Safety may mean staying out of romantic, friendship, or family relationships that are destructive to you. A destructive relationship is one that dismantles your sense of self-worth through verbal, emotional, or physical abuse, coercive demands, control, or intimidation. Safety may also mean staying out of environments that are unsafe, and staying away from behaviors that put you at risk, such as the abuse of alcohol or drugs.

Incorporating self-nurturing into your present-day life includes getting adequate sleep, exercise, and nutrition. Self-nurturing means taking care of yourself when you are ill. It includes finding healthy friendships, and reaching out for help when you need to. Self-nurturing includes saying no when necessary. And it includes finding time each day to relax or meditate, as well as time each week to do something you enjoy. Self-nurturing includes finding the right balance between time spent meeting your responsibilities, nurturing your children and your other relationships, and time spent doing those things that recharge and revitalize your energy. If your life is continually out of balance, your energy will be chronically depleted and you will be more vulnerable to stress. As you focus on adopting a more balanced, self-nurturing lifestyle you will gain more energy and resilience for all that you do—especially for your very demanding and vital role as a parent.

Exercise: Write out a schedule of your typical week. Create a plan that will help you create a better balance and incorporate more healthy self-care into your life. Balance time spent meeting responsibilities with time for your children, time for your spouse, and time that is just for you to do whatever helps you get reenergized and revitalized.

Chapter Nine

Forming Healing Connections

Adults with insecure attachment styles have an imaginary connecting cord between themselves and others that is thin and frayed—it feels like it will snap with the slightest tug. An important part of healing that frayed cord is experiencing relationships that are trustworthy and healthy. Therefore, even if you learned early in life that you could not depend on others to meet your emotional or physical needs, positive relationships later in life can help you *learn* to trust others. As you develop an imaginary cord that is strong and elastic between yourself and others, the resulting sense of a secure base will buffer you against the stresses of life. You will find yourself naturally more capable of supplying your child with the same sense of security and strong cord attachment.

1. RELATIONSHIP OBSTACLES

There are obviously some obstacles to developing healthy relationships when your earliest relationships were not the best. The following questions can help you identify patterns of relating that may be presently interfering with the development of healthy friendships or relationships:

1. Do you tend to either put people on pedestals or dismiss them completely?
2. Do you put people through pass/fail tests?
3. Do you find yourself making negative judgments of whomever you are with?

4. Do you tend to assume others are making negative judgments of you?

5. Do you feel like a chameleon—changing your attitudes or beliefs to suit whomever you are with?

6. Or are you the opposite, overreacting and arguing with any opinions that are different from your own?

7. Do you find yourself drawn toward others who are critical and controlling of you?

8. Or conversely, do you find yourself drawn toward others with low self-esteem whom you can easily control?

9. Do you avoid any but the most superficial relationships?

10. Or do you desire close relationships, but find that others complain that you are too smothering, clingy, or controlling?

11. Do you desire close relationships, but sabotage them or push them away at the same time?

2. IS IT WORTH IT?

At this point you may be thinking, *Those are some pretty big obstacles. It's not going to be easy to get past these old patterns. Will it really be worth it?*

In a word—yes. Dr. Scott Henderson, researcher at the Australian National University, found that individuals who *perceive* that they can depend on the people in their environment to be there for them and *feel a sense of connection* have a decreased risk for depression and anxiety. A close bond with another person *who is trusted to be supportive* is a tremendous buffer against stress.[1] Furthermore, if you grew up without secure attachment relationships and you have an insecure type of attachment status in your adult life, experiencing healthy relationships in adulthood can help you move closer toward the secure end of the attachment continuum. A relationship with a trustworthy, healthy other can help you to change your most core beliefs about trust and closeness, even though you may have to work at not running away from those relationships initially. Core beliefs such as *Others will not respond to me positively* can gradually shift to *Others can care about me* and *I am good enough* as you experience healthy relationships. *Others are not trustworthy* can slowly change to *Some others can be trusted.*

Naturally, as you internalize healthier, more positive beliefs about yourself and others and create healthier connections in your life, there will be great benefits to your child. As she observes you interacting with others, she, too, will learn how to reach out and connect with people. Through observation she will form core beliefs about how *she* should expect to be treated by others. As you find more emotional fulfillment in your adult relationships, your support network can become your external holding environment giving you a greater sense of a secure base in your life. You will have more to give to your child emotionally, strengthening your attachment relationship and giving her a greater sense of security in her life.

3. IF AN ADDICTION SUBSTITUTES FOR PEOPLE IN YOUR LIFE

In my clinical practice I have observed time and time again that adults who have a frayed-cord connection with others are addiction-prone. In his book, *The Addictive Personality,* Craig Nakken, therapist and addictions counselor with the Family Therapy Institute in St. Paul, Minnesota, describes why individuals who do not have trusting, close relationships with others are vulnerable to developing addictions. He explains that when the addicted person uses his chemical or behavior of choice, he experiences a very intense mood change, or a "high." The feelings accompanying this mood change are so intense that they are mistaken for the intensity of feelings accompanying an intimate relationship. Therefore, the adult forms *a seemingly intense and intimate relationship with his addiction.* Furthermore, the addicted person finds he can *count on* the intense mood change created by his addiction. The effect is *predictable* and *reliable.* Nakken writes, "What makes the addictive relationship so attractive is the mood change it produces. It works every time, it's guaranteed. No human relationship can make this kind of guarantee."[2] Because of this, the addicted person comes to trust his addiction. He achieves a sense of power and control knowing he can depend on his addiction to give him the high he wants. His trust in his addiction is in sharp contrast to his distrust of people.

Both the intensity and the predictability are extremely seductive to individuals who grew up without secure attachments and who now have frayed-cord connections with others. However, as Nakken writes, "Finding emotional fulfillment through an object or event is an illusion."[3] The feelings of intimacy and control achieved by acting out addictions are no more real than a desert mirage. The harsh reality is that there is *no* control. There is no intimacy, either—no connection anywhere. The mood change, although predictable, is just temporary. Following each high there is an inevitable painful emotional crash. Each type of addiction is accompanied by its own set of very painful consequences, which result in one's life steadily becoming more and more unmanageable and out of control as the addiction progresses. The shame and resulting pain can be enormous. As the shame and pain grow, the addicted individual turns to the only strategy for coping he knows—the addiction. He becomes trapped in a vicious, unending cycle.

As an addiction progresses, the addicted person becomes more and more cut off from whatever real relationships he has, including his relationships with his children. Anyone caught in the vicious roller coaster ride of addiction cannot have the emotional energy required to be attuned to a child or to provide a secure holding environment. As the relationship with the addiction becomes more and more central in the person's life, all other relationships get pushed further and further to the periphery. There just isn't room for anyone or anything else.

If you have an addiction, seek a treatment program or a professional with expertise in the area of addiction. In addition, find a Twelve Step group where you can begin to learn how to connect to others and to a Higher Power along with other people who have been there and who know what you are going through. Yes, meeting people and forming connections will be frightening for you. That's why your addiction was so seductive to you in the first place! But everyone else in your Twelve Step group has felt the same way. That's why they are there as well.

Do not underestimate the power of addictions. Recovery for your addiction must be a top priority. If you have an active addiction, you will not be able to address any other issues. All self-growth and change will be at a standstill. You will not be able to mend your parental instincts or strengthen your relationship with your child. Your relationship with your child and your mate will deteriorate steadily as your addiction progresses.

4. HEALTHY FRIENDSHIPS—WHAT ARE THEY LIKE?

As mentioned earlier, one of the problems you may be encountering in forming healthy connections is that in forming a friendship you may have expectations that are either too perfectionistic or too low. You may have no idea what a healthy friendship is supposed to be like because you haven't had enough experience with good relationships to know.

The following is a list of characteristics of any good friendship:

1. Friends enjoy time spent together and feel relaxed and able to be themselves.
2. Friends don't put one another down for their feelings or opinions. It's all right if they don't share the same views.
3. Friends give each other encouragement.
4. Friends do not engage in manipulative, controlling, or abusive behavior with one another.
5. Friends respect one another's needs for space and separateness.
6. When friends experience conflict they communicate and work together toward some kind of compromise or resolution.

You may have an unrealistic idea that you shouldn't have to work at friendships—that they should just happen effortlessly. However, just like romantic and parent–child relationships, friendships do take effort. It takes effort to pick up the phone, to plan a get-together, or to resolve a difference.

You may have put all your energy into your romantic relationship and let your friendships go. However, putting all your emotional eggs in one basket, so to speak, is pretty risky business. It's not fair to your partner to expect him or her to meet all of your emotional needs. This kind of setup can put immense pressure on a romantic relationship.

5. SOCIAL ANXIETY

If you feel anxious and uncomfortable around other people, Dr. David Burns, Director of the Institute for Cognitive and Behavioral Therapies at the Presbyterian University of Pennsylvania Medical Center in Philadelphia, suggests that you focus your energy on making the people *around* you comfortable.[4] This technique really works—for a very simple reason. Almost all people feel somewhat anxious in social situations. When you are imagining yourself to be the only anxious person in a social setting, you are merely comparing your insides to other people's outsides! When you focus on making others comfortable, you will keep the focus of your attention off of your own discomfort and lessen your self-consciousness. And by focusing on making others comfortable, you will find that others will be drawn to you.

The following suggestions have been adapted from the very practical, useful ideas for making friends outlined in much more detail in Burns' book, *Intimate Connections: The Clinically Proven Program for Making Close Friends and Finding a Loving Partner*[5]:

1. Smile and say hello. People who are uncomfortable socially often tend to look very serious and glum. People around them often perceive their serious faces as evidence of a bad mood or a judgmental nature and so naturally they keep their distance! Practice smiling and saying hello to each person you come into contact with—at the store, at work, at church, or on the street. Even though it probably feels extremely uncomfortable at first, if you keep it up, it will eventually become easier, especially as you notice positive responses from others! Don't expect everyone to smile or say hello in return, but many people will. Through this one very simple skill you will automatically cause others to perceive you as warm and approachable.

2. Show interest in others. Think about people you have met that you felt the most comfortable with. Did they spend the whole time talking? Or did they ask questions about you, and appear interested in what you had to say? Burns suggests observing talk show hosts. At the time of this writing Rosie O'Donnell is a very popular host. As I watched her show the other day it dawned on me that she is a true *appreciator* of people. She seems genuinely in awe of the talents of each guest she invites to her show. She is focused, attentive, and sincerely interested in what each guest has to say. The viewer senses that her guests feel immediately at ease, which even makes the viewer comfortable.

3. Learn how to chat and make small talk. Small talk is light and fun. You don't have to be a genius or lead the life of a Mata Hari in order to make interesting small talk. Catch the nightly news, or browse through the magazine or newspaper stand. There is always something interesting going on in the world of politics or entertainment. It can be fun to discuss the latest foibles in the news, the current gossip about the entertainment world, or the latest movies, television shows, or music.

4. Lighten up. People will be most comfortable around you as they're still getting to know you if you stay light-hearted and keep a sense of humor about things. Most people feel nervous when a discussion becomes too serious before they have really gotten to know and trust the other person. Stay nonjudgmental and accepting. Generally people feel threatened or offended and will distance themselves if their point of view is criticized or if unsolicited advice is given unless the source is someone they know well and trust. Remember Rosie. She has a light-hearted, fun approach that is almost kidlike. She makes people feel warm and safe.

5. Be human. A big mistake many people make is feeling the need to present themselves in a perfect way. Many people fear that they will be disliked because of their personal flaws. Nothing could be further from the truth. People are intimidated by others they perceive as "perfect." In general, people feel most comfortable with others who are not afraid to let their "humanness" show. Look at Rosie again. She talks about her weight, her "chin hairs," her crooked nose, and her therapist. These things make her human—imperfect—and lovable!

Don't be afraid to let people know the real you. Take down the facade. It only pushes people away from you. There can be no real connection between people who are not real. Even if it feels like you are taking a big risk, be yourself with others. You will find that others will appreciate your genuineness, and the bonds you make with others will be more authentic. Besides, as one of my clients commented to me one day, "There is nothing that takes more energy than trying to be someone you're not!" And to think, it only works against you!

6. CATCH YOUR THINKING ERRORS

Burns describes several types of thinking errors that can cause us to turn tail and run from social situations. The following thinking errors have been adapted from Burns' suggestions for combating social anxiety outlined in detail in his book, *Intimate Connections*.[6] If you find yourself hiding from people, look for these errors in your thinking.

6.1. Fortunetelling

Do you tend to predict that you will make a fool of yourself, be ignored, be rejected, or experience some other form of social mishap before you even get to the social gathering? If so, you are probably vividly visualizing the awful event in your mind and already experiencing the terrible feelings. You're ready to go home and crawl in bed before you've even arrived at the setting.

Practice *catching* yourself. Identify the fortunetelling. Imagine a great big red stop sign, while thinking STOP! Then visualize the upcoming social situation going well. Imagine yourself smiling and saying hello, making small talk, and being interested in the person you're talking to. Notice the change in the way you feel.

6.2. "Should" Statements

Do you have rigid standards or rules by which you judge yourself or others? Practice catching your judgmental thoughts and consciously let go of them. Practice letting go of judgments about appearances—either yours or others. Practice letting go of judgments about others' points of view, or judging your own conversation. Do you go back over and examine everything you said after each conversation? Do you find yourself thinking, "I *should* have said . . ." and "I *shouldn't* have said . . . ," time and time again? And then on top of that, do you judge yourself for being anxious or self-conscious? Practice accepting all of your feelings as O.K., and remember that others feel the same way on the inside. When you notice the "should" statements, catch them and then let them go. Practice lightening up on yourself and on others, too! The less you judge others, the less you will judge yourself and vice versa. Others will pick up on your more relaxed attitude, and they will feel more comfortable and relaxed, too!

6.3. Overgeneralization

Do you tend to focus on any negative experiences you have, and generalize from those experiences? As an example, if you encounter a rude parent at a PTA meeting, you might avoid returning ever again, assuming that "*all* those parents are rude!" If a friend breaks a confidence you might assume, "I can *never* trust him again!" Furthermore, you might think, "*No one* is trustworthy in this world!" or, "People *always* hurt me!"

Practice catching yourself using the words, "always," "never," "all," or "no one" in your thinking. Generalizations like these are usually inaccurate, and tend to come out of emotional mind. Ask yourself, "What would my wise mind say about this?"

6.4. Mind Reading

Do you tend to assume that people are making negative judgments about you? Do you imagine their negative thoughts or imagine them making critical remarks about you behind your back? One way to combat "mind reading" is to catch yourself imagining the critical thoughts of others, and then ask yourself, "Why do I think I am *so* important that other people are spending their energy and time thinking and talking about me?" Take the idea to its extreme. Imagine the people you know calling a special meeting just to get together and evaluate and discuss you. This might help you see how ludicrous it is. Again, ask yourself, "What would my wise mind say about this?"

On the other hand, if your suspiciousness is fueled because you are involved in a gossipy group of people who like to make themselves feel big by putting other people down, you may want to disassociate yourself from this unhealthy group. Certainly, you wouldn't want to waste energy worrying about what this type of group is saying about you!

6.5. Labeling[7]

Do you find yourself name-calling yourself or name-calling others, even if only in your thoughts? Labeling, or name-calling, is very destructive. The language each one of us uses, whether it is in our thoughts or spoken aloud, is very powerful. Labeling fuels the inner critic and judgmental thinking. Name-calling can erode your self-confidence and your self-esteem, adding to your avoidance of social situations. Labeling and judging of others can result in actions that may alienate the people around you. If you find yourself using words like jerk, stupid, idiot, imbecile, etc., toward yourself or others, catch yourself and substitute a nonjudgmental remark instead.

7. KEEPING YOUR SENSE OF SELF WITHOUT DRIVING OTHERS AWAY

Whether you are too controlling or you let others control you, or you vacillate between these two extremes, you can learn some skills that will help you find a better balance. In her Dialectical Behavioral Therapy (DBT) program, Marsha Linehan has systematically outlined skills that can help you preserve your relationships without giving up your sense of self in the process. Again, even though her program was designed to help individuals with borderline personality disorder, I have found that most people find Linehan's skills very useful and therefore I have adapted them here. They are described in much greater detail in Linehan's *Skills Training Manual for Treating Borderline Personality Disorder*, although the workbook is meant to be used with the help of a trained therapist.[8]

The following list of three main goals in any relationship is adapted from Linehan's workbook[9]:

1. Getting your objectives met. (Either asking for something you want from the other person or refusing to agree to an unreasonable request from the other person.)
2. Preserving the relationship.
3. Keeping your self-respect.

Goals sometimes conflict with one another, making their attainment difficult. For example, acting in a way that ensures that you get what you want may damage the relationship. Acting in a way that ensures the other person will still like you may mean giving in and/or losing your self-respect.

Therefore, Linehan teaches that in any relationship situation where it isn't clear what you should do, the first step is to identify the relative importance of each goal. Determine your priorities. For example, if not getting what you want would lead to buildup of so many resentments on your part that you would consider leaving the relationship, it may be preferable to tolerate short-term conflict in order to try to get your objectives met. On the other hand, if the relationship is important to you, but it is too tentative to tolerate conflict at the moment, you may need to focus more on the skills for enhancing the relationship and focus less on getting your objectives met right now. If the other person makes a request and saying "yes" will make you feel like a doormat, but saying "no" will damage the relationship, you need to determine whether focusing on the relationship or your self-respect is most crucial to you right now.[10]

8. GETTING WHAT YOU WANT—IT'S NOT AN EITHER/OR PROPOSITION

Getting what you want in a relationship is not a black-or-white proposition according to Linehan. Don't ask yourself whether you should insist on your way or not. Rather, ask yourself with how much *intensity* you should try to get what you want.

If you are making a request, you can hint (low intensity), you can ask (moderate intensity), or you can absolutely *insist* on getting what you want (high intensity). If you are refusing an unreasonable request, you can express hesitancy (low intensity), you can express unwillingness (moderate intensity), or you can downright refuse (high intensity).[11]

9. HOW INTENSE SHOULD YOU BE?

When you are unsure with how much force or intensity you should try to get what you want, consider the following questions adapted from Linehan's workbook before you go after what you want or refuse an unreasonable request[12]:

1. How important is it to me to get my way right now versus keeping a good relationship versus keeping my self-respect?
2. Is he capable of giving me what I want? (Or) Am I capable of giving him what he wants?
3. Is this an appropriate time for me to ask? (Or) Is this a good time for me to say no?
4. Do I have the right to make this request? (Or) Does he have the right to make this request of me?
5. Am I willing to do as much for him as I am asking? (Or) Does he do for me as much as he is asking of me?
6. Will asking or not asking create more problems in the long run for this relationship? (Or) Will saying no or saying yes create more problems in the long run for this relationship?
9. Do I often make requests for things I could actually do myself? (Or) Does he typically make requests for things he could do himself?
10. Will asking or not asking make me feel badly about myself? (Or) Will saying no or saying yes make me feel badly about myself?

10. HOW TO ASK FOR WHAT YOU WANT

The following six steps for asking for what you want or saying "no" in a relationship are also adapted from Linehan's workbook.[13] Remember that the force or intensity with which you try to get your objectives met will depend on your answers to the questions in the previous section.

For example, let's say you want to ask your employer for more responsibility at work. You have decided that your objective is important, it's a good time to ask, you have the right to ask, and if you don't, you'll feel badly about yourself. On the other hand, the job and preserving the relationship with the employer are also important, so you want to ask with moderate intensity.

The steps to follow are:

1. Describe the situation as you perceive it.
2. Describe your feelings or opinions.
3. Ask for what you want clearly. Don't expect the other person to read your mind.
4. Let the other person know in advance how appreciative you will feel if you get what you want.
5. Consciously stay focused on your objectives. Ignore any diversions from the topic at hand or suggest they be discussed later. Like a broken record, keep repeating your original point. (This is aptly called the Broken Record Technique!)
6. At the same time, if necessary, negotiate. If the other person is not even willing to strike a bargain, hand the problem over to him: "We have a problem here, and you don't care for the solutions I have suggested. What do you suggest we do to solve this problem?"

Imagine that you state to your employer, John Smith, "My skills have not been adequately utilized. I have more to offer this company. I would like to take on some of the larger accounts. I will feel enthusiastic about my work, and the company will benefit as well." When John Smith responds by pointing out that you joined the company only last year, you respond by stating with conviction in your voice, "I am certain that I have the ability to do the job. The company will benefit, and I will feel more positive about my work."

11. PRESERVING THE RELATIONSHIP

Following is an adaptation of Linehan's steps for approaching someone in a way that will help preserve the relationship.[14] The more important the relationship, the more closely you will want to attend to these simple steps.

1. Use a gentle tone of voice and a courteous manner. Avoid criticizing or threatening.

2. Listen and be sensitive to the other person's viewpoint. Validate his or her feelings nonjudgmentally, even while you are continuing to maintain your own point of view.
3. Keep the discussion light. Smile and use a little humor. Avoid behaving in a manner that is overly serious or heavy-handed.

Although you feel strongly about taking more responsibility at work, you also value your relationship with your employer. You don't threaten to quit or raise your voice. You smile and validate John's point of view while continuing to maintain your own: "John, I recognize that you're taking a gamble by giving those accounts to someone who has been with the company for only a few months, and I want you to know, I won't let you down."

12. KEEPING YOUR SELF-RESPECT

Following are Linehan's steps for approaching someone in a way that will maintain your self-respect[15]:

1. Treat yourself and the other person fairly. Either taking advantage of another person *or* letting another person walk all over you will cause you to lose self-respect.
2. Avoid apologizing if you have done nothing wrong. Make amends if you have done or said anything that has harmed the other person.
3. Hold onto your values. Stay honest and above board. By keeping your actions consistent with your values, you will enhance your self-respect and your self-image.

In your discussion with John you stay assertive and maintain your opinion that you can handle the accounts because to give up too easily would cause you to lose respect for yourself and to feel resentful toward John which would damage your relationship with him.

No matter how skillful you become, remember that you will not be able to preserve every relationship and/or get what you want in every relationship. There will always be factors that are not in your control, such as the other person's objectives, values, personality, and current emotional state. Separate what you can control from what you cannot control. You can learn to control yourself, your actions, and your responses. You can generally learn to act in ways that preserve your self-respect. Keep in mind that although you may have some *influence,* you do not have *control* when it comes to other people. Practice the art of acceptance about people and situations outside of your control. The more you can learn to accept the facts of life you cannot change, the less frustrated you will feel.

13. YOUR RELATIONSHIP WITH YOUR PARTNER

All of the skills and suggestions outlined in this chapter can be applied to romantic relationships as well as friendships. Look over the list of characteristics of a healthy friendship. These same characteristics should form the foundation of any romantic relationship. In addition, it takes extra effort on the part of mates to negotiate their differences *and* keep the interest and spark alive as they manage the day-to-day problems of running a household, earning and managing money, and raising children together.

Most marriages go through similar phases. In the romance phase both partners see only the best facets of one another and bring out only the best in one another. As time goes on, however, each partner begins to recognize characteristics in the other that they do not care for, and often a phase of disillusionment ensues. Often the disillusionment leads the couple to either divorce or to stay married, but without the emotional connection. In marriages that make it through and become satisfying, both partners work through their problems together. The working-through phase takes real willingness and effort. It is often a long and arduous process with many ups and downs. If both partners stay with it, the working-through phase can lead to real growth and a lasting phase of deeper intimacy and commitment.

The state of your relationship with your partner will have a direct bearing on the emotional security of your child. Children are naturally intuitive and sensitive and will become extremely stressed when there is chronic tension and conflict around them. Furthermore, parents in conflict are definitely not the most effective parenting team. If your partnership has reached the phase of disillusionment and you feel stuck there, consider enlisting the services of a marital therapist to help you work through this painful phase. If your partner won't go with you, go without him or her. When you're in the middle of the disillusionment phase it is difficult to see the forest for the trees. You need someone standing outside the forest who can see the big picture to help guide you through.

14. CONNECTING WITH A POWER GREATER THAN YOURSELF

An adult who has an imaginary frayed cord connecting herself with others often has the same frayed-cord connection with God. Her earliest attachment figures become the prototypes for her image of God. As a result, God may be perceived as untrustworthy, judgmental, critical, abandoning, rejecting, controlling, or harsh. Yet, if God represents ideal love, the qualities God embodies should be the same qualities embodied by a secure-cord attachment figure. He/She should be accepting, unconditionally loving, forgiving, trustworthy, dependable, tender, gentle, kind, and understanding.

Confront any misperceptions you hold of God that may be rooted in your own experiences with attachment figures. Through the power of prayer and meditation let God help you understand God. Take time each day to make conscious contact with the God of your understanding.

The ultimate connection is the connection to a Higher Power. You become connected to the greater universe beyond the narrow scope of what you can see in this plane of existence when you are "attuned" to God.

15. IN CONCLUSION . . .

If your attachment with your parents was not secure, issues of trust and self-worth may have interfered with your ability to form healthy, supportive relationships in adulthood. With insight into the core beliefs that have stood in your way, you can strengthen the security of your attachments and make connections with others that will help increase your ability to trust and form bonds, buffering you against the stresses of life. Your relationships with others will become your external "secure holding environment." The support you feel will enable you to give more to your child emotionally, and your child will learn to seek and establish healthy relationships by your role modeling. In addition, all parents seeking recovery from the effects of a painful past or from addictions or depression need others in their lives. Recovery should not be a solitary venture. You will find there is indeed strength in numbers as you reach out and make connections with supportive others and with a Higher Power on your personal journey.

Chapter Ten

A New Life Story

Changing Your Core Beliefs

The intent of this chapter is to help you get a new perspective on your life. You will discover some new and different methods to help you reconstruct any deep-down negative core beliefs or attitudes you adopted as a child. You will be guided in installing healthier, more positive thoughts about your life. You will learn to tell the story of your life in a way that will help you develop a different perspective on where you have been and to feel a sense of satisfaction in how far you have come. Of course, who you are as a parent is a very important part of your life story, and you will be guided in creating an internal image of yourself as the parent you are becoming.

1. THE UNLIVABLE AGREEMENT

You began creating your life story during the very earliest experiences in your life. To understand the circumstances in which you began developing your story, it is important to fully understand the vulnerability of infancy. Every baby born possesses an innate sense that his life is dependent upon his parent—that he needs that parent or he will die. In every infant there is a deep primal fear of abandonment, and to an infant, abandonment equals annihilation. Therefore, every baby born focuses every ounce of spare energy he has on getting his parent to bond with him. He is biologically programmed to pick up on every nuance of his parent's body language and verbal cues. The parental frown, the aversion of the head, the stiffening of the body, can all trigger waves of anxiety in the infant or toddler. Although it is all done on a nonverbal, unconscious level, the child is constantly figuring out what he needs to do to get Mom and Dad to stay with him and to bond with him.

Landry Wildwind, LCSW, a psychotherapist and consultant in private practice in Richmond, California, originated a concept called the "unlivable agreement." Landry describes the unlivable agreement as the agreement the baby makes "during the most threatening moments for the child . . . when the parent appears to withdraw love or caretaking, or threatens the child's sense of selfhood, safety, belonging or value."[1]

At such moments, the baby makes a nonverbal, unconscious agreement to be a certain way—whatever seems to best keep Mom or Dad there for him. Through trial and error the baby or young child figures out what works. Landry states, "The terms of such agreements typically include sacrifice of the child's authentic feelings, needs and development."[2]

Bertrand Cramer, Professor of Psychiatry at the University of Geneva, also writes about the infant's contract with his parents: "One could say that a kind of contract is negotiated. Babies learn what terms they must respect to maintain their relationship with their mothers. This contract is binding, since a baby needs to be reassured at every moment by the mother's expression or tone of voice that she is pleased with him or her."[3]

As much of the agreement is determined even before the child has a vocabulary, the terms are never given conscious examination. Once the terms of the agreement are worked out so that the child can get the best bond possible, even if it is only a partial bond, this agreement becomes permanently embedded within the child's unconscious mind. It becomes a part of his private logic system. Thus, the unspoken agreement can remain unaltered in the unconscious mind into adulthood without any conscious recognition of the agreement whatsoever. Without knowing why, every time the adult veers from the agreement, he may experience intense anxiety. The anxiety he experiences as an adult is the biologically programmed response he had to breaking the agreement when he was an infant. In other words, the adult experiences the innate fear of abandonment and annihilation of the infant self—even when his survival is no longer threatened.

There are many types of unlivable agreements that infants and small children develop. Some young boys and girls agree to shut down their feelings and emotional needs because they have learned that their feelings and needs cause the parent to retreat. Some children who have agreed not to have needs learn to virtually "blend into the woodwork" to keep the parent from rejecting him or her. Some boys and girls agree to take care of the parent's emotional needs in order to keep that parent close by. They may learn to cheer the parent up when she is down or calm the parent when she is distressed. These children grow up worrying about the parent, molding their own behavior in whatever way makes the parent happiest. They can completely lose sight of who they really are, or what makes them happy. For many children, the terms of their agreement include the agreement to not be happy. These children have noticed that any noise, even happy sounds like laughing and playing, cause the parent to distance from them. Some children agree to be the scapegoat for their parent's problems—in other words, to be the "naughty child" and the receptor of the parent's anger. These children found this role provided them with much-needed attention and interaction from their parents. Some children, unfortunately, have to agree to have no ownership of their bodies—to allow their bodies to be used to meet the sexual needs of a parent. The young boy or girl adopting an unlivable agreement has little choice about it. He or she must agree to whatever is necessary to keep that parent close by— to get that parent to bond in whatever partial way is possible. The fear of total annihilation biologically programmed into the child motivates the child like nothing else can.

Melissa, whose story is told in Chapter Sixteen, had worked through several traumatic memories of childhood physical, emotional, and sexual abuse. She wrote out the unlivable agreement she had with her mother as follows:

The Unlivable Agreement

> *If you will just bond with me, Mom, and not reject or abandon me, then I promise I will:*
> *Give up my freedom to be myself, give up my soul, so you can have complete and total control over me.*
> *Give up my right to be real outside of my relationship with you.*
> *Give up my right to enjoy things, to laugh or be happy because that would give me too much of a sense of self and deprive you of control.*
> *Give up my right to have my own needs or to get my needs met because I must subjugate myself to your needs only.*
> *Give up my right to be a sexual person, to enjoy my femaleness or to own my sexuality because my sexuality, too, must be owned by you and controlled by you. I must allow you to use my sexuality to get your needs met.*

I know, Mom, that I have no choice but to live by this agreement or you won't
be my mom and I will die.

Melissa's mother had been dead for several years, but Melissa realized that even after her mother's death she had continued to function according to the rules of the agreement she had made with her mother when
she was just a young child. Of course, this agreement had never been ver-
balized, and in fact was followed by Melissa on an unconscious level. But
when she sat down and tried to figure out exactly what her agreement
was, it became quite obvious to her on a conscious level and the words just
flowed.

Next Melissa thought about what kind of contract she would now like
to establish with her mother. She wrote "Null and Void" across the old
contract in big red letters. The new contract looked like this:

The New Contract

My new contract with you, Mom, says that I will:
Take back my freedom to be myself, own my own soul, and no one will have
total control over me.
Affirm my realness at all times. I no longer need your blank mirror.
Let myself enjoy things that make me happy. I will laugh when I want to. I
will be happy just to be.
Allow myself to have emotional needs and acknowledge that they are impor-
tant. I will allow myself to get my emotional needs met through myself
and others.
I'm not doing this to hurt you, Mom. Just like I had no choice but to follow
the old contract for survival, I have no choice now but to adopt the new
contract for my survival now. I don't want you to be hurt, but I can't
take care of you anymore. I need to turn you over to God's care now.
Our original contract has now expired. I am not renewing it. Everything that
I need to survive and live is inside me. I don't need anything from you
anymore.

Next Melissa did a visualization in which she imagined reading the
terms of the new contract to her mother. She told me she pictured a court-
room where they were in the presence of God. But Melissa became fearful,
and imagined her mother becoming angry and screaming at her. I asked
Melissa to close her eyes and imagine watching from a safe place as I approached her mother. I spoke out loud to her mother about the old con-

tract and the new contract, as I would if her mother had bodily been sitting in my office and I were conducting a family therapy session. I acknowledged the pain that Melissa's mother must have suffered in *her* childhood and adult years, and offered her a chance to stop the generational cycle of hurt in her family—a chance to redeem herself and heal Melissa. At that point Melissa gasped, and said that she could visualize her mother letting go and drawing into the presence of God. Melissa was tearful, and said that for the first time she felt at peace with her mother. She also said that it was the first time she had ever experienced anyone defending her to her mother.

Melissa's work was not over, as now she had to learn how to follow the new contract, and make it a habit in her life. This meant changing habits that had been in place for 40 years, which required some real concerted effort. But identifying her old agreement and claiming her rights in her new contract was a real turning point for Melissa.

Janet came into therapy due to overwhelming anxiety about being a mother. She had two young children and felt tormented by the idea that she was going to make some kind of drastic mistake. Every time the children became ill she became terrified that she would do the wrong thing and they would die. In addition, she was afraid to express her real feelings, even with friends. She constantly questioned her own motives and feared that inside she was really a selfish and a bad person. One of the things that most helped Janet was writing out the terms of the unlivable agreement she believed she had made unconsciously as a child. She remembered that she had grown up in a family where it was very important to assign blame. It had been important to her parents that she admit she was bad over and over again, and to accept responsibility for anything that went wrong. She remembered that her parents were always suspicious of her, and as a result she had become suspicious of herself. For whatever reason, in order to be accepted in her family she had had to take the role of the "bad one," or "the one to blame." Sometimes therapists refer to the member who takes this role in a family as the "family scapegoat." A family with a scapegoat can pin their problems on the scapegoat, allowing the rest of the family to feel exonerated.

Janet's unlivable agreement and new contract read as follows:

My Unlivable Agreement

> *To get the acceptance, and bonding I need to survive I agree to:*
> *Not be myself.*

Be less than others—stay in my place.
Have badness in me.
Be responsible for everything.
Remain hypervigilant.

My New Contract

> *The above is null and void. Now I agree to think with my heart because I know it to be true and not be afraid to be myself or be responsible for only my actions.*

Janet began working very hard at looking into her heart and expressing true feelings and thoughts. She began expressing herself in her watercolors, and painted according to what she felt, not according to what would please other people. She began taking actions in her life that expressed her values, not the values of her parents. She made the decision to stick to her guns even in the face of criticism, although she balanced this decision with a willingness to take an honest look at criticism first and assess if there was something she needed to change or improve in herself. She decided she would not take responsibility for negative feelings or problems that did not belong to her. Some of these changes made waves in her family of origin and in her own nuclear family. But she found when she stayed true to herself and took care of herself in this way she had more energy, and more of herself available to give to others in a loving way. The greatest benefit was that she began taking care of her children, even when they were ill, with more confidence. Her anxiety lessened as she realized that she was not a bad person who caused bad things to happen.

Joe, recovering from post-traumatic stress disorder, addictions, and depression, tells his story in Chapter Sixteen. His alcoholic mother had been physically and sexually abusive to him. He wrote his unlivable agreement with her as follows:

My Unlivable Agreement

> *If you will not reject me openly, mom:*
> *I will keep the secret.*
> *I will not force you to face the truth about what you did to me.*
> *I accept responsibility for the abuse I received from you.*
> *I realize I was unworthy of your love and protection.*
> *So if you will pretend I will pretend that everything is O.K.*

My New Contract

I will be happy.
I will be responsible for me.
You will be responsible for you.
The cycle of abuse is broken.
I am worthy of love and I am capable of love because I lay this old agreement
down.

As Joe freed himself from the terms of the old agreement which had kept him tied up in shame and fear, he found he was better able to live in the present. He discovered he had the freedom to really love and enjoy his present family, and he could actually feel their love for him.

Exercise: See if you can put your own "unlivable agreement" into words, and write it out in your notebook. Refer back to any negative self-beliefs you listed in the exercise in Chapter Two. Are any of those beliefs part of the terms of your unlivable agreement? Think about how you would like to change your agreement now. Write out the terms of your new contract.

Creating a new contract is an important step in creating your new life story. Adopting your new contract will have very positive effects on your life, including your parenting. Unlivable agreements are generally not helpful to adults who want to be good parents. Unlivable agreements often prevent people from feeling they have the right to have feelings or needs, get their needs met, or take care of themselves. By truly acknowledging their rights to have needs and feelings, their right to enjoy things, and their right to get their needs met in healthy ways *and* making changes accordingly in their lives, they are able to live happier, more balanced lives. Happier parents are naturally able to create a happier, more enjoyable and secure environment for their children.

2. A NEW CONTRACT FOR YOUR CHILD

In addition, if you can revise your own bonding contract and adopt an agreement that is healthy for you, you will be better equipped to be able to offer your child an "unconditional bonding agreement"—one that offers your love and affection without conditions, along with acceptance and appreciation for who he or she is.

Exercise: In your notebook, write out the terms of the bonding contract that you wish your own children to have with you.

Dan wrote out this contract for his one-month-old baby, Dillon: Dad and Mom, I agree to accept your unconditional love and to be whoever I am. I agree to express my needs, my thoughts, and my feelings. I agree to depend on you to meet my emotional needs, to keep me safe, and to give me guidance. I agree to experience all kinds of feelings—happiness, sadness, love, anger, and to know that you will always be there no matter what.

3. PUTTING YOUR NEW CONTRACT INTO EFFECT

Revising your unlivable agreement can be an important step toward changing deep-down core beliefs that have distorted your sense of who you are. After creating your new contract, read it often. As you consciously practice taking actions in your life that are consistent with the terms of your new contract, your new life story is taking form. You can feel satisfaction in knowing that you are consciously choosing your story out of the wisdom you have gained in your adult years. You can also feel pride in knowing that you are providing your child with a personal story that affirms his or her specialness and offers love with no strings attached.

4. AFFIRMATIONS TO GOD

I continually learn from the clients I work with. Sophia had been raised with rigid, critical parents who had been unable to offer her unconditional love and acceptance, leaving her with a deep-seated belief that she was defective, and a severe, chronic depression. Following is Sophia's unlivable agreement and her new contract:

My Unlivable Agreement
> *I will agree to be unlovable and defective.*
> *I will agree not to ask to get my emotional needs met.*
> *I will agree to believe I deserve mistreatment.*

The New Contract
> *I am lovable and am not defective.*
> *I deserve to ask others to get my needs met.*

I do not deserve to be mistreated.

While Sophia was coming to therapy with me, she also began attending an informal support group of women seeking spiritual growth. From this group she developed the idea of turning her new contract into affirmations to God. The next week she came in with the following affirmations that she had been writing out every day in her notebook.

Affirmations to God

> *Thank you for making me perfect and lovable in every way. I will honor this gift by being mindful of and not judging my feelings and thoughts.*
> *Thank you for putting people in my life that meet my emotional needs. I will honor this gift by not allowing others to mistreat me.*

Sophia then began adding more affirmations to her list. She wanted to develop a more positive outlook at home and at work, become less judgmental, stop worrying about money, and begin eating correctly. She wrote:

> *Thank you for the gifts of positive attitude and gratitude. I will honor these gifts by not judging myself or others.*
> *Thank you for a job I enjoy and all the money to do whatever I want. I will honor this gift by being productive.*
> *Thank you for the willingness and courage to change the things I can. I will honor this by writing daily affirmations and recording my food each day.*

Sophia found that the important thing was that she write the affirmations to God *as if they already felt true for her,* even though in the beginning they did not feel that way at all!

Sophia underwent an amazing transformation! She became much more positive, more self-confident, and for the first time in years and years she was able to stop compulsively overeating. I was sold on her idea, and began sharing Sophia's idea with other clients who also found that praying in this way on a daily basis helped them transform their beliefs, feelings and actions.

Following are more examples of affirmations to God:

> *Thank you for making me a patient and caring parent. I will honor this gift by giving myself credit for the good things I do.*
> *Thank you for giving me all of the time and energy I will need today. I will honor this gift by staying calm and relaxed.*

Thank you for making me a valuable, worthwhile human being. I will honor this gift by taking good care of myself today and not harming myself in any way.

Thank you for putting so many loving, good people in my life. I will honor this gift by loving others today.

Thank you for giving me love, protection, and guidance. I will honor this by staying in today and letting go of useless worries.

Thank you for giving me the gift of sobriety. I will honor this gift by calling my sponsor today.

Thank you for giving me a strong and healthy body. I will honor this gift by ingesting only healthy food today.

Thank you for giving me the gift of serenity today. I will honor this gift by letting go of things I cannot change.

Writing out or praying affirmations to God on a daily basis can help you change old negative beliefs and actions and connect to more positive energy in your life. Affirmations to God have greatly enriched my own daily meditation and prayer time. I often make up new affirmations to God to fit the need of the day. The prayers help me achieve a greater level of serenity and connection to my Higher Power and create more positive energy and attitudes in my own life.

Exercise: Look at your new contract and try writing out your own list of affirmations to God. Try thanking God for your new beliefs and attitudes as if you already have them in the present, and describe how you will honor each gift. Carry them with you. Write them out or repeat them each day. Make your affirmations your personal mantras.

These affirmations can help you tap into more positive energy and create a more positive outlook as part of your new life story. You may be surprised at how they enrich your life through a deeper sense of spirituality and connection with your Higher Power.

5. MAKING SENSE OF YOUR PAST

After interviewing a large number of adults and assessing their attachment styles, Mary Maine, a researcher at the University of California at Berkeley, and her colleagues made some interesting observations. They noticed there were some major differences in the way these adults told their personal stories. Adults with secure attachment status in adulthood were made up of two main groups. The first group of secure adults experienced healthy, close relationships with their parents as they were growing up. These adults maintained secure attachment styles throughout their whole lives. The second group of secure adults was made up of adults who had achieved a secure attachment style in adulthood even though their early relationships with parents had not been happy. This group of now secure adults had worked through their feelings about their early lives by talking with therapists and supportive others. They were subsequently able to tell a cohesive story of their lives in a way that made sense of their past and gave them a feeling of mastery over their early experiences. They were no longer either overwhelmed by their emotions or disconnected from them. They had worked through their feelings related to their parents to the point that they were able to see their parents realistically. They acknowledged both the positive and the negative characteristics of their parents. The adults in the study who remained insecurely attached had difficulty telling a cohesive story of their lives and became either emotionally overwhelmed or emotionally disconnected during the telling of the story.[4]

Sorting out our memories, making sense of our life story, and coming to terms with it appear to be important in moving us along the continuum toward a more secure attachment style. If you have a hard time telling your story without sounding confused and disjointed, it may be a good idea to let a therapist help you put your story together. One helpful technique is to create a time line. Draw a line on a long sheet of butcher paper, and make a mark for each year of your life. Fill in each event you can remember next to the year it happened. This may help you create some order out of the chaos of confusing memories. If you get overwhelmed with feelings when you tell your life story or feel emotionally disconnected, find a professional who can help you practice the emotion management skills in Chapter Seven before you attempt to finish putting your story together. If you experience vivid nightmares or daytime flashes of memories that seem vividly real during the day, you may suffer from post-traumatic stress disorder and will need a skilled professional to help you with the resolution of past trauma.

As you practice telling your story, eventually you will reach a point at which you can tell it in a way that makes sense. You will know you have worked it through when you have emotions connected to your early experiences, but you do not feel overwhelmed by them. As you practice telling your story, compare where you have been in your life with where you are now. Acknowledge the progress you have made in overcoming the difficulties of your past and honor whatever you had to do to survive. As you put the pieces of your story together you will develop a sense of mastery over the past and anticipation for the journey ahead.

6. MEDITATION FOR THE PARENT YOU ARE BECOMING

If you are taking the time to read this book, your role as a parent is an important part of your life story and your sense of identity. However, as the ghosts of your past intruded in your relationship with your child, your self-image as a parent may have taken a beating. A damaged self-image as a parent can create feelings of failure and low self-worth. In addition, just as our behavior impacts our self-image, our self-image impacts our behavior. The following meditation can help you create a more positive parent self-image and enlist the help of your unconscious mind in becoming the parent you want to be. Add this meditation to your other taped meditations and listen to it often.

As you are relaxing there . . . noticing your breath, in, and out . . . you body and your mind just know . . . how to help you relax . . . how to help your muscles let go of their tension . . . in your head and neck . . . your shoulders and your back . . . your arms and hands . . . your legs and feet . . . You can feel this feeling of comfort . . . in your mind, peaceful, and relaxed . . . that's right, and as you rest there . . . you can imagine yourself walking . . . down a magical path in a forest . . . a beautiful forest with green leaves . . . the sun forming patterns as it filters through . . . onto the path in front of you . . . and up ahead there is a clearing . . . As you get closer you can see your future self . . . You see the parent you are now becoming . . . there, with your children . . . the parent you have always wished to be . . . Notice how serene and confident you look . . . Notice your relaxed and confident face . . . Notice your body, calm and easy-going . . . Notice what you are doing . . . how you are responding with your child . . . very adult, very in charge, self-confident . . . secure, firm, loving, accepting, touching, hugging, smiling . . . enjoying yourself, enjoying your child . . . Feel yourself now, moving into this scene . . . notice how you feel, in your wise, adult mind . . . as the parent you are becoming . . . and enjoy this experience for as long as you would like . . . and when you are ready, bring back with you . . . whatever resources you need . . . and wake up your arms, your legs, and open up your eyes, feeling refreshed and rested.

7. IN CONCLUSION . . .

Remember that your story is one of progress, not perfection. Perfectionism is immobilizing. Perfection is an unattainable goal, and is a setup for feelings of failure and low self-worth. Perfectionism is about judging and criticizing, and is fueled by an oversized critical parent. Identify it for what it is, acknowledge it, and choose not to listen to it. Your new life story is a human story. It is a story about overcoming a difficult past to become more whole, more healed, and more effective as a parent. It is a story of courage and determination. Give yourself permission to feel good about the progress you are making as you incorporate your new contract in your life, connect with more positive, spiritual energy, and image yourself as the parent you are becoming.

Chapter Eleven

Parents with Additional Challenges

Coping when It Seems Like Too Much

Imagine if every baby could be born at the perfect time to a couple who was happily married and completely compatible, had plenty of money, and all the time in the world to do what they needed to do and be with their baby. What a terrific fantasy!

Now let's get real. Most babies are born to couples or singles somewhere between adolescence and early 40s. In real life, many of these parents are often still struggling financially, barely making it from paycheck to paycheck, or not making it financially at all. Many of these parents are still trying to find their "niche" in the world—one in which they can both feel competent and make a decent living. Many of these parents are struggling with their relationship—working through issues related to trust, anger, money, household chores, and time together. Many of these parents are not in a committed relationship at all. Many babies are conceived unexpectedly—and arrive at times which are really not at all convenient for the parents.

New babies often find themselves in a stress-filled world. That's reality.

1. STRESS—LET'S FACE IT!

Yes, it is possible to deal with the realities of a stress-filled life and be a good parent, too. The first step is to take stock of your life and identify where your external stress is coming from. Is your relationship with your mate conflicted? Do you have conflict with other significant others in your life—parents or siblings? Are you going it alone? Are you short on support from others in your life? Do you have financial worries? Are there stressful problems at work? Is your job by its very nature stressful to you?

The second step is to be aware of how these stresses are affecting you. Use your distress cue card from the exercise in Chapter Seven. Do you find yourself preoccupied with worry thoughts, making it difficult to concentrate or remember things? Do you find that you have trouble winding down and going to sleep at night? Do you feel tension in your chest or suffer from stomachaches or headaches? Do you find yourself nervous and anxious, or irritable and grouchy? Do you find yourself losing your temper far too easily? Are these things also negatively affecting your self-esteem?

The third step is to examine how your stress may be negatively impacting your child. If you are preoccupied with worry thoughts and have trouble concentrating, you may have trouble "tuning in" to your child's feelings and needs. Your anxiety may interfere with your ability to hear your child and read her expressions and body language. If this is an ongoing problem, your child may be lacking that feeling of "attunement" from you that is so helpful to a secure attachment.

If stress is causing you to feel tense and anxious, you may have trouble soothing and calming your child when she feels distressed. You may be more likely to lose your temper with your child and say and do things you later regret. If these problems are ongoing, your child may lack a sense of a secure holding environment.

The fourth step of course is to find some healthy outlets and healthy self-soothing activities to help you cope. As you practice the skills taught in Chapter Seven you will find out which methods of relaxation and outlets work for you. Stay consciously and mindfully aware of your stress level. Use your distress cue card to help you stay aware of your stress level, and continue to write down the outlets and the techniques for relaxing and letting go of stress that work for you.

The fifth step is to *find support*. Do not try to manage your anxiety and cope with your situation alone. If you are in a stressful situation like single parenting, a divorce, a relationship conflict, financial distress, or job stress, you need supportive others to talk to.

1.1. We All Need Someone to Lean On

We all need someone to lean on—*especially* if we are parents. We can't provide the solid, steady holding environment our child needs if there is no one upon whom *we* can lean. We cannot be attuned to our child's feelings and needs if no one is tuned in to what *we* feel—especially when we are under stress.

Find some other adults upon whom you can lean. You need to be able to talk about your feelings. You need others who will listen without giving advice if that's what you need—and who will understand. You need others with whom you can discuss your problems who will help you figure out solutions.

There is no one perfect support person. There is no one person who will be able to be emotionally available every time you need support, or who will always give you just the kind of listening ear you need. Resist the urge to put all of your emotional eggs in one basket! One person can never be everything to someone else. Even if you have a supportive wife or husband or supportive parents, you still need a supportive network of friends.

Consider attending a support group. One of the Twelve Step groups listed in Appendix C may fit for you, such as Adult Children of Alcoholics, Al-Anon, or Alcoholics Anonymous. If you are single, consider Parents Without Partners, listed in Appendix B. Many parents find a supportive community of people within a church setting. Many single parents find a network by joining a singles' group or a couples' group associated with a local church. Remember that most people feel uncomfortable the first few times in a new group of people. Feeling a sense of belonging takes time. Attend a group at least five or six times before you decide whether or not it is for you.

Even when life isn't anywhere near picture perfect, just knowing there are others on whom you can lean for support will help give you the strength you need to be the pillar for your child. Knowing there are others who will listen to you will help you "tune in" to what your child is telling you by her words or body language. When you are finding comfort in relationships with other adults you will feel better able to offer comfort to your child.

2. TEENAGE MOMS AND DADS

If you are over 20, you can pretty safely skip this section. But there are many teenage moms and dads out there, and you have some very specific risk factors that need to be addressed so that you, too, can give your child what she needs to grow up feeling secure and worthwhile.

What makes being a teenage parent difficult is that developmentally you are at a stage in your life where you are (just like every other teenager on the planet) trying to figure out who you are—what you think about things—what you feel—and what you want out of life. In the middle of all this, you suddenly have a new task—to help your baby figure out who *she* is, what *she* feels, and what *she* wants! Actually, teenagers and babies are working on some of the same developmental issues! It's just that teenagers are working on figuring out who they are at a much more advanced level than the babies and toddlers. So even though you worked on this task when you were a baby, you couldn't finish the work because your brain wasn't developed enough.

Developing your own identity and helping your baby develop her identity are two jobs that actually conflict with each other quite a bit. Why? Because as you are developing your identity you are very focused on yourself. This doesn't mean you are a selfish person by nature. It just means that right now you are very absorbed in this task. At the same time, however, your baby has the same kind of task to do, which is very important to her future well-being, and her parents are the most important people in the world to help her. In order to help her, you have to be attuned with what she is feeling and needing. You have to be able to show her that she is a very special and important person so that she will grow up feeling she has a self and that it is a very special self. Therefore, somehow you have to learn how to be both self-absorbed *and* baby-absorbed all at the same time!

The other reason being a teenage parent is difficult is because becoming a parent has not happened at a very *convenient* time in your life. You may not have a solid relationship with a mate. You may not have a place where you and your child and possibly a mate can live on your own. You may not be finished with school. You may not have the capacity to support yourself and your baby. You are still trying to accomplish all of these very fundamental things *and* raise a child! What's more, you may have conflicted relationships with your parents, or the child's other parent, and you may find your old friends drifting away. Most teenage parents are in extremely stressful circumstances. In fact, psychologist Joy Osofsky and her colleagues at Louisiana State University have found that teenage parents are more vulnerable to depression and low self-esteem than older parents.[1] No wonder it's tough for a teenage parent to give his or her baby the secure holding environment the child needs!

More than anything, teenage parents need emotional support. You still need someone to nurture you, to be attuned with your feelings, and to give you a secure holding environment. If you can find others to whom you can confide and where you feel understood and cared about, more than anything else this will help you to be able to give your child the loving attention she or he needs. Finding supportive others does not mean finding someone who will take care of your responsibilities for you. You need someone who will listen and who will give you guidance and emotional support. Find someone who is older—someone who is not in the same developmental stage, and who is experienced with kids. If your relationship with your parents is too strained right now, perhaps there is an aunt, uncle, grandparent, or neighbor with whom you could spend more time.

In addition, it would be a good idea to find a counselor to give you professional guidance. Even if you have no money or insurance, universities offering graduate programs in counseling and social work often offer community counseling services at low fees. Social services affiliated with religious organizations also often offer counseling for a sliding scale fee. Also check out the services offered through the local YWCA. A counselor can provide guidance and resources to help you with parenting, child development, relationships, finances, education, and careers.

Osofsky and her colleagues identify some common problems to teenage parents, which I have adapted as follows:

1. *Teenage parents have trouble tuning in to what their babies are feeling.* To avoid this pitfall, practice observing your baby closely. Listen to the different types of cries, and notice the different facial expressions that your baby makes. Spend time with older adults who have raised children and ask them what they think your baby is feeling at different times.

2. *Teenage parents have trouble giving their babies the feeling that they are safe, secure, and loved.* Experiment with different ways to play with your baby. What makes her smile? What makes her laugh? Try talking to her in "baby talk." The research shows that babies respond more to baby talk than to normal voice tones. Experiment with different ways to soothe your

baby when she is upset. Does she like to be rocked or walked? What is her favorite position to be held? Observe people you think are good with children, and try to imitate them. Don't think this is silly. This is the best way there is to learn to be a good parent! Remember that the most important thing you can teach your baby is how to have a close relationship with another human being. This is *far* more important than teaching her not to touch the glass vase on the coffee table! For more ideas about how to get close to your baby, read through Chapters Twelve and Fifteen.

3. *Teenage parents often have unrealistic expectations of how babies and children act and what they are capable of doing.* Teenage parents often expect more of their children than is realistic. Get a book from the library on child development, read parenting magazines, or talk to your pediatrician or to a counselor to find out what is normal. Observe other children who are the same age as your child and notice how they act and what they can do. Remember that there is a wide variance for what is normal because different children develop in different areas at different rates! The more your child feels that you accept her for the little individual she is, right where she is, the better able she will be to develop her potential emotionally, intellectually, and physically.[2]

2.1. If You Are the Teen Dad

If you are the dad, don't think for a minute that you aren't important, because you are. Even if you are not now in a relationship with the mother of your baby, you will always and forever be a very important attachment figure in the life of your child. The research shows that if you maintain positive involvement with your child, you will positively impact your child's emotional well-being for the rest of her or his life. If you are an absent father, or interact only in negative ways with your child and her or his mother, you will have just as much of an impact, but it will be negative.

And yet you, too, are stressed out. You are in an extremely tough situation financially and emotionally. All of the advice given about seeking support and talking about your feelings is for you as much as it is for your child's mother. Sometimes talking about feelings is more difficult for men. Our culture seems to portray "real" men as emotionally distant or the "strong, silent type." But men who try to conform to this stereotype build unhealthy walls around their emotions. They have trouble maintaining relationships, and their children find them unavailable emotionally. The best thing you can do for your child is to avoid building walls, and talk to someone about what you are going through.

3. POST-TRAUMATIC STRESS DISORDER

Many individuals who were subjected to severe types of physical or sexual abuse in childhood suffer from post-traumatic stress disorder (PTSD.) Symptoms include intrusive memories that surface as visual pictures, body sensations, or recurring dreams. Sometimes the abuse is repeated or reenacted in some way in one's present life. Both intrusive memories and reenactments are the trauma survivor's way of trying to get some mastery over the trauma. The unconscious mind is replaying the trauma over and over like a stuck record with the purpose of finding a better ending. Unfortunately, the sought-after feeling of resolution and mastery never comes and the survivor is stuck in an endless nightmare of reliving the original event or events.

Another symptom of PTSD is a chronic feeling of hypervigilance and anxiety. The trauma survivor becomes stuck in the feelings of fear related to the trauma and is not able to self-soothe and calm down.

The individual with PTSD tries very hard to avoid the painful memories and the anxious feelings. Blocking memories through the use of drugs, alcohol, or food are all common ways of trying to avoid the pain. Dissociating, which is kind of a "splitting off" internally, is a common method of coping. There are many ways to dissociate. Some survivors describe "spacing out" mentally, "going numb," or describe a feeling that they are no longer in their bodies. Some survivors will dissociate so thoroughly at times that they will lose time. The skill of dissociation is usually learned during the childhood trauma, as children are most capable of learning to dissociate. Many survivors remember "leaving their bodies" during the traumatic childhood event. Some survivors have lived through situations so far beyond human endurance that they dissociated to the point of creating "alter" personalities to endure the painful situations and carry the memories for them.

People who suffer from PTSD as adults have limited control over their emotional responses and reactions. Trauma memories are stored differently in the brain from other types of memories. They are stored in the limbic area of the brain, which is the emotional center. Any type of stimulus in the environment that resembles any aspect of the trauma can trigger an intrusive memory that may surface in the form of picture, sensation, or pure emotion. Because during flashbacks the left side of the brain, including the center for speech, becomes inactive, individuals with PTSD have great difficulty describing their memories or flashbacks in words. It is easy to see why some individuals with PTSD get to feeling pretty hopeless at times.

If the traumatic abuse was inflicted by a parent, the person with PTSD will usually have a fearful type of attachment style. Any close relationship can trigger feelings of fear, anxiety, lack of control, unsafety, and lack of trust. Spouses and children of PTSD survivors are often left feeling hurt and confused by the reactions of the trauma survivor in the context of their relationships with him or her.

If you are a trauma survivor and a parent, you are facing a challenging situation as you try to cope with traumatic memories and overwhelming emotions while trying to stay emotionally connected with your child. It is no surprise if you have difficulty soothing and comforting your child when you are enduring such overwhelming emotional storms of your own! For your own emotional well-being and for the well-being of your family, you need to find a support system, and you need to find a professional skilled in trauma resolution. Before working with memories your therapist should help you learn techniques to help you ground yourself when you become dissociated and to manage your intense emotions.

One method of treatment that has been proven helpful for trauma is called Eye Movement Desensitization and Reprocessing (EMDR.) It is not the only method available for working with PTSD, but it is one that I have found to be effective. Researchers do not yet understand how it works, but the eye movements may somehow help the parts of the brain work together to process the traumatic material. If your therapist uses EMDR, he or she will first establish with you which traumatic images and emotions need to be processed. Your therapist will also help you identify the negative thoughts that are connected to the trauma and the positive thoughts you would rather have associated with the trauma. Most people have three primary core negative beliefs that must be addressed. These are, "It was my fault," "I am not safe," and "I am not in control." Your therapist will help you process the painful images to bring down the level of distress and change the negative beliefs to rational, more positive ones. EMDR can also be used to help change negative core beliefs associated with earlier experiences that were disturbing or upsetting, even when they would not fall under the category of true trauma.

4. DEPRESSION

People who have never suffered from a clinical depression have a very difficult time comprehending what it is like to be genuinely depressed. Even though their intentions are probably good, people who have never experienced depression will make comments such as, "You just have to snap out of it," or "Look on the bright side of things." A clinical depression is not the same as "having a down day" or "feeling out of sorts" for a few days. Whether a clinical depression has been inherited, is the result of early childhood deprivation or trauma, or is due to overwhelming losses, brain chemistry is altered. Sometimes therapy alone seems to be enough to straighten things out, but often some kind of antidepressant medication is required along with the therapy to help get the chemistry back in balance. Often therapy isn't beneficial without medication because the depression clouds the thinking. Antidepressant medication is not addictive. It will not give you a "high" and it will not do a thing for you if you are not depressed. Many people with a mild to moderate depression are benefiting from the herb, St. John's Wort. This herb was used in Europe to treat depression for years before it was approved for use in the United States.

Symptoms of clinical depression include the loss of interest in things one used to enjoy, feelings of lethargy and apathy, and feelings of irritability. Sometimes depression includes tearfulness, problems with memory and concentration, sleep problems, problems with eating too much or lack of appetite, feelings of hopelessness, and sometimes thoughts about suicide.

If you suffer from a clinical depression, seek help both for your sake and for the sake of your child. Obviously, if you are depressed you probably have great difficulty being "attuned" with your child or experiencing light-hearted, playful, emotional exchanges with her. Your child may experience you as overly serious, preoccupied with your thoughts, or even irritable and reactive. You can't control the fact that you suffer from depression or that the depression affects your responses to your child. What you can control is seeking help and getting the appropriate treatment so that you don't have to suffer from this any longer than necessary. To lessen the impact of your mood on your child, find a support system. When you don't have it emotionally to give, ask someone else to take your child for awhile both to give you some respite and to give your child another outlet for social interaction.

If your child is old enough to talk with about it, validate her feelings and perceptions. Of course you don't want to give her information she is too young to understand or make her think she has a responsibility to make you feel better. But you *can* say, for example, "I must seem pretty grumpy to you. You're right, I have been grumpy. It has nothing to do with you, though, and it's not your job to make me feel better. I love you, and I'm going to go talk to someone who can help me feel better so we can start having fun again. It might take a little while, but it will get better."

5. POSTPARTUM DEPRESSION

Most new mothers have a short period of feeling blue after giving birth that is called "postpartum blues." This may be related to sleep deprivation, feeling worn out from the delivery, or hormone changes. Postpartum blues are not serious, as they go away in just a few days.

About ten percent of new mothers experience a more serious depression following delivery. This is called "postpartum depression." Postpartum depression may be triggered by sudden changes in hormones or by changes in thyroid level after giving birth. Other factors may include lack of rest and the stress of caring for a new baby and adjusting to the change in lifestyle. "Feeling memories" related to the mother's childhood as described in Chapter Two also negatively impact a mother's mood. Mothers who lack supportive partners or supportive families are more vulnerable to postpartum depression. New mothers may experience the symptoms of depression following the birth of their baby for weeks, months, or even longer. Sometimes postpartum depression is accompanied by scary thoughts and fears about harming the baby and fears about not loving the baby. It is important to recognize that these unsettling thoughts and fears are symptoms of the depression.

If you think you are suffering from postpartum depression discuss your symptoms with your doctor. Make a conscious effort to get as much rest as you can. If you lack a supportive partner or supportive family members, ask for help from friends, your church, or a counselor. Find a friend or hire a babysitter who can give you respite from caring for your baby on a regular basis. This will help you and your baby, because after a break you will return to her more refreshed, and with more energy to interact with her. Check out the resources for postpartum depression listed in Appendix B that may be helpful to you.

6. BORDERLINE PERSONALITY DISORDER

People who grew up in families where they didn't experience adequate emotional nurturing, and where feelings were discounted as not valid or unimportant, are vulnerable to the development of borderline personality disorder. Often individuals with this diagnosis also have posttraumatic stress symptoms and/or symptoms of severe depression. Individuals with borderline personality disorder often have chronic feelings of emptiness, worthlessness, and despair that just seem to go on and on. They may resort to self-harming such as cutting or burning themselves as a way of releasing pent-up tension. They may also have trouble with compulsive behaviors in other areas that are harmful such as drug or alcohol use. Individuals with this diagnosis often lack a strong sense of self. They may experience chronic suicidal thoughts, and may have acted out on these thoughts more than once in the past. Individuals with this diagnosis usually have a fearful attachment style, resulting in unstable relationships with other people.

If you identify with these symptoms, you probably also find it very difficult to provide your child with a secure holding environment or to be attuned to her feelings and needs because your emotions are so overwhelming to you.

Because your childhood experiences did not teach you healthy skills for managing your emotions and coping with distress, first and foremost you need to learn skills for managing your emotions in addition to proper medical treatment for your depression. Marsha Linehan's Dialectical Behavioral Treatment Program was designed for treating individuals with borderline personality disorder, even though most of us can benefit from learning the skills that her program teaches. The skills workbook, intended to be used with a therapist, teaches how to regulate emotions, cope with distress, develop healthy relationships, and apply Zen mindfulness skills for better mind control.[3] (See Chapters Seven and Nine.)

You will want to include your children in some of your therapy sessions, or enlist another therapist to work separately with them so that they can begin learning some basic skills for identifying, verbalizing, and coping with feelings right along with you. If you are lacking in these skills, they probably are, too, so why not give them a head start on learning them now? As you and your children learn about managing feelings and learn better relationship and communication skills, the family will become a more secure holding environment for them and parenting will become more rewarding for you.

7. ADDICTIONS

As discussed in Chapter Nine, if you grew up in an environment where you learned not to trust other people, you will be more vulnerable to forming an attachment relationship with alcohol, drugs, food, gambling, sex, or some other substance or behavior. If you are addicted, you chose the substance or behavior as a substitute for close, trusting relationships because it gave you a predictable mood change, whereas in your early attachment experiences you learned not to depend on people for emotional fulfillment. You found you could count on your addiction to either soothe and comfort you, or thrill and excite you. It made your painful feelings go away. You found your addiction to be predictable, dependable, and trustworthy. It made you feel like you had control. It became the secure holding environment you could not find anywhere else. It became your primary attachment relationship. You loved it intensely and it seemed to give you what you needed in return. What a perfect relationship! It's no wonder your life began to revolve around this relationship. Of course, all your other relationships got pushed to the periphery, including your relationships with your children!

Unfortunately, soon after you were sucked into this attachment relationship with your addiction, the illusion of the perfect relationship most likely began to crumble. You probably found that the positive affects were short-lived, and you found yourself desperate to act out with your substance or behavior again and again. As your life began to revolve around using or acting out, your real-life relationships probably began to fall apart. As the short-term feeling of control wore off you most likely discovered your life was becoming more and more out of control. The painful consequences related to your addiction may have caused you to feel increasingly ashamed and distressed, only to bring you back to your addiction for comfort, and around and around the cycle you went.

In addition, as you have experienced the roller coaster ride of intense, short-lived peaks and valleys of despair, your child has been there in the seat next to you. There is no such thing as a secure holding environment on this ride. There has been no one attuned with your child as she or he has endured the peaks and valleys with you, because your energy has been focused on holding on for your own dear life.

If you are not yet in recovery, don't try to handle your addiction on your own. Seek both professional addictions counseling and a Twelve Step support group to help you. Other types of support groups may also be helpful such as church-based recovery groups. Groups are essential in helping people with addictions trust and connect to others.

Be aware that denial will be an obstacle for you. Denial is one of the biggest reasons why people stay addicted. Denial works in many ways, including denying to oneself that there is a problem. Denial includes convincing others that there is no problem, and it includes believing that one can deal with it alone ("I can stop whenever I decide to"). Denial includes believing that other people are to blame and includes telling oneself, "It's really not hurting anyone but me."

As you work on your own recovery you can help your children by involving them in some counseling so that they can learn about addiction and recovery. Al-Anon, the Twelve Step group for family members of alcoholics, has Al-Ateen meetings in many areas. Al-Ateen can be a great way for teenagers to become part of the recovery process. Many areas even have Al-Anon groups for younger children. It is vital that you do not attempt to hide the facts of your addiction and recovery from your children. Claudia Black, author of several books for adult children of alcoholics, has identified three typical rules in alcoholic families. They are, "Don't talk, don't trust, and don't feel."[4] Show your children that it's O.K. to talk about the addiction and that it's O.K. to trust others to help them when they have problems. Show your children that it's O.K. to talk about their feelings, even if they talk about how scared, sad, and angry they feel about your addiction. The more open and accepting of their feelings you can be, the less negative impact your addiction will have on their lives.

8. BIPOLAR DISORDER

Bipolar disorder is a mood disorder that seems to be primarily biological. There are many levels of severity and different types of bipolar disorder, so that two individuals with this disorder may seem quite different in the way that their moods affect them. Basically, an individual with bipolar disorder has experienced both periods of depression and one or more periods of mania or hypomania. Hypomania may include an increase in activity level, emotional lability, and feelings of euphoria or grandiosity. Mania may include extreme hyperactivity, emotional lability, explosive anger, grandiose or paranoid delusions, incoherent thought processes, or even psychosis. Bipolar disorder must be treated with the right medication. Therapy can be helpful in learning to manage the symptoms and coping with other associated problems. If you are a parent with bipolar disorder, it will be important to work with your therapist on identifying when you are entering an episode of severe depression or mania, and to have a plan that will lessen the impact on your child. Having one or preferably more support people that can step in and be a support for your child during those periods will be a vital part of your plan. Your child will develop a sense of a more secure holding environment when your backup support people can supply her with the structure and security she needs during your difficult times.

If you have a diagnosis of bipolar disorder, like the parent with major depression or an addiction you can also help your child by getting her involved in some counseling. A counselor can help your child understand the disorder and develop her own plans for coping when you become less emotionally available to her.

Refer to Appendix B for further resources.

9. IN CONCLUSION . . .

God, grant me the serenity to accept the things I cannot change, to change the things I can, and the wisdom to know the difference.

True wisdom is sorting out what can be changed from what cannot be changed, and focusing on the things that we *can* do instead of dwelling on things outside of our control. As parents, most of us would love to give our children an ideal world in which to live, but we must all realize that an ideal world just doesn't exist—not for anybody. Divorce, financial problems, emotional problems, conflict—most children are born into families that run into some type of difficulty at one time or another. We live in a stressful and complex society. Try to forgive yourself for not being able to provide a fairy tale life for your child and focus your energy instead in a more helpful direction. Zero in on what you *can* do, such as getting more support for yourself and for your child, getting proper treatment for a depression, or getting help for an addiction, to reduce the negative impact on your child. As your children observe you changing the things you can, they will learn from your example how to tackle the problems in their own lives head on.

Part Three

The Third Key

Strengthening Your Relationship with Your Child

Congratulations! Through the first part of this book you have gained an understanding of any misperceptions or emotional responses that may have interfered with your relationship with your child. By working through the second part you have begun developing a more secure inner "holding environment" for yourself and overcoming the effects of your past by practicing visualizations, acquiring emotions management skills and relationship skills, and changing beliefs and perceptions. You are now ready to adopt a healthy approach to parenting that will allow you to establish a more secure attachment relationship at the same time that you teach your child discipline and responsibility. Special techniques offered later in this part will help you to do any repair work in your attachment relationship with your child that may be needed.

Chapter Twelve

Adopting a Healthy Philosophy for Parenting that Works

As mentioned in the introduction to this book, parenting is a sensitive issue for all parents. Being a parent has become a very important part of your identity—a part of who you are. Reading this book might have triggered feelings of inadequacy or guilt at times. If so, it is only because parenting is so important to you. Remember that you always did the best you could with whatever tools and understanding you had at the time. What's more, all parents make mistakes. What is really important is that you have had the courage to look into yourself and examine your responses with your child. You have had the courage to begin the work to heal and mend your parental instincts. And now you are at a place where you can focus on strengthening your relationship with your child so you can break the generational cycle that may have begun long ago in your family.

1. CREATING A SECURE HOLDING ENVIRONMENT FOR YOUR CHILD

A secure parent–child attachment relationship is impossible without a secure holding environment. A secure holding environment is like a home. A good solid structure with firm walls, floor, and ceiling are requirements for a home that is secure and safe. Equally important to a secure home is the warm, nurturing interior.

1.1. The Holding Environment as Structure

Like standing in a home with crumbling walls, a child who is not pro-vided adequate structure does not feel safe. If a parent's responses to mis-behaviors change as the parent's moods change, the child will be unclear about the limits and will feel more anxious. Have you ever been in a work situation where you had no idea what would be expected of you from one day to the next and where the rules were always changing? Or have you been in an adult relationship where communication was poor and you couldn't figure out where you stood with your significant other or what was expected of you in the relationship? Even adults get anxious when the rules and boundaries are unclear. To provide clear limits for your child, think carefully about what the expectations are in your family. Then sim-plify those expectations into just a few important family rules that you can reinforce. Keep it simple and be consistent. For children who can read, post the rules on the refrigerator. If they can't read, draw pictures. Use simple wording. And then be prepared to repeat, and repeat, and to follow through with reinforcing those rules.

As you set limits with your child, reinforce those limits with firm, steady responses. Parental misperceptions and parental stress can trip us up here, causing us to either overreact or underreact. Remind yourself that there is probably something seriously wrong when a child never acts out. Every child who has an ounce of spirit and drive to be independent will be a challenge at times. The most effective approach to misbehavior is a busi-ness-like, no-nonsense response. Although there is a place for parental anger as discussed later under the "Sixty Second Scolding," for the most part you will want to save the intense emotionality for the good behavior and remain firm, yet calm when your child misbehaves.

When your child does not respond to a firm reminder or redirection a good rule of thumb is to give him a choice of some kind. "You are welcome to either stay and eat with good manners or you may take your yelling to your room." "You may take turns with your sister or you may play by yourself in the other room." "You may come along with me to the car now or you can be carried to the car." If your child does not make the choice for good behavior, swiftly and perfunctorily dispatch him to where he needs to go. Do not give him an ounce of extra attention or emotionality, as this will only reinforce the negative behavior. With very young children who have trouble following a request in a timely manner you can simply say, "I am going to give you to the count of three to please do as I ask." A consequence such as a timeout or removal of a privilege can follow if your child still does not comply.

Dr. Stanley Greenspan, child psychiatrist and Clinical Professor at George Washington University Medical School, and Nancy Greenspan write in their book, *The Essential Partnership*, "Intuitively sensing their parents' resolve and intensity, most children pick their spots carefully. They usually misbehave where they think they can get away with it." It is appropriate to be flexible and willing to negotiate on some things, but we must know which things we are not going to be flexible about and then clearly convey our resolve to our child. With a toddler Greenspan suggests you get eye contact first and then use exaggerated gestures and facial expressions to get your point across. At the same time it is important to show empathy by letting your child know you understand how difficult it can be to follow the rules.[1]

A structured holding environment is safe, dependable, and predictable. When his parents leave, a child in a secure holding environment can trust them to prepare him for their departure and to return when they say they will return. He can trust that things will happen fairly regularly in his life. He has a daily routine on which he can depend. After all, even as adults we feel more secure when we have some sort of routine to our lives. Getting up each morning to a regular ritual such as coffee and a newspaper, or a morning shower, becomes an emotional security blanket. We like having some idea of what we can expect from the day. Can you remember a time when your life was in a state of transition of some kind, such as a new job or a move? Most of us feel anxious during times that involve change and we yearn for a return to stability. We like the familiar and the predictable. Franchise restaurants like McDonald's are successful because no matter where we are, even in a foreign country, we can walk into one and know what to expect. Children thrive in environments they can count on with predictable people, places, and routines.

1.2. The Holding Environment as Nurturing

Remember the metaphor of the home as a holding environment. The walls and roof are firm and the foundation is solid. But the house is not a secure holding environment without a warm and comfortable interior. In the same way, discipline must be balanced out with an abundance of nurturing and warmth. A song we all remember from childhood, "A Spoonful of Sugar" from *Mary Poppins*, is a wonderful metaphor for the balance of discipline *and* nurturing provided by the secure holding environment. Medicine *does* go down much more easily when it is sweetened with sugar. Structure and discipline alone, without the sweetness, will not satisfy the requirements for an attachment relationship between parent and child. As you practice your inner child imagery you will be able to draw upon your wellspring of nurturing experiences to nurture your child. For every limit-setting interaction there should be at least seven nurturing interactions to keep a good balance. Nurturing includes having fun together, sharing thoughts and feelings, and holding or hugging. Nurturing includes giving your child affirming messages such as *you're lovable, you're special, you're capable,* and *it's O.K. to make mistakes.* When your child misbehaves, separate your child from his behavior. Convey again and again as you set limits, *I love you—I just don't like this particular behavior.* If the child feels loved, the child will *care.* He will care how you feel about his behavior and he will care about himself. A child who has been taught to see himself as a good person will try to live up to his own self-image. A child who believes he is inherently defective and unlovable will see no use in trying.

A secure holding environment also provides a child with a safe place to experience his feelings. A child feels safe when he can trust his parent to accept and validate his feelings. He feels safe when he can depend on his parent to remain steady and give him comfort when his emotions become overwhelming.

2. DISCIPLINE AS TEACHING

T. Berry Brazelton, M.D., renowned pediatrician and author, reminds us in his book, *Touchpoints,* that "discipline means 'teaching,' not punishment," and that teaching is a long-term process. Brazelton adds, "What you do about any single incident is not as important as what you teach on *each* occasion."[2] Keep in mind that there are no quick fixes or magic wands when it comes to rearing children. For every responsible young adult on this planet, years and years of parental teaching, guidance, and love have been consistently provided.

With this in mind, it becomes obvious that the key to effective discipline is providing the response that will most help the child learn over the long haul.

Children learn appropriate behavior when the following three factors are in place:

1. They have come to care about themselves and others.
2. They have come to understand how their misbehaviors lead to negative outcomes for themselves or others.
3. They have been helped to learn a new way to behave that works better.

2.1. The Problems with Spanking

Corporal punishment, including spanking, slapping, or hitting, interferes with all three of the factors required for learning appropriate behavior. Corporal punishment has long been an accepted form of discipline in our society. Although the majority of parents use spanking, slapping, or hitting, there is solid evidence now that corporal punishment, even the kind that is accepted by society, *is* harmful to children.

First, hitting of any kind interferes with the child developing caring and trusting feelings for himself or others—factor 1 above. Hitting of any kind naturally weakens the attachment relationship. Remember that the attachment figure is the person to whom the child automatically wants to go when he is hurt. When the pain has been inflicted by the attachment figure the child is immediately caught in a Catch-22—the person to whom he wants to go for comfort is the source of the pain. The automatic response of the child is to feel both hurt and rage, because he has no one to whom he may go. In response he may shut down his attachment system and bury his needs for comfort. This interferes with trust of the attachment figure and with trust of self. The child may conclude that the parent is untrustworthy, that he himself is defective, or both.

As a result of the inner turmoil, hurt, and rage the child feels, his focus is not on his misbehavior. He does not think about what he did that was wrong, why it was wrong, and what he should do better next time. He may associate his misbehavior with the consequence of getting hit, but if the parent is not present to hit next time, he will likely repeat the misbehavior because he will have no reason not to. Thus, hitting interferes with factor 2: understanding why the misbehavior is harmful to himself or others.

Third, hitting does not teach appropriate and effective ways to behave: factor 3. Even if the parent follows the hitting with a lengthy discussion of appropriate vs. inappropriate behavior the parent's actions will speak much louder than any words he or she may use. Hitting the child demonstrates to the child that hitting is the answer to conflict and frustration.

Murray Straus, codirector of the Family Research Lab at the University of New Hampshire and author of *Beating the Devil out of Them,* has documented some compelling evidence that corporal punishment indeed has long-term negative effects. His research shows strong correlations between the type of corporal punishment in childhood that is normally accepted by society and problems later in life including depression, suicidal thoughts, violence toward family members, violent crimes, alcohol abuse, and job problems.[3]

Corporal punishment is very seductive to frustrated parents for three reasons:

1. It stops the misbehavior for the moment. (Although it causes behavior to become worse in the long run.)
2. It provides a release for parental frustration and anger, so the parent *feels* better afterward.
3. It is accepted by society.

Often we believe that if a certain action makes us feel better, it must have been the correct action. Parents who were spanked or hit in childhood were taught by example that spanking or hitting is an appropriate reaction to oppositional behavior. Parents who were raised in very authoritarian households may hold the common misperception that "the parent should have absolute authority over the child," therefore they are *supposed to* do whatever it takes to achieve this all-important objective. In addition, the common misperceptions "my child is shameful" and "I am not safe with my child" put parents in the state of emotional mind where they are more likely to respond out of emotions that are disconnected from rational thought. Obviously, parents who lacked adequate nurturing or received harsh punishment growing up will be more vulnerable to resorting to corporal punishment.

2.2. Letting the Consequences Do the Teaching

You will be more prepared to provide the kinds of responses that will best help your child learn appropriate behavior if you are regularly disputing your parental misperceptions and practicing the emotion management skills to stay in wise mind. A child learns the most from his mistakes when the parent lets the consequences do the teaching because it keeps the child's attention focused on his behavior instead of on *mom's* or *dad's* behavior. Think about this: When children misbehave or make poor decisions, we want children to think, "Why did I make that dumb decision? It didn't work out for me at all! My poor decision led to a poor outcome for me!" However, as soon as we turn into screaming meanies our children stop thinking this way immediately! Instead, they begin thinking, "Why are my mom and dad so mean to me? I have the meanest mom and dad in the whole world!" The only cause and effect conclusion this child can come up with is, "Having a mean mom and dad leads to a bad outcome for me!"

2.3. Empathy

How can we help our children best learn from their mistakes? Dr. Foster Cline and Jim Fay, authors of *Parenting with Love and Logic*, suggest *empathy* as the vehicle with which we can help our children learn. Indeed, I have discovered that empathy is a superb tool for parents, and one that parents find quite easy to use once they have a handle on their parental misperceptions. Empathy allows the child to learn from the natural and logical consequences of his behavior. Empathy removes from the child the opportunity to focus on *his parents'* behavior instead of his own. Empathy allows the child to feel the parent's attunement with him, strengthening the attachment relationship even while dealing with misbehavior. Cline and Fay state, "Letting the consequences do the teaching isn't enough. We as parents must show our empathy—our sincere, loving concern—when the consequences hit. That's what drives the lesson home with our children without making them feel we're not on their side."[4]

How does a parent show empathy? Let your child know that you understand it is hard, that you feel for him, and that you care about him as he faces the consequence of his behavior. This will help your child to stay focused on his own behavior as the problem and will help him understand that you are on his side. It is extremely important that you not convey your empathy in a sarcastic manner. When you are feeling angry, you may be tempted to show sarcastic empathy, such as, "Oh? You didn't do your homework and you had to stay after school? Well, isn't that just too bad. I really feel sorry for someone that makes such stupid decisions!" Obviously, this is not an example of genuine empathy! This response will not effectively allow the child to learn from the consequence of his behavior, as he will immediately begin thinking about what a sarcastic parent he has!

Make sure your child does have some kind of consequence to deal with as the result of his poor decision or misbehavior. This consequence may come the child's way naturally. You have it made when your child suffers natural consequences caused by the choices he made. Be grateful for these natural consequences.

Examples of Natural Consequences

Your child spends all his allowance in one day and has no more money to purchase treats for the rest of the week.
Your child won't share, and as a result his friend goes home.
Your child talks in class, and as a result he has to stay after school.
Your child tarries and misses the bus. As a result he has to walk the long walk home.
Your child stays up too late and feels tired and miserable the next day.

When your child experiences natural consequences from his behavior, all you have to do is *not fix* the problem for the child, and then apply empathy. If there are no natural consequences resulting from the misbehavior, then you must supply a consequence that is appropriate and logical. The more reasonable the connection between his behavior and the consequence that follows, the more likely your child will connect the cause with the effect.

Examples of Logical Consequences

Loss of a privilege or an activity.
A timeout to get the behavior under control.
An extra chore.
Doing something to make amends to someone.
Giving up part of his allowance to pay someone for doing his chore or for breaking or losing something.

Whether the consequence is a natural result of the behavior or a logical consequence that you have provided, you can show genuine empathy for your child's plight. Tabetha described to me how she had used empathy very effectively one day with her eight-year-old son:

"Danny came home from school last Tuesday with a note I had to sign from his teacher stating that he had thrown food at lunch and as a result would have to miss recess the rest of the week. In the past, my misperception, My child will make me worthwhile would have gotten in the way. I would have been so embarrassed that he had misbehaved that I would have totally blown up at Danny! He would have ended up stomping off to his room thinking about how mad he was at me. But Friday I remembered that Danny's behavior at school was not about me, and I was able to put my arm around him and say to him with real genuineness in my voice, 'Gee, Danny, I feel so *sad* for you. The weather is going to be so great this week and I know how much you love recess.' He looked really sad then, and I know he was wishing he had never misbehaved. Then I said, 'On the bright side, Danny, I know how smart you are and I'm sure you won't ever make this mistake again!'"

Tabetha was able to overcome her misperception and her automatic emotional response to respond in a way that helped Danny most effectively learn from his mistake. Granted, the bigger the issue, the more challenging it can be to remain empathic. Mark described how his son Daryl had had an accident with the family car.

"The accident was his fault. He wasn't paying attention and he ran right through a yield sign, colliding with the car that had the right-of-way. Thank God no one was hurt, but when he came home that night and I saw the car I had so many feelings! I felt afraid of what could have happened to him, and angry about my car at the same time! Thankfully, I was able to let him know how frightened and upset I felt at that moment pretty appropriately—I just raised my voice a little bit. Then I calmed myself down and put my arm around Daryl and said, 'Son, I realize this is hard for you too. It's a scary thing having an accident. It's going to be real tough for you to earn the money to pay for the deductible and the extra cost when your insurance rates go up.' Daryl looked shocked, like he hadn't even thought about the fact that he would be paying for this accident financially. But I could see that his focus was on his own carelessness. He was upset with himself, not with me."

2.4. Whose Problem Is It?

The misperception, "My child will make me whole," may cause you to believe that your child's behavior is a reflection of you. As a result, his problem becomes your problem. Instead of a firm, business-like response, you subsequently respond with a desperate need to fix your child immediately. As long as you are owning the problem, however, your child sees it as your problem and yours alone. He will remain about as unmotivated as you are desperate to solve it.

The misperception, "The parent should be the absolute authority over the child," will also make the child's problem yours. Holding onto this belief will cause you to become emotionally invested in proving your authority. This then becomes a problem for you—but not a problem for your child. The intensity with which you try to get him in line will be equal to the lack of caring about the problem your child will have.

Cline and Fay write, "children who know their problems are the concern of their parents don't worry about them. This can be explained partly by the 'no sense in both of us worrying about it' syndrome. Most of us don't worry about something if somebody else will do the worrying for us."[5]

As you dispute your misperceptions it will become easier for you to allow your child to be the sole owner of his problems. Give the child's problems to him with the help of natural or logical consequences, plenty of empathy for his plight, and the message that he is capable of handling it: "It must feel just terrible to know your teacher is very unhappy with you! But I have confidence in you. I know you'll figure out what to do. Let me know if you need some help to think it through. Good luck, honey!" Sending your child off to solve his problems with your good will and good wishes will plant the problem firmly where it needs to be located—in your child's mind and heart.

According to Cline and Fay, there are two times we should make our child's problem our problem: "(1) We step in when our children are in definite danger of losing life or limb, or of making a decision that could affect them for a lifetime; and (2) We step in when the children know that we know that they know that they cannot cope with their problem, and the consequences are very significant."[6] Examples of such a situation would include a child who needs treatment for a drug problem, a child who is in over his head with a dangerous group of kids, or a child who is suffering from depression or anxiety.

Sometimes the nature of the problem causes it to be owned by the parent. Then the parent must impose a consequence (with plenty of empathy of course!) that will make the problem a problem for the child. For example, if your teenager borrowed your best sweater and lost it, it is not a problem for him. It becomes a problem for him only when you tell him with great sincerity that you know how hard it will be for him to earn the money to replace the sweater. Of course, you would add, "Although it will be difficult, I have confidence in your ability to find a way to earn the money you will need!"

2.5. Sharing Your Feelings

It *is* O.K. to let your child know how his behavior has affected you. Part of learning about the consequences of his behavior is learning how his actions affect other people. Mark did a good job letting Daryl know how crashing his car affected him while keeping the focus of Daryl's thoughts on his own behavior. Mark did not give Daryl the opportunity to focus instead on how angry and mean his Dad is! Mark expressed his hurt and fear without yelling, shaming, threatening, or name-calling. He simply told Daryl, with feeling in his voice, how his actions had made him feel. His feelings were logical and natural considering the facts. They were not out of proportion to the situation at hand.

It's O.K. to tell your child, "I feel hurt," "I feel angry," or "I feel disappointed." As you practice your emotion management skills you will more easily be able to express your feelings using "I feel" statements without yelling, threatening, or shaming. When you use "I feel" statements with your child, you are modeling the best way to convey feelings. From your example he will better learn to identify and express his own feelings—a skill that will benefit him all his life.

2.6. Sixty Second Scolding

Cline and Fay describe a technique they call the "Sixty Second Scolding." This technique allows the parent to express her anger in a way that ensures the child will learn from his mistakes. The technique avoids giving the child the opportunity to focus on the parent's misbehavior instead. The approach is effective because the parent stays appropriate and in control. It is also effective because it avoids shaming the child, and because the negative interaction is followed by a positive interaction. It works like this: For up to 60 seconds it is O.K. to "scold" your child. Use "I feel" sentences with the purpose of conveying to your child your feelings of anger, irritation, frustration, hurt, and disappointment. Avoid sentences that begin with the word "you," because "you" sentences bring up the defensive wall. Avoid name-calling or shaming and avoid use of the words "always" or "never."[7]

Examples of Effective "I Feel" Statements

"I feel very hurt and angry that you would take money from me without asking!"

"I feel so sad that you would say something so hurtful to your sister."

"I feel very angry and disappointed right now. That was a very poor decision that has very negative consequences for both of us. I know you are capable of much better decisions than this."

"I am so frustrated right now I feel like I could explode! I'm very angry with you about this behavior!"

Examples of Harmful "You" Statements

"You always screw up! You never think! When will you ever do something right?"

"You are an idiot! What were you thinking?"

"You'll never amount to anything! You're lazy and good for nothing!"

"You are a little brat! I can't take you anywhere!"

To successfully use the Sixty Second Scolding technique with appropriate "I feel" statements it will be important to stay on top of your parental misperceptions and practice your emotion management skills in order to stay out of "emotion mind."

The most important part of the technique is the genuine nurturing that follows the scolding. Put your arm around your child or give him a hug. Let him know how much you love him, even though you didn't love the behavior. Tell him how smart he is, how capable he is, and that you know he'll be able to make a better decision next time. Give the positive interaction *at least as much time* as the negative interaction. If your child is going to suffer a consequence for his behavior, use empathy and let him know that you really feel badly for him because you realize the consequence will be difficult.

The 60 second scolding allows you to share your genuine feelings with your child without taking the focus of your child's thoughts off of his behavior and onto your behavior. It helps the child learn how his actions can hurt others, and maintains the attachment relationship.

3. REMOVING POWER AS THE HOLY GRAIL

If you have always disciplined with an authoritarian style, you may hold the misperception described in Chapter Five that "the parent should have absolute authority over the child." You may have grown up in a family where the parents had the power and the children had none. Thus, power may have become the Holy Grail for you—the coveted, but unattainable prize. The parent who grew up in that type of atmosphere naturally believes that she must have the power now that her parents once had, and will tend to rule with the same authoritarian style. As a result, her children will learn to covet power as the supreme god in the same way. If you have held this parental misperception, it will be very important for you to continually dispute your misperception so that you can remove power as the Holy Grail in your family. Keep the focus on communication, cooperation, negotiation, and learning to be responsible for self as family goals. Remember that this does not mean that as parent you don't have the final say or the right to say no and set limits. Of course you do. But take a minute right now and think about past employers or teachers that you have had. Have you ever had a boss or teacher who seemed to enjoy lording her power over her employees or students? She probably made decisions arbitrarily without thought for the feelings or opinions of those she supervised. She made it a point to make sure everyone knew that she was the boss and she had the right to do as she pleased. On the other hand, have you ever been lucky enough to work for a boss or take a class with a teacher who was so self-assured she did not seem to feel the need to demonstrate her power? This employer or teacher probably listened to the opinions of the people she supervised, gave choices, and democratically shared the responsibility for some of the decision-making. In which type of setting did you notice more cooperation, more motivation, and more positive attitudes?

3.1. The Family Meeting

Having weekly family meetings can be very helpful in developing a more democratic type of family. It can be helpful to establish a set time each week, such as after Sunday dinner, or first thing Saturday morning. You may want to use a laid back approach, setting a time to get together as a family each week to discuss any concerns and figure out solutions to problems in the family. Or you may want to formalize the meeting, taking turns "chairing" the meeting and taking notes, and running the meeting according to parliamentary procedure. Remember that the goal is for the family to learn to communicate and work together in solving any problems that arise in the family. All the family members should have a chance to share their views and voice their opinions.

3.2. Choices

Another way to remove power as the Holy Grail in the family is to give children choices wherever possible. Cline and Fay state, "Winnable war is waged through choices, not demands. Choices change the entire complexion of the control struggle. They allow us to give away the control we don't need and gain the control we do. With choices kids have no demands to react against, and the control we need is established."[8] The main rule about giving choices is, don't give any choices that you can't actually live with. A sane parent obviously is not going to give her child the choice, "You may either hold my hand as we cross the street or run ahead and deal with the oncoming truck!" A choice is not a real choice unless you are able to let your child actually experience the consequences of whatever he chooses. Of course children cannot make all of their own choices; that comes with adulthood. But the older your child becomes, the more choices he should be making as he moves closer toward living responsibly and independently in the world. A young adult leaving his childhood home who has never had to make any decisions or choices for himself and has never dealt with any real-life consequences from his decisions is going to be inexperienced and ill-equipped to face the many hard choices life has to offer.

Examples of Choices that Can Be Given to Younger Children

"Feel free to either play quietly in the living room while the adults are visiting or play loudly in your bedroom."

"Would you rather have a shower or a bath tonight?"

"You may cooperate with me while I finish this shopping or I'll run you home so that you can stay with Dad while I finish."

"You may brush your teeth before the bed-time story or after the bed-time story."

"You may pick out your own outfit to wear to school today or I can pick out an outfit for you."

"The two of you can choose to figure out a way to play together nicely or you can play the rest of today in separate rooms."

Examples of Choices for Older Children

"You may finish mowing the lawn tonight or finish the lawn first thing in the morning."

"This is how much money I have to spend on your school clothes. You decide how we can best provide you with the most for the money we have to spend."

"Would you like to finish your job or pay me to finish it for you from your allowance?"

"Why don't you talk to your counselor about your future career ideas, and then you can decide which courses you should take this year."

"As long as I see that you are a leader and not a follower I trust you to choose your own friends because I know you will make good decisions no matter who you are with."

3.3. Thinking Words, Not Fighting Words

The words and tone of voice we use with our children can help tremendously in removing power as the Holy Grail in our family. Cline and Fay suggest using "thinking words" instead of "fighting words" to encourage children to think and cooperate instead of argue.[9] Thinking words treat children respectfully. Think again about different employers you have had in the past. Remember the employer who liked to lord her power over the workers? How did she speak to them? Did she bark orders? Did her voice sound irritated, impatient, or sarcastic? Compare her style of speech to the style of the employer or teacher who had the most success motivating her employees or students to give their very best effort.

When we use fighting words with our children we are lording our power over them and challenging them to either give up any sense of their own power in the family or fight with us for it. Thinking words treat children respectfully, raise morale, and motivate. Fighting words treat children disrespectfully and lower motivation to do well.

Examples of Thinking Words

"Feel free to join us for dinner as soon as you're finished cleaning up your room."

"Gee, I'll bet you feel awful about that D on your report card. What do you think you can do about that?"

"We'd love to have you back at the dinner table just as soon as you've gotten the behavior under control."

"A detention, wow. You must feel really badly about missing your playtime after school. I wonder if there's something you could do differently to avoid this problem next time?"

"I'd love to give you a ride to school, but I do need to leave in five minutes. If you're not ready, walking may be your only option today."

"I'd be glad to give you a ride to soccer, but I need some help from you first in finishing that chore you started."

Examples of Fighting Words

"No dinner until you finish cleaning that room!"

"I told you you needed to do more studying at night! Now you've got a D on your report card, just like I predicted!"

"Get to your room and don't come back to the table until you're ready to behave!"

"A detention? You'll never learn will you?"

"Serves you right for being so slow! Now you'll just have to walk to school because I'm leaving!"

"Get that job done right now or there will be no ride to soccer practice!"

4. TEACHING YOUR CHILD HOW TO COPE WITH FEELINGS

Can you imagine anything that is more important to getting along in this world than the ability to handle emotions? Our feelings are what make us human. We may have no problem upon experiencing certain feelings such as comfort, joy, love, wonder, or excitement. Other emotions are more difficult to handle, such as boredom, sorrow, fear, anger, loneliness, despair, and shame. Every day of our lives we walk through a myriad of emotions, positive and negative, whether we try to suppress them, act on them, or allow ourselves to just experience them.

In order to be able to teach our children to cope with emotions we need to be able to respond in a calm but empathic manner to their emotions, and to role-model handling our own emotions in a healthy way as well. As you continue practicing the emotion management skills in Chapter Seven you will more easily be able to respond to your child's emotions in ways that will teach him how to cope.

There are three main points to remember in responding to your child's feelings:

4.1. Use Reflective Listening

Practice listening intently to your child, especially to the feelings behind his words or behaviors, and then nonjudgmentally share with your child what you are understanding. Each time you respond to your child in this way you are accomplishing several things.

First, you are helping him learn how to identify what he is feeling and how to describe his feelings with words. The child who has learned how to express feelings with language has less need to act out his feelings in harmful ways.

Second, when you reflect what you hear without judging your child's feelings as good, bad, right, or wrong, you are teaching him the mindfulness skill of accepting all feelings nonjudgmentally. If he can learn to accept feelings as just feelings and not judge them, he will not feel the need to search for methods to bury his feelings or avoid his feelings. He will not "beat himself up" for having certain feelings because he perceives them as "weak" or "bad." Through nonjudgmental reflective listening you can help your child become at home with all of his feelings.

Third, as you respond nonjudgmentally to your child's feelings you are providing *attunement*, vital to forming a secure attachment. When your child senses you are tuned into him he feels understood, accepted, and validated. When you truly know your child and you still love him, he is able to believe that he is worthwhile. When he bares his soul and finds acceptance it frees him to continue to be true to himself. With this freedom there is no need for him to hide behind a mask or a false self.

Reflective listening does not mean telling a child what he feels or what he does not feel or what he should feel. Reflective listening means really listening. Sometimes we are listening to our child's words. Sometimes we are listening to feelings behind a behavior.

Following is an example of reflective listening.

Ann described to me one day how John had come home from fourth grade, had thrown his book bag on the floor, and flung himself onto his bed in his room:

> "He began screaming, 'I hate school! I am never going back there! I quit!' In the past, I think I might have responded by angrily shouting back, 'You have to go to school! You're only in the fourth grade!' But instead I just went into his room and sat on his bed. His eyes were

teary, and I said, 'Wow, you sound really angry.' He said, 'I am! And I'm not going back!' So I said, 'Do you want to tell me more about it?' He told me how some kids were throwing gravel after school. Apparently some of the gravel landed in his hair, and so he picked up a big handful, just as the principal walked out. He was the only one she saw actually holding the gravel, so he was the only one who got a detention. I said, 'It sounds like you feel really angry that you were the only one who got a detention, but you weren't the only one throwing gravel.' He said, 'Yeah, it's really unfair.' I just sat there with him, rubbing his back. I wanted to say something about how he's probably gotten other kids in trouble plenty of times in the past, but I didn't. Then he just said something like, 'What's for snack?' After that it seemed like he'd just accepted the situation and it wasn't such a big deal."

4.2. Soothe

When you soothe and comfort your child, you are providing a nurturing holding environment, calming him and helping him feel safe with his feelings. The more your child experiences soothing and comforting, the better he will be able to internalize this skill and keep himself calm, or comfort himself when he is distressed.

Soothing may mean holding or touching silently, or it may include soothing, nurturing words, like "You're going to be O.K.," "Your feelings are all right with me," "I love you," "It's O.K. to cry," "I know you're mad, and it's O.K.," and "I'm here for you, it's O.K. to tell me what you need." With an infant, examples of soothing behavior include rocking, massaging, swaddling in a blanket, or rubbing the head gently and speaking soothing words in a soft, tender tone. No child is too young or too old to be taught to manage his emotions by providing him with the experience of a secure holding environment.

4.3. Encourage Your Child to Talk, Think, and Problem Solve

The child who is old enough to verbalize can be helped to learn how to talk about his feelings, talk about the situation, and problem solve. As in the example above, a child may find his painful feelings dissipate once he believes his feelings have been understood and validated. At other times, when a child feels his emotions have been understood he may be open to talking more about his feelings and exploring alternatives. You may find it helpful to ask an open-ended thinking question like, "Do you suppose there might be something you could think of that would help?" You may suggest, "Let's work together and try to think up some possible solutions that you could choose from next time." Sometimes the situation cannot be changed, but a child can be helped to find a new perspective on it. You may be able to "wonder aloud" to get the child thinking, making statements such as, "I wonder if there is another way to look at this situation." This doesn't work unless the child feels his feelings are totally understood first. Avoid communication-stopping responses like lecturing or advice giving: "You're making a big deal out of nothing . . ." "You need to stop letting it bother you, it's not that big of deal . . ." "What you should have done is . . ." "Why in the world did you . . . " These kinds of responses create a defensive wall. By providing an environment where he feels his feelings are accepted nonjudgmentally you can help him learn how to cope with distress by talking and thinking things through.

5. TEACHING COPING THROUGH ROLE MODELING

As you continue to develop your own internal holding environment your child will also learn healthy ways to manage his emotions as he observes you. As you practice the skill of verbalizing your feelings and experiences into words he will imitate you. As you demonstrate an accepting attitude toward your own range of feelings he will learn from your example. As you learn to cope with crisis or distress through self-soothing or positive activity your child will learn to cope from watching you. Your child will also learn about healthy self-care through watching as you practice nurturing yourself and taking care of yourself in healthy ways. When he sees you reaching out when you need help, saying no when you need to, and taking time to relax, he is finding permission to do the same for himself. Imagine what kind of learning takes place when a child observes his parent isolate, rage, or use alcohol or drugs to cope with stressful emotions. Now think about what a difference it could make in the life of this child if he observes the same parent turn his life around, attend support meetings, and take care of himself in healthy ways.

6. WHEN YOUR CHILD IS ANGRY WITH YOU

Part of providing a secure holding environment is setting limits and not letting a child do damage. When a child is throwing a tantrum and striking out at you, throwing things, or kicking it can be helpful for the parent to hold the child securely—not angrily—and to say to him, "It's O.K. to be angry, but I cannot allow you to hurt me, hurt yourself, or hurt our things. I'll keep you safe until you get back in control." Later, when the child is calm, encourage him to talk about what he was feeling when he became out of control. Let your child know it's O.K. for him to tell you he is angry with you. If you can hear your child's angry words and respond by talking with him calmly about his feelings, you are teaching him to appropriately express anger and talk through his problems. When a child can learn how to express his anger appropriately, he has less need to act out his anger in damaging ways.

If you believe your child might be acting out anger toward you in less direct ways, it may be helpful to give him permission to express his anger in words. You might say to him, "If you are feeling angry with me, it's O.K. to tell me you're mad. I won't get mad at you for being mad at me. We can talk about it." Remember, too, that anger is often a secondary emotion to underlying feelings of hurt or rejection. Again, "wondering aloud" can be useful. For example, "I'm just wondering if you might be feeling hurt because I took that trip last weekend and you couldn't go," or, "I have a feeling you might be upset with me. Why don't we talk about it?" Reinforce your child for sharing his angry feelings with you appropriately—"It makes me feel good that you can be honest with me and talk to me about your feelings."

7. CHANGING NEGATIVE ATTENTION SEEKING

Similarly, if your child is acting out and seems to just be "asking for" negative attention from you, you may be caught in a vicious negative cycle. Your negative responses to your child's behavior may have become reinforcing for the acting-out behavior just because it's attention—and for a child, any attention is much better than no attention. Remember the attachment system described in Chapters Three and Four. When the attachment system kicks in, children will naturally signal their attachment needs through whining, clinging, or other attention-getting misbehaviors.

So how can you break the cycle? The first rule of thumb is, reduce the emotional intensity of your negative responses, and increase the intensity of any positive interactions you can initiate when he is not acting out.

In other words, when your child acts up, stay as low key as you possibly can while redirecting your child or giving him a consequence. Remain no-nonsense and business-like. Do you remember the two deadpan characters on the old *Dragnet* show? Try to be as lacking in emotion as Joe Friday reading a criminal his rights. It is also helpful to remember the acronym KISS—Keep It Short and Simple! The more you lecture and carry on, the more attention you are giving your child for his misbehavior.

Conversely, when your child is showing good behavior, up the intensity of your responses by tenfold. Give him a squeeze, and tell him how TERRIFIC it is to be with him. Arrange plenty of one-on-one time with him, make eye contact, and talk with him. Think about those things you most enjoy doing with your child and initiate some of those activities so that you can spend plenty of time together that you both enjoy.

Teaching your child to verbalize his feelings can help him learn to ask for what he needs more directly. If you suspect he is acting out to get attention, you might say lightheartedly, "Hey, if you are needing some attention from me, just TELL me, O.K.? Around here, we can just ask for what we need!" It might be helpful to do a little role play with your child, letting him practice asking you directly for some attention.

8. MANIPULATION TO "GET STUFF"

Remember that all kids do this. When it is a problem, it is usually because the manipulation has been rewarded in the past, so be sure not to reward it. Teach your child how to ask directly and appropriately with the understanding that if it is not reasonable or doable, even asking appropriately won't work. I can very politely and directly ask my husband to drive to Kansas City and buy me some special Kansas City barbecue ribs, but it won't do me any good. However, show your child that when the request is reasonable, a direct request will be much more effective than whining, pouting, or any other type of manipulation.

9. MEDITATION FOR PROBLEM-FOCUSED COPING

Remember that adults who had to deal with very difficult circumstances as children have often naturally fallen into a habit of emotion-focused coping. If you habitually have used emotion-focused coping, your automatic response to the discomfort of feelings has been to try to rid yourself of them.

Your responses to strong emotions have been automatic, whether discharging feelings, blocking them, or escaping them. Emotional mind has been in charge. As you continue changing core beliefs and misperceptions and learning to manage your emotions you will be more capable of responding to your child from your adult wise mind. Many parents have found the following mindfulness meditation helpful in adopting problem-focused coping in the face of strong emotions and challenging situations with their children.

Get into a comfortable position . . . and close your eyes . . . Take a deep breath, and exhale . . . Hold in mind the word relax, relax . . . as you continue to breathe, in and out . . . Notice the feeling of relaxation . . . spreading throughout your body . . . Allow your head, and the muscles in your face . . . to become heavy and relaxed . . . Let your shoulders droop...Allow your arms and hands to become . . . heavy and relaxed . . . relaxed and heavy . . . Allow your back to sink down . . . into the cushions beneath you . . . Notice as the tension drains . . . from your legs and feet . . . as they become heavier and heavier . . . relaxed and heavy . . . Your whole body feels heavy . . . You can enjoy that relaxed and comfortable feeling . . . Take a deep breath again . . . and exhale, as you hold in mind . . . the word relax, relax, relax . . . I invite you now, to visualize . . . a situation that has occurred in the past . . . between you and your child . . . that triggered feelings of frustration or anger . . . a situation that you wish . . . you could have dealt with differently . . . Imagine that the situation is repeating itself...Watch the situation unfold...but this time, imagine yourself . . . observing your own feelings of anger or frustration . . . Hold in mind the thoughts . . . I can ride out these feelings . . . These feelings are temporary . . . These are just feelings, and these feelings won't hurt me . . . I can acknowledge my feelings . . . but I don't have to act on them . . . I can ride out these feelings . . . like riding on a raft in a stormy sea . . . These feelings will pass . . . I can slow down and think rationally . . . about how I want to act . . . I can choose to act in a way . . . that will be effective . . . That's right . . . Now visualize yourself responding . . . to your child in a manner . . . that will manage the situation effectively . . . take a minute now, to visualize your response . . . (pause) and then imagine how you will feel . . . after it is all over . . . competent, and masterful . . . and when you are ready . . . wake up your arms, and your legs, and open your eyes, feeling relaxed, and refreshed.

10. HAVE A PARENT TIMEOUT PLAN!

For those situations where your emotions are too intense to ride out without acting out of emotional mind you need to have a timeout plan.

Having a timeout plan ready can prevent you from losing control and saying or doing something you will later regret. When you feel your blood boiling, say to your child, "I need to cool down before I decide what to do," and get out fast! Your plan might be to go to your bedroom, take a walk, or jog around the block. Your plan might be to dig in the garden or lock yourself in the bathroom and take a bath. Decide on your timeout plan right now so that you won't have to think about it when you're in the middle of the overwhelming feelings. Once you have given yourself the time you need to cool down you will be able to find your way back to wise mind and return to the situation with a more rational and effective response.

11. IN CONCLUSION . . .

As you continue disputing your misperceptions, learning emotion management techniques, practicing your visualizations, and so on, it will gradually become easier to permanently adopt the philosophy of parenting described in this chapter. As you parent more and more often from your adult wise mind you will become more capable of using empathy with your children and allowing them to learn from the consequences of their mistakes. You will become more capable of tuning into their feelings and needs and supplying the right balance of nurturing and limits. As a result, you will begin to see positive changes in your children as they become more secure with you and more secure in the world.

Chapter Thirteen

Parenting the More Challenging Child

Almost every parent, when asked about his or her child's personality, will claim that his or her unique traits were evident even in the newborn nursery. Moms and dads can often be heard making comments like, "He was feisty and stubborn from day one! He knew what he wanted and he couldn't be persuaded even as an infant!" Or, "She has always been such an easy-going kid. Even as a baby she slept well, ate well, and was easy to please—nothing like her temperamental brother!" Some mothers will even describe the child as exhibiting their natural personality characteristics *in utero!* "I knew he was going to be an active one. He kicked and kicked so much during my pregnancy I couldn't even get a decent night's sleep!"

1. INBORN TEMPERAMENT

It's a fact. Children are not unformed clay that we as parents can simply mold into the types of personalities that we would like them to be. Every child is born with certain aspects of his or her personality preprogrammed well before delivery day. Dr. Stella Chess and Dr. Alexander Thomas, professors of psychiatry at New York University Medical Center, have studied the role of inborn traits in personality development through a long-term study that began in 1956 and continues today.[1] In their book, *Temperament in Clinical Practice,* they explain how the infant "brings her own characteristics actively to the interaction with parental attitudes and practices."[2] Stella and Chess refer to the mesh between a parent's innate temperament and her child's innate temperament as the "goodness of fit" between the parent and child.[3] They have identified nine categories of traits that seem to be innate.

Stanley Turecki, M.D., author of *The Difficult Child,* describes the nine basic categories of personality traits identified by Chess and Thomas:

"1. Activity level. How active or restless is the child generally, from an early age?
2. Distractibility. How easily is the child distracted? Can he pay attention?
3. Intensity. How loud is the child generally, whether happy or unhappy?
4. Regularity. How predictable is the child in his patterns of sleep, appetite, bowel habits?
5. Persistence. Once involved with something, does the child stay with it for a long time? (Positive persistence) How relentless or stubborn is he when he wants something (Negative persistence)
6. Sensory threshold. How does the child react to sensory stimuli: noise, bright lights, colors, smells, pain, warm weather, tastes, the texture and feel of clothes? Is he easily bothered? Is he easily overstimulated?
7. Approach/withdrawal. What is the child's initial response to newness—new places, people, foods, clothes?
8. Adaptability. How does the child deal with transition and change?
9. Mood. What is the child's basic disposition? Is it more sunny or more serious?"[4]

2. THE DIFFICULT TEMPERAMENT

Looking again at these nine dimensions of temperament, Turecki defines the traits that tend to make a child more "difficult" to handle for parents and teachers:

"Difficult Traits

1. High activity level. Very active, restless, fidgety; always into things; makes you tired; 'ran before he walked'; easily overstimu-

lated; gets wild or 'revved up'; impulsive, loses control, can be aggressive, hates to be confined.

2. Distractibility. Has trouble concentrating and paying attention, especially if not really interested; doesn't 'listen'; tunes you out; daydreams; forgets instructions.

3. High intensity. Loud and forceful whether miserable, angry, or happy.

4. Irregularity. Unpredictable. Can't tell when he'll be hungry or tired; conflict over meals and bedtime; wakes up at night; moods are changeable; has good or bad days for no obvious reason.

5. Negative persistence. Stubborn; goes on and on nagging, whining, or negotiating if wants something; relentless, won't give up; gets 'locked in'; may have long tantrums.

6. Low sensory threshold. 'Sensitive'—physically not emotionally; highly aware of color, light, appearance, texture, sound, smell, taste, or temperature (not necessarily all of these); 'creative' but with strong and unusual preferences which can be embarrassing; clothes have to feel and look right, making dressing a problem; doesn't like the way many foods look, smell, or taste; picky eater; bothered and overstimulated by bright lights and noisy settings; refuses to dress warmly when the weather is cold.

7. Initial withdrawal. Shy and reserved with new people; doesn't like new situations; holds back or protests by crying or clinging; may tantrum if forced to go forward.

8. Poor adaptability. Has trouble with transition and change—of activity or routine; inflexible, very particular, notices minor changes; gets used to things and won't give them up; has trouble adapting to anything unfamiliar; can want the same clothes or foods over and over.

9. Negative mood. Basically serious or cranky; doesn't show pleasure openly; not a 'sunny' disposition."[5]

Keep in mind that these traits are not good or bad, right or wrong. By "difficult," researchers simply mean that in general these are the traits that most parents tend to find more difficult to handle in terms of raising their child. It does not mean that these so-called "difficult" traits might not actually have positive aspects, or even be useful for the child in many ways, especially in adulthood. A "serious"-tempered adult may become a serious journalist, a lawyer, or work hard for causes important to him or her.

An adult with a low threshold to stimulus may become a musician with an ear for fine nuances in music or an interior designer with an eye for color. A child with negative persistence may become an adult who will not give up and who accomplishes things most others would not. A highly active child may become a superb athlete or dancer.

In a very general way, however, the more "difficult" traits a child is born with, the more challenges a parent will face in managing the child from infancy on.

3. THE DIFFICULT CHILD AND ATTACHMENT

A critical factor in developing a secure attachment with a child is attunement. Attunement, as discussed in Chapter Three, is the ability of the parent to "tune in" to a child's feelings and needs, giving the child the feeling that she is understood. Attunement presents a special challenge for a parent with a child who is irregular, especially in infancy. The parent naturally will have more trouble "tuning in" to what is wrong with the cranky baby who never naps at the same time from one day to the next and never gets hungry on schedule.

Attunement is also more challenging with the child who is very intense and negative in mood. This child cries louder and more often than other children. When she is not crying she is often whiny and cranky. Her parent knows there is no good external reason to be this loud and this cranky all the time. It becomes very difficult then for this parent to "tune in" and show empathy with his child's intense emotions. It's much more tempting to "tune her out!"

Also critical in developing a secure attachment are touch, eye contact, and positive emotional exchanges between parent and child. But the highly active child, even as an infant, may be wiggly and squirmy. As a preschooler she may not want to sit on Dad's lap and listen to a story. The infant with a low threshold for stimulus may scream if you rock her and talk to her simultaneously. She doesn't like tickle games and is so fussy about her food that feeding time is stressful, not fun.

Another important factor to attachment is the secure holding environment that provides a consistent, steady response to the child's emotions and behaviors. Yet even the most patient parent has trouble responding firmly, but calmly when a child with a difficult temperament has had several tantrums in one day or an infant has slept only two hours at a stretch for weeks!

4. MANAGING THE CHILD WITH A DIFFICULT TEMPERAMENT

It is more challenging for *any* parent to develop a secure attachment with a child who has a difficult temperament. A secure attachment will not change a child's inborn temperament. Yet a child with a difficult temperament will be in general more cooperative, more social, less aggressive, and have higher self-esteem with a more secure attachment. If your child has anywhere from one to all nine of the "difficult" temperament traits, it will be important for you to learn some special techniques that will help you provide the attunement, the consistency, and the positive interactions your child needs to develop a secure attachment with you.

4.1. Identify Your Child's Temperament-Related Behaviors

Turecki writes, "In learning to deal with your child, half the battle is to recognize the temperamental issues that often cause problem behavior."[6] Take a day or two to observe your child closely, keeping a notebook and pen handy to jot down all of your child's behaviors that you find troublesome. Also make a list of what you observe to be your child's strengths.

Turecki suggests developing a "temperamental profile" of your child.[7] You can do this by examining your list of your child's troublesome behaviors to determine which ones may be related to a difficult temperament trait. If you live with a partner, include her or him in this process as well. Then go back to the list of temperament-related behaviors and your list of your child's strengths, and rate your child on each of the nine difficult temperament traits as severe, moderate, mild, or no problem.

4.1.1. Stacey and Miranda Stacey observed her child, eight-year-old Miranda, and compiled this list of troublesome behaviors and related temperament traits:

Often "whiny," nothing seems to ever satisfy her (negative mood, high intensity).

Gets a new toy or candy at the store, and before you know it she's whining for the next thing (negative mood, high intensity, negative persistence).

Doesn't seem to be able to entertain herself. Doesn't play with her toys. If she can't play outside with other kids, she's restless, fidgety, under my feet, and complaining (high activity level, distractible).

Stomps her feet and slams her door when she doesn't get something she wants (negative persistence, negative mood, high intensity).

Aggressive with her four-year-old sister—yells at her, calls her names (high activity level, negative mood, high intensity).

Gets "hyper" and "wound up" at night and won't settle down and go to sleep. Keeps getting out of bed—"I'm hungry, thirsty, etc" (high activity level, irregularity).

Doesn't listen when I tell her to pick up her toys, get her coat on, come to dinner, turn off the T.V., get her pajamas on, brush her teeth (poor adaptability, distractible).

Refuses to eat at dinner, says she is not hungry, but then whines for something to eat later (irregularity).

Very grumpy every morning. Whines and won't get dressed or eat breakfast. She is often late for school (irregularity, negative mood, poor adaptability).

Has fits about practicing piano (distractibility, high activity level).

Teachers complain she talks too much, gets out of her seat, and races through her schoolwork (distractibility, high activity level).

Stacey then listed Miranda's strengths:

1. Loves animals.
2. Loves sports, swimming, dance classes.
3. Although teachers complain she fidgets and talks, and she has trouble getting ready for school, she loves school once she gets there.
4. Likes to help with vacuuming, leaf raking, snow shoveling.
5. She is very sociable.
6. She is enthusiastic and excited about all new experiences.

Next Stacey listed the nine difficult temperament traits and rated them:

1. High activity level—severe.
2. High distractibility—severe.
3. High intensity—severe.
4. Irregularity—severe.
5. High negative persistence—moderate.
6. Low sensory threshold—no problem.
7. Initial withdrawal—no problem.
8. Poor adaptability—severe.
9. Predominantly negative mood—severe.

4.2. Identify Behaviors that Can Be Ignored

Dr. Turecki points out, very correctly, that parents of difficult-temperament children often find themselves punishing their children and exhibiting anger toward their children all too frequently. The problem with parental anger and overpunishing, of course, is that it interferes with the attachment relationship, increasing the child's level of anger and resentment. Also, as Dr. Turecki states, "Excessive attention, even if it's negative, is such a powerful reward to a child that it actually reinforces the undesirable behavior."[8] When parents are reacting and disciplining every annoying behavior, they wind up disciplining or reacting to their child so often that parent and child get locked into a negative pattern of relating.

Dr. Turecki suggests identifying those behaviors that are irrelevant and can be ignored.[9] For example, you may have already discovered that punishing or scolding a child for being "grumpy" or "having a bad attitude" just never works. The child usually winds up even grumpier and feels resentful toward you for "picking on her." Chalk up her bad attitude or her whiny, grumpy mood to inborn temperament, and remind yourself that your child cannot help it. It is just the way she was born. Then ignore the grumpiness.

If you have a highly active child her loud noises as she runs her toy across the floor may annoy you, but is this something you can ignore? Remember that a child who is highly active needs to discharge some of that energy in some way. The more opportunity you give her to run her energy off outdoors or in a gym the better. Chess and Thomas found in their study that highly active boys in New York City who lived in small apartments and had nowhere to run and play had more behavior problems in school. The highly active boys who had yards or a park to run around in exhibited far fewer behavior problems.[10] Sports can be a great positive outlet for highly active children to channel their energy.

If you have a child who is irregular—who gets hungry at irregular times of the day and perhaps also has low sensory threshold for taste—the dinner table can be a war zone. Try to remember that no child has ever starved to death because of her refusal to eat green beans. When parents become overly concerned with their child's eating habits, however, food can become a highly charged emotional issue for the whole family. This type of atmosphere can lead to the development of eating disorders. In *Touchpoints: Your Child's Emotional and Behavioral Development,* Brazelton writes, "Pushing a child to eat is the surest way to create a problem. In order for feeding to be a pleasure for a child, *she* must be in control—of choices, of refusals, and of when she can stop eating."[11] To ensure that your child develops a healthy relationship with food, take the negative emotions out of mealtime. Relax and enjoy your own food and enjoy the company of your child whether she eats or not. Ask that your child sit with the family and share about the day's events. Put nutritious food on the table. Ask your child to put on her plate only what food she will actually eat so that it doesn't go to waste. Keep some nutritious snacks in the refrigerator your child can help herself to later. Beyond that, don't worry about it.

4.3. Stacey and Miranda

Stacey decided that she needed to accept that she could not turn Miranda into an easy-going, relaxed, and cheerful child. She decided to stop lecturing Miranda about her grumpiness and her whining. Stacey decided to pull out of the battle over practicing piano, since Miranda's personality obviously wasn't suited to the instrument, and decided she would even let Miranda drop piano lessons if she wanted to. Since Miranda had so much energy and liked sports, Stacey began enrolling Miranda in more sports activities and became an enthusiastic parent spectator, even though she had never been interested in sports before. Stacey also pulled out of the battle over food and only required that Miranda sit with the family and talk about the day's events.

4.4. Identify Relevant Behaviors that Need Coaching

Look over your list of your child's problem behaviors that are related to temperament. You can help your child with many of her temperament-related behaviors by taking the role of a supportive coach.

Turecki points out that one way to help your child learn to manage her own temperament is by labeling for her in a caring, understanding way those things that are hard for her. Turecki writes, "Labeling, which is essentially an on-the-spot statement in response to a behavior, is one part of showing your child that you understand her. Once the child is able to recognize some of her temperamental features, she will gain more self-control."[12] Labeling your child's temperament difficulties in a caring manner will give you more attunement with your child, enhancing your attachment relationship with her. Lets look more specifically at how you can use the techniques of labeling and coaching in each of the difficult temperament areas:

4.4.1. High Activity Level   If your child gets easily overstimulated and revved up, and then becomes out of control, impulsive, or aggressive, you will need to practice staying "tuned in" to what is happening and intervene early. When you notice your child becoming hyper, step in and *label*. Again, labeling does not mean name-calling or describing the problem in a negative way. The purpose of the labeling is to help your child gain insight into what is happening herself, so that eventually she can self-monitor. The labeling also will help your child feel understood. As an example, you might say, "You are starting to get wound up. I know it is hard for you to stay calm. Let me help you." Invite your child to sit on your lap while you rub her back or arms, sing a song, work a puzzle, or recite a poem together. You might suggest that she take a timeout or a cooldown in her room for a little while—*not* for punishment, but just to get herself calmed down. I discovered a long time ago that a soak in the bathtub had a nice calming effect on my own children when they had become wound up, a technique that Turecki also suggests.[13] I have also discovered that having a nightly "cuddle time" has a twofold benefit: It calms and relaxes a child who is wound up, and it enhances the attachment relationship at the same time. You and your child may be able to think of some more ideas of your own for helping her get relaxed and calmed down when she is beginning to zoom out of control.

4.4.2. High Distractibility   If your child tunes you out, doesn't listen, and can't follow directions, again *label*, but, as Turecki suggests, make sure you have eye contact when you are speaking with the highly distractible child.[14] When I am working with a distractible child in my office I find it helpful to say something like, "I know it is hard for you to pay attention and concentrate. Let me help you. Here, look me right in my eyes. That's right. O.K., now here is what I would like you to do." Gently put your hands on your child's shoulders, or sit her on your lap as you get eye contact, and then carefully and slowly tell her what you need from her. Give just one or two directions at a time. If she is working on homework, but not getting it done, again show empathy: "I know it is hard for you to concentrate for a long time." Ask her what she thinks might help. If she doesn't have any ideas, you might suggest she get up and run around the yard for a few minutes and then come back and try again. Don't own your child's problem. If she doesn't like your suggestions, give the problem to her by saying, "You are a very smart girl and I trust that you will be able to figure out a way to get the homework done."

4.4.3. High Intensity Parents often get into a vicious cycle with highly intense, negative-mood kids because it is so difficult to *validate* a child's feelings when they are always so *extreme*. A parent may have no problem validating a child who quietly expresses his moods: "Oh, Tommy, I am sorry you're feeling so sad!" But when sister Susie starts shrieking and carrying on loudly about having no one to play with this same parent may react in an invalidating way: "Please stop carrying on about nothing! Be quiet and find something else to do!" As parents, we have to be very careful about this, because if we discount a child's feelings repeatedly, she will eventually learn to either repress her feelings, which will be harmful, or up the intensity even further in an attempt to get the validation she needs.

Even when the reason for a child's misery is not apparent, the child can be validated by responding, "Gee, I'm sorry you're feeling so unhappy." By labeling her feeling you are teaching her the vocabulary of feelings, which is vital to emotion management. She might calm down if you rub her back and talk in a low, calm voice. Remember, however, that it is not your job to get rid of her feelings or to solve her problem for her. Express your confidence in her ability to figure out a solution to her problem and wish her good luck.

Superintense kids tend to tantrum more than other kids. If the tantrum is due to out-of-control feelings she can't manage, Turecki suggests holding her if you are able, or stay near, and speak in a calming voice. Tell her you know she feels out of control, but that you'll keep her safe until she feels better. Don't give in to a child who is tantrumming to get something she wants.[15]

4.4.4. Irregularity When a child is very irregular regarding sleeping and eating, you will want to find the right balance between being overly controlling and overly lax. Being overly controlling does not work because you cannot force a child to eat when she is not hungry or to sleep when she is not tired. At the same time you cannot let a child dictate when the family eats or when the family goes to bed. A happy medium is to ask the child to join the family at dinnertime for family sharing, whether or not she chooses to eat. And a child can be given a regular bedtime when she needs to be in bed, whether she chooses to sleep or not. Turecki suggests giving the child a small night light and some small toys or books to look at in bed until she feels sleepy.[16] If the child has fears, give her a special "brave bear" (or other animal) just for bedtime use to watch over her while she sleeps.[17] Develop a regular bedtime routine leading up to bedtime that is calming and relaxing for your child, such as a book and a "cuddle time" with you. You might want to include a back rub and an arm rub to help your child calm down and get relaxed.

4.4.5. High Negative Persistence   If your child gets "locked in" to something she wants or something she wants to do, it is again helpful to label the problem for the child by saying, "You're getting locked in to this. I know it is hard for you, but . . ." If the child is locked in to something she wants, Turecki suggests you tell the child, "You have asked for —— three times already. You are not going to get it. You can ask two more times and then you must stop!"[18] I have found this technique to be a Godsend when my own children have become overly persistent!

Be firm with the child who gets locked in and do not give her the idea through experience that tantrumming or whining is the way to get what she wants. Do express empathy with her for how difficult it is for her to let go, but be firm about your answer if her request is not reasonable.

4.4.6. Low Sensory Threshold   If your child becomes upset by the feel of the tags in her clothes or the seams in her socks, remember that she is indeed overly sensitive to tactile sensations and that it is something she cannot help. The same is true for the child or infant who has strong reactions to sounds, bright lights, or new tastes. The use of empathy and labeling will prevent these issues from escalating and turning into power struggles: "I understand that this bothers you because I know that you are very sensitive to things you feel . . . hear . . . see." If your child becomes hyper or cross in stores, she may be on sensory overload from the bright lights, stimulating objects, crowds, and loud noises. If your child has a low sensory threshold, you may want to avoid these situations as much as you can until she is mature enough to handle them.

My youngest daughter, Hannah, has a low sensory threshold. At age two she refused to wear underpants for about a year, because they "bothered her." I told her I understood, and kept her in soft knit sweatpants that year. We cut the tags out of her shirts, and spent many minutes each morning getting the seams straight in her socks so they didn't bother her toes. It was easy for me to be patient with this, because I, too, have always had a low sensory threshold! I still remember when I was ten and I wore a new slip to school my mother had bought for me that had smocking all the way down the front. I suffered the entire day—not a minute went by when it wasn't bothering me. Luckily, my mother was a very patient woman and she spent that evening carefully removing all of the smocking from my new slip. I still can't wear things that are scratchy or tight and I still remove labels that make me itch.

Babies with low sensory threshold will be cross and agitated unless parents take care to avoid stimulating noise, lights, and rough textures. Parents with sensitive babies must avoid crowds and must learn to interact very gently and quietly with their babies. I discuss attachment with sensitive babies further in Chapter Fifteen.

4.4.7. Initial Withdrawal   Parents with children who have initial withdrawal must take care again to be empathic, and to remember that this is a temperament trait that the child cannot help. At the same time, the child with initial withdrawal needs you to occasionally give her that push forward to help her overcome her fears. A child who is shy and slow to warm up with new people and new situations can again be helped by putting words to her feelings, but also remind her that her feelings are temporary: "I know new situations make you feel shy and a little scared, but I'll stay with you awhile until you feel more comfortable. Remember when you felt shy the first day of nursery school? Later on you wound up having lots of fun." When you can, introduce a new situation gradually: "Today we'll go see your kindergarten room and visit your teacher. Tomorrow will be your first day of school, and I will walk you to your room."

When a child continuously balks at going to school, Turecki points out that it is important to make it clear that although you understand it is hard to get up and go some days, staying home is not an option.[19] You can walk her to the door, or put a special surprise note in her lunch box that she can look forward to. But let her know that no matter what, all children must go to school each day.

4.4.8. Poor Adaptability   The child with the poor adaptability trait will have problems with any kinds of changes or transitions. Moving from playtime to mealtime will be a struggle. Moving from T.V. to bath time will be difficult. So will bath to bed. As you struggle to get your child from the house to the car to run errands you may find yourself thinking, "What should take two seconds is taking 15 minutes and now I'm too exhausted to go!"

For the child who has trouble with transitions, preparation is the key. Put words to the problem, show empathy, and then give her fair warning: "Tammy, I know you hate leaving your toys, but in five minutes we must leave the house to go to the store. You may bring one toy along in the car, but pick out which toy you want to bring now so you'll be ready to go." Turecki suggests using a "Changing Clock." The changing clock "gives them a chance to prepare for a transition within a limited time frame set by something neutral (the clock) and not you."[20] The changing clock is a battery-powered, digital clock that you use only for help with transitions. Set the clock in front of your child and write down for her what the clock will look like when it is time to stop what she is doing and do whatever she has to do next. I have found the Changing Clock to be a very effective approach.

The child who has trouble adapting to new foods can also be prepared gradually. A toddler can be given just a bite or two of a new food until she feels comfortable with it and asks for more. If you prepare a new dish which you expect your older child will refuse, put it on the table and tell her that this new dish is really for Mom and Dad, but that if she wants to have a taste of it, it will be O.K. with you. If she doesn't want to taste it, that's fine, too. She can just help herself to the other foods on the table. Over time, if you don't turn it into a power struggle, she will begin tasting and getting used to a wider variety of foods.

4.4.9. Predominantly Negative Mood   As I mentioned under the category of high intensity, it is most difficult for parents to validate feelings and be attuned with children who have highly intense, predominantly negative moods. Yet by acknowledging and putting words to her feelings you can help your child manage her strong emotions. This does not mean you need to fix your child's feelings or "cheer her up." If you have this idea, you are only setting yourself up for frustration and are at risk for blaming and becoming angry with your child when she doesn't "cheer up" like she's supposed to. You cannot discipline a child out of a negative mood. "Put a smile on your face or go to your room right this minute" will only cause an escalation of your child's negative mood. It is important to try to accept your child as she is. Acknowledge her feelings, give her a little empathy, and then let go of it! For example, when Susie comes in from school scowling and grumbling about "those stupid idiots on the bus," Mom says, "Susie, it looks like you're feeling a little mad today. Sorry you're having a bad day." Then she gives Susie a quick hug and goes back to whatever she is doing—unless Susie seems to want to talk about it, in which case Mom listens empathically.

If, however, Susie begins taking her negative mood out on Mom or a sibling with hurtful remarks or aggressive behavior, then it's time for Mom to set some boundaries. "I'm sorry you're in a bad mood, but it's not O.K. to take it out on others."

4.5. Stacey and Miranda

Stacey began giving Miranda more empathy and hugs when she was grumpy instead of lecturing her. She didn't make a big deal about Miranda's moods or try to fix them. She reminded herself, instead, "This is just who Miranda is. And it's O.K."

Stacey became more cautious about letting Miranda get all "wound up" at night. She began getting Miranda into the tub early in the evening, as this tended to calm her. Each evening at bedtime she rubbed her back and talked softly with her for a few minutes before tucking her in.

As Miranda tended to fall asleep sooner this way, Stacey was able to get her up a little earlier in the mornings so she didn't have to rush her. She said to Miranda, "I know it's hard for you to get ready for school on time, so I have bought a special Changing Clock. If you are ready by the time it says 7:30, you can come downstairs and watch 30 minutes of television before we have to leave for school." Because Miranda wasn't usually hungry for breakfast, Stacey said, "I know you don't always get hungry at the same times the rest of us do, but if you can just drink a glass of juice with a piece of toast, I'll know you have had enough nutrition to get through the morning."

Stacey also found the Changing Clock to be very helpful when it came time to transition Miranda to the car, to dinnertime, to bath time, or any time she needed to bring Miranda in from playing outdoors.

She found that channeling Miranda's energy into helping her around the house, and expressing her appreciation for what a great helper she was, seemed to help Miranda feel good about herself.

4.6. Design a Behavior Modification Plan for Specific Misbehaviors

Specific behaviors that are definitely problematic need a planned approach. When parents have no preconceived plan for dealing with specific problem behaviors with a difficult temperament child, they are more likely to find themselves responding with frustration and anger. This does nothing to help any child change, but it is especially ineffective with the difficult temperament child. If you become angry and begin shouting, for instance, at the difficult temperament child, the intensity of your negative mood will trigger *her* intensity and negative mood. If she is a low-sensory-threshold child, the loudness of your voice will cause her to become agitated. As her feelings become even more intense, she will become even less able to control her behaviors.

Behavior modification is a straightforward approach that is effective with the difficult temperament child. Behavior modification simply means increasing positive behaviors by reinforcing them with some type of praise, attention, or reward. Negative behaviors are decreased by either ignoring them or using a consequence.

Sit down with any other caregivers your child has and make a list of specific behaviors you wish to increase. Design a simple reward system. For example, you might want to give your child a sticker, a happy face, or a chip each time she exhibits specific desired positive behaviors. It is best to use the reward system to focus on just one, two, or three very important desired behaviors. Decide how many stickers, chips, or happy faces your child will need to earn a reward of some kind. The reward can be a small item she wants or it can be a special outing with you, which also enhances the attachment relationship.

Next make a list of the specific most troublesome behaviors that your child exhibits—those behaviors you do not feel you can simply ignore. Make a list of specific consequences for the specific misbehaviors you want to decrease. The consequence may be losing the sticker or chip she could have earned. The consequence may be an extra chore, the removal of a privilege, or a timeout. When you and any other caregivers involved have completed your plan, share the plan with your child, presenting it in a positive way: "We are going to use this plan to help you get better control over your behaviors." When your child exhibits one of the misbehaviors on your list, you will find the plan will help you avoid reacting with anger as you apply the planned consequence. Stay firm, business-like, and brief, with a dose of empathy. For example, you might say something like, "Woops! Jumping on the furniture breaks the rule about being careful with our things. You have a time out on the stairs for five minutes. I know it's difficult—but off you go—now!" If your child child doesn't do what she is asked right away, get the "I mean business" tone in your voice. Are you able to get her to get back on the sidewalk when she steps out into the street? Then use that same tone of voice if she refuses to do as she is asked. Follow-through and consistency are absolutely essential to making your plan effective.

4.7. Stacey and Miranda

Stacey decided that the three specific behaviors she would like Miranda to increase were (1) cooperative behaviors while getting ready for school in the morning, (2) sharing and cooperative behaviors while playing with her four-year-old sister, and (3) listening and cooperative behaviors with her teacher. Stacey decided to set up a reward system for these three areas to help motivate Miranda to try harder. She discussed the plan with Miranda's father and with Miranda's teacher at school. Then she explained to Miranda that each day she was kind to her sister she could earn a sticker, and she could earn a sticker each day she was ready to leave for school by 8:00 A.M. In addition, she could earn a sticker for each day she brought home a note from her teacher stating that Miranda had been cooperative in class. Stacey explained to Miranda that when she had earned a total of 12 stickers, she and Miranda would go on an outing to the arcade together.

Stacey and Miranda's father also made a list of Miranda's most troublesome behaviors: Yelling at her four-year-old sister and calling her names, uncooperative behavior in the morning, and uncooperative behavior at school. Stacey decided that she did not need to set up consequences for misbehaviors at school, as that would be in her teacher's hands. Plus, if she was uncooperative at school, she would not get a positive note from her teacher and she would not receive a sticker. She also decided that losing her sticker was enough of a consequence for Miranda when she was late in the morning. She wanted to motivate Miranda without being overly harsh, as she knew Miranda was struggling against her natural inborn temperament in the mornings. However, she did decide that each time Miranda called her sister a name or yelled at her Miranda would receive an eight-minute timeout on the stairs. Miranda's sister, in turn, would receive a timeout of four minutes for the same type of behavior. (Most experts agree that a timeout equal to one minute per year of age seems to be about right.) As soon as Stacey observed Miranda becoming frustrated while playing with her sister, Stacey found it helpful to suggest to Miranda that she play in a separate room for awhile to cool herself down. In this way she was teaching Miranda to monitor her own mood and manage her own anger before it got out of control.

Stacey found that following the plan with her difficult temperament child helped her provide Miranda with a more secure holding environment. Miranda also sensed that her mother was more attuned to her emotions and needs because Stacey stayed more aware of Miranda's level of intensity and coached her in a supportive way. When the negative cycles of interactions between mother and daughter decreased, there was more room for positive interactions between them, further strengthening their attachment. Stacey also applied some of the techniques outlined in Chapter Fifteen, such as remediation touching and holding. She noticed as time went on that she was enjoying Miranda more, and Miranda seemed to have improved self-esteem and self-confidence.

4.8. Identify the Parental Misperceptions or Temperament Traits that Might Trip You Up

In addition to having a specific plan for dealing with your child's misbehaviors, it will help you to avoid either overreacting or underreacting if you can dispute the parental misperceptions that might interfere with a neutral, business-like response and consistent follow-through. It is especially easy for the parent of a child with difficult temperament traits to compare his child to other children and think, "My child exhibits more troublesome behavior than other children. She must have inherited some kind of badness from me," "She must not love me," or, "She is abusive like my mother." A difficult temperament child is also more likely to trigger anxious feelings of unsafety or anxiety about not being in control. These parental misperceptions can result in overreacting with shame or anger or responding with too much leniency as an attempt to win her love or approval. However, identifying a child's inborn difficult temperament traits can often help put the situation back into perspective. If you have a child with a difficult temperament, it will be important to use your reminder cards to help you dispute your parental misperceptions. Use your cards to remind yourself that your child's behaviors are related to her difficult temperament.

As you read about the difficult temperament traits you may have identified some of these traits in yourself. This is not an unusual situation, as these temperament traits tend to be genetic! Sharing similar difficult traits with your child can be helpful, as in the case of a parent who shares his child's low threshold to stimulus and who subsequently has more empathy for his child's agitated response to scratchy tags or bothersome noises. On the other hand, if you share your child's trait of expressing emotions with high intensity, you may naturally respond to your child's intense reactions with a very intense expression of your own emotions. Your intensity may then add fuel to your child's intense emotions, creating vicious cycles of reacting and overreacting between you. In this case it may be a good idea to enlist the help of a professional to coach you in managing your own difficult temperament traits so that you can respond more effectively to your difficult temperament child.

5. ATTENTION DEFICIT HYPERACTIVITY DISORDER

There is a great deal of controversy about attention deficit hyperactivity disorder (ADHD) not only because it is a problem that can look quite different in different children, but also because researchers have not been able to isolate one specific cause for ADHD. Many children with a very difficult temperament style may wind up being diagnosed as ADHD, even though there is nothing actually abnormal about their condition. Some children with symptoms that resemble ADHD may actually be experiencing a psychological response to trauma or excessive stress in their environment. There is scientific evidence, however, that many children diagnosed with ADHD have an abnormal neurobiological condition. An imbalance in the neurotransmitters—the chemicals in the brain that allow the nerves to communicate—most likely plays a role in the symptoms. There is evidence that ADHD does run in families, although problems in the pregnancy or the birth process, drug or alcohol used during pregnancy, environmental toxins, or nutritional deficiencies may all affect the developing brain. Paul Wender, Professor of Psychiatry and Director of Psychiatric Research at the Utah School of Medicine, offers a thorough review of the research available on the biological studies of ADHD in his book, *Attention-Deficit Hyperactivity Disorder in Adults*.[21]

Lisa Bain, a science and medical writer who worked with the doctors at The Children's Hospital of Philadelphia to write her book, *A Parent's Guide to Attention Deficit Disorders*, describes other disorders which often accompany a diagnosis of ADHD.[22] Other problems that also seem to be related to abnormal brain physiology include learning disorders, tic disorders including Tourette's syndrome, obsessive compulsive disorder, depression, bipolar disorder, and anxiety disorders. Often children with ADHD are exceptionally oppositional and uncooperative with their parents and teachers, and are diagnosed with oppositional defiant disorder or a conduct disorder in addition to the ADHD.

The following diagnostic criteria for ADHD are from the *Diagnostic and Statistical Manual of Mental Disorders, Fourth Edition* (pp. 83–84), published by the American Psychiatric Association[23]:

"A.   Either (1) or (2):

(1)   six (or more) of the following symptoms of **inattention** have persisted for at least 6 months to a degree that is maladaptive and inconsistent with developmental level:
Inattention

(a)   often fails to give close attention to details or makes careless mistakes in schoolwork, work, or other activities

(b)   often has difficulty sustaining attention in tasks or play activities

(c)   often does not seem to listen when spoken to directly

(d)   often does not follow through on instructions and fails to finish schoolwork, chores, or duties in the workplace (not due to oppositional behavior or failure to understand instructions)

(e)   often has difficulty organizing tasks and activities

(f)   often avoids, dislikes, or is reluctant to engage in tasks that require sustained mental effort (such as schoolwork or homework)

(g)   often loses things necessary for tasks or activities (e.g., toys, school assignments, pencils, books, or tools)

(h)   is often easily distracted by extraneous stimuli

(i)   is often forgetful in daily activities

(2)   six (or more) of the following symptoms of hyperactivity-impulsivity have persisted for at least 6 months to a degree that is maladaptive and inconsistent with developmental level:

Hyperactivity

(a) often fidgets with hands or feet or squirms in seat
(b) often leaves seat in classroom or in other situations in which remaining seated is expected
(c) often runs about or climbs excessively in situations in which it is inappropriate (in adolescents or adults, may be limited to subjective feelings of restlessness)
(d) often has difficulty playing or engaging in leisure activities quietly
(e) is often "on the go" or often acts as if "driven by a motor"
(f) often talks excessively

Impulsivity

(g) often blurts out answers before questions have been completed
(h) often has difficulty awaiting turn
(i) often interrupts or intrudes on others (e.g., butts into conversations or games)

"B. Some hyperactive-impulsive or inattentive symptoms that caused impairment were present before age 7 years.
"C. Some impairment from the symptoms is present in two or more settings (e.g., at school or work and at home).
"D. There must be clear evidence of clinically significant impairment to social, academic, or occupational functioning."

A child can be diagnosed with ADHD predominantly hyperactive-impulsive type, ADHD predominantly inattentive type, or ADHD combined type.

5.2. ADHD and Attachment

Forming a secure attachment with a child with ADHD can be a tremendous challenge, because the symptoms of ADHD are so challenging to manage. When so much of a parent's energy is spent focusing on the child's behaviors, correcting the child, and consequencing the child, less energy is available for "tuning in" to the child's feelings or engaging in positive emotional interactions. When a child won't sit still for a minute it is more difficult to hold the child or get eye contact. Providing a positive, secure holding environment becomes very difficult when a child who is hyperactive, impulsive, and uncooperative frequently provokes her parents to frustration and anger. Unfortunately, without enough positive interactions to balance out the negative interactions, the attachment relationship can become less and less secure, resulting in a vicious cycle of increased negative behaviors on the part of the child and increased anger and frustration on the part of the parent.

However, although a secure attachment cannot prevent or cure ADHD, a secure attachment does improve the overall functioning of a child with ADHD. Soleil Gregg, in a research review for the Appalachia Educational Laboratories, writes in regard to children with ADHD, "Perhaps the most critical factor influencing the development of prosocial behavior is attachment to at least one prosocial adult who believes in the child and provides unconditional acceptance and support."[24] The question becomes, in light of the difficulty of parenting a child with ADHD, how can a parent improve the quality of the attachment relationship while at the same time managing the child's very challenging behaviors?

5.3. Medical Management

If you suspect your child may have ADHD, make sure he or she is assessed by a psychologist, pediatrician, or psychiatrist for whom ADHD is a specialty. If your child is diagnosed with ADHD, a pediatrician or a psychiatrist can prescribe medication that may help control your child's symptoms. Ritalin is probably the most widely used medication to treat ADHD, but it is not the only medication used. For some children and adults with ADHD, medication is a lifesaver giving them more ability to focus and control their impulses. Medication does not cure ADHD, but it changes the chemistry in the brain in such a way that the individual simply has more control over the symptoms. When a child receives the proper medicine to combat the symptoms her behavior can become less difficult for parents and teachers to manage. In turn she often finds new acceptance from adults and peers, improving her self-esteem. Proper medication often allows the parent to enjoy more positive interactions with her child, thus improving the quality of the attachment relationship. The increased security and emotional connection with her parents in turn positively affects the child's overall functioning.

Medication should be prescribed only by a qualified physician and must be carefully monitored by the parent to make sure it is being used exactly as prescribed. Parents can have access to on-going up-to-date information on research, medical management, and behavior management through two national organizations, the Attention Deficit Disorders Association (ADDA) and Children and Adults with Attention Deficit Disorders (CHADD), listed in Appendix B.

5.4. Counseling and Support Groups

The ADHD child, the parents, and siblings can all be helped by talking with a counselor who is experienced with ADHD. Counseling can help the child learn strategies to better cope with her symptoms, improve her self-esteem, and learn to express her feelings of frustration and anger appropriately. Siblings can be encouraged to talk about their own feelings of frustration related to having a brother or sister with ADHD, and they can learn strategies to better cope with the provocative behaviors as well.

Counseling can help parents plan behavior management strategies, avoid taking their child's behavior personally, improve the attachment relationship, and take better care of themselves and their marriage. A skilled counselor can help you identify any parental misperceptions that may be causing your emotions to interfere with effective behavior management such as, "My child is abusive," or "My child doesn't love me enough."

Also, as ADHD often appears to have a genetic component, many times parents of ADHD children had ADHD themselves and some still have symptoms as adults! Sometimes adults get diagnosed only after they have a child with the same symptoms. This can be an especially trying situation, as a parent's ADHD symptoms can make it even more difficult for him or her to respond to the child's behaviors in a structured, consistent manner. In this case a counselor who has expertise in ADHD has a very important role as coach to both the parent and the child in managing the ADHD symptoms.

Many parents of children with ADHD find support groups extremely helpful for gaining the latest information about medical treatment and behavioral management strategies. In addition, it can be helpful to find out you are not alone, to share feelings with others who understand, and to even share laughter with other parents about shared experiences. Contact the Attention Deficit Disorders Association (ADDA) and Children and Adults with Attention Deficit Disorders (CHADD) listed in Appendix B for information about support groups in your area.

5.5. ADHD and Behavior Management

The strategies for managing the behaviors of a difficult temperament child are also the most effective strategies to use to manage the behavior of the ADHD child. Following is a summary of each point. Refer to the section on difficult temperament for more detail.

1. List your child's ADHD-related behaviors. List her strengths.

2. Identify which behaviors are not relevant and make a commitment to simply ignore those behaviors. "Don't sweat the small stuff" becomes a very useful motto here. Like the difficult temperament child, the ADHD child can become increasingly demoralized and angry when the parent and child have become locked into a pattern of punishment, punishment, and more punishment.

3. Identify which behaviors need "coaching." Monitor your child's emotional state and intervene early, putting words to what is happening as you see her becoming increasingly hyper, inattentive, or impulsive. Use empathy as you intervene to help her regain control of herself.

4. Identify the priority problem behaviors and design a planned, strategic approach that rewards positive behavior and gives consequences with consistent followthrough for misbehaviors. To avoid getting locked into an increasingly negative pattern of relating and maintain the attachment relationship, correct her behavior with a calm, but firm tone and plenty of empathy for how difficult it is. Positive reinforcement for appropriate behavior is especially motivating for the child with ADHD and enhances self-esteem.

5. Continue disputing your parental misperceptions and healing your past so that you can give your ADHD child the steady, secure environment she needs for optimum functioning. If you suspect that you may have ADHD symptoms, find an experienced professional to evaluate you and become your "coach."

6. IN CONCLUSION . . .

With proper medical management, professional support for you and your child and a planned, strategic approach to behavior management you will be able to enjoy your child more, which will in turn strengthen your attachment relationship. Practice separating the behaviors from the child, and make sure you let your children know they are always loved even when you don't like their behaviors. Give them positive affirmations every day. Chapter Fifteen will give you more ideas for improving the quality of your attachment relationship. Use what fits for you and your child, or adapt my techniques in any way that works for you!

Chapter Fourteen

Special Issues Related to Adoptive Families

Adoption can be a rewarding way to form a family, providing a viable solution both for the child whose birth parents are unable to provide a home, and for the parents who have the desire to parent a child. Some adoptive parents have chosen adoption due to infertility, and other adoptive parents already have birth children, but find parenting a rewarding experience and so feel compelled to adopt a child who needs a family. The adoption experience does pose some unique challenges, however. Overall, adoptive parents increase their chances for developing a secure attachment between themselves and their child by acknowledging and addressing the special issues related to adoption.

Following are several common misperceptions of adoptive parents that can unnecessarily interfere with the adjustment of the adoptive family.

1. SIX COMMON PARENTAL MISPERCEPTIONS RELATED TO ADOPTION

1.1. As an Adoptive Parent I Must Prove Myself Worthy

Lou Shilton, an Adoption Specialist with the Nebraska Department of Health and Human Services, described this misperception to me. Lou helps place children who are older or who have special needs. She stated, "Many adoptive parents share the notion that they must prove themselves as worthy to be parents. Often adoptive parents seem to believe that they must be superparents. They think they should not have any problems and should not have to ask for help." Sometimes adoptive parents think that if their child is having problems adjusting, or if they are having problems managing their child, it must mean they are not good enough to be adoptive parents. Some adoptive parents think that if they talk about any problems or seek help, someone will say to them, "Well, you were the ones who chose this!" as if making that decision somehow takes away their right to need help with it. The fear about admitting to problems or asking for help sometimes can be related to infertility—to the belief that somehow because they were infertile, they weren't really "good enough" to be parents. On the other hand, if a couple has birth children, but just want more children to raise, they can feel an even stronger pressure to prove themselves as good enough to take on more, or to handle the challenges of a special-needs child. Another reason adoptive parents believe they must prove themselves worthy is the experience of going through the evaluative process with the agency in order to receive the stamp of approval to become parents. All of these factors together seem to contribute to the parents' belief that if there are any problems following placement, it means they aren't good enough to be adoptive parents. This is a very unrealistic notion when it comes to adoption, and it is harmful when it prevents parents from being open about the problems that exist and accepting help from outside. Infertile couples need to remember that their infertility is a purely physical problem and has nothing to do with their emotional capacity to parent. Couples who choose to adopt "just because" often adopt a child who is older or has special needs. They should expect that problems in adjustment are likely to arise for which they will need some professional guidance.

If you are an adoptive parent and you have a large "internal critic" you may be especially vulnerable to unrealistic expectations about parenting an adoptive child. If you are struggling with old negative messages such as "I am not good enough" or "I am not worthy," you may feel an even stronger need to prove yourself worthy to parent your child. You may tend to misinterpret common adjustment problems as evidence of your defectiveness.

It is important that you acknowledge your critical messages, and remind yourself that part of becoming an effective parent is knowing when there is a problem and when it is time to seek some help!

1.2. If I Don't Automatically Feel a Strong Attachment with My Child, or If He Doesn't Automatically Attach to Me, It Must Mean I'm Not a Good Enough Parent

Even a new parent bringing home a baby that has been born to him or her often goes through a stage of feeling unsure and wondering silently, "Was I really ready for this?" Naturally, adoptive parents have the same feelings and fears. I remember the first days after we brought our adopted two-year-old daughter home, I was excited and joyful, yet also felt strange and very scared to suddenly find myself Mom to a little girl I didn't even know! She definitely felt equally unsure about me! In the beginning, adoptive parents often secretly fear they won't have the capacity to love their adopted child as they would love a birth child, or fear that he won't be able to love them as he would his birth parents. All of these fears cast doubt upon the parents' belief in their ability to be a good parent to their adoptive child.

It is important for adoptive parents to remember and to expect that the attachment process will take time for both the child and the adoptive parents. Feelings of love usually do not develop instantaneously. Although the attachment/love relationship may take time to develop, it can become just as strong between adopted children and their parents as it can become between birth children and their parents.

The suggestions for strengthening attachment in the last chapter should be very helpful to you. But don't set a deadline on the calendar. Just look for the little signs of progress each passing day and delight in those signs. Find enjoyment in watching the process happen gradually for you and your child.

1.3. Love Is an Automatic Cure-All

If your child is older and had experiences with attachment figures early in life that caused him to be mistrustful, the attachment process will be much more difficult for both of you because the closer he feels to you, the more anxious he may become. Consequently, as you get closer he may act out and push you away. This can create a Catch-22 situation, as the child who needs love the most can't accept it. A child who experienced abuse may act out in ways that reenact his script, seeking the only kind of attention he feels comfortable with at this point—negative attention. Outside help from a professional trained in working with both trauma and attachment problems will be very important in working through these kinds of difficulties. If your child is unattached and therefore is exhibiting severely disturbed behavior, you and he will need some very intensive help as described in more detail at the end of this chapter.

1.4. If My Child Holds Anger or Grief about His Early Losses, or Wants to Search for His Birth Parents, It Means He Doesn't Love Me

You may be especially vulnerable to this misperception if as a child you experienced rejection and you struggle with trusting that people really care about you. It will be important for you to remember that your child's issues of loss have nothing to do with his feelings about you. In general, children placed after six months of age tend to have the most difficulty with core abandonment, but even those placed at birth can struggle with intense feelings related to the early loss of their birth mother. Even a wonderful home and a loving relationship with you cannot erase your child's earliest experiences of loss, although you can provide the secure holding environment that will help give your child the security he needs to work through his painful feelings. And yes, he may direct his anger about his early losses toward you. Why? Because you are there. You are safe. And his intimate relationship with you may trigger feeling memories of the first, most intimate relationship of his life. Those feeling memories can be very painful. No matter how rejecting your child behaves toward you, he desperately needs your constancy in his life. Keep in the very forefront of your mind the realization that his anger and grief are not about you, even though it may feel that way.

The desire to search for birth parents is also a very natural response for an adoptee in his quest for finding a sense of completion and understanding of who he is. If your child begins a search, he is not rejecting you. A parent who loses a child, after all, will grieve and mourn the loss of that child intensely even though she may have other living children whom she loves. In the same way many adoptees have a natural yearning for what has been lost that cannot be erased by even the most wonderful relationship with their adoptive parents.

1.5. My Child Will Be Grateful that We Gave Him a Family and a Good Home

Sometimes adoptive parents assume that an adopted child will be grateful to them for giving him a home when he had none, or that a child adopted at an older age will be grateful to the adoptive parents for giving him a family that treats him well as opposed to, say, a birth family that neglected or abused him. Sometimes adoptive parents assume that the child will be so grateful for what he has in the adoptive home that he won't feel the loss of his birth parents or he won't ever act out in his new home. The truth is, these ideas generally do not occur to an adopted child, and why should they? We need to remember that all children are entitled to a good family and a good home just because they are children. Believing that an adopted child should be grateful to us is equivalent to believing a birth child owes us for bringing him home from the hospital. Additionally, if a child does end up feeling he "owes" his parents, the indebtedness he feels can interfere with his drive toward autonomy and separation. This does not mean that when either an adopted child or a birth child reaches adulthood he might not look back and feel grateful to his parents for the good home they provided. In fact, this is quite likely! But when we point out to an adoptive child, "Look at all we've done for you" or "Look where you would be without us," we discount and deny the very real pain the child feels about his separation from his birth family, no matter what the situation was. Furthermore, we are failing to acknowledge every child's inherent right to have a loving home and caring parents.

1.6. Adoption Will Automatically Heal My Grief over Infertility

Just as you cannot take away your child's earlier losses no matter how loving you are, adopting a child does not automatically take away feelings of grief related to infertility. Resolve, Inc., is a wonderful organization for parents dealing with infertility, and is listed in Appendix B.

2. COMMON ISSUES OF THE ADOPTIVE CHILD

Becoming attuned to your adopted child's feelings will enhance your relationship and help him feel supported and understood. However, adopted children often do not express their innermost feelings directly. Having a clear understanding of issues common to many adopted children will help you have a more intuitive understanding of what your child may be feeling when he expresses his feelings indirectly.

2.1. The Primal Wound

In Chapter Three I described how the mother provides the mirror in which the baby gets to know himself. He sees himself reflected in her gaze, and so he knows himself to be real, and to be loved. Imagine now that the mother, the mirror to the self, is suddenly removed. There is no mirror; there is no self. The adoptee often describes this lack of self as a "hole inside" or a "feeling of emptiness." He often tries to fill this hole with sweets, "things," or alcohol or drugs in the teen years. Therapist and adoptive mother Nancy Verrier explains in her book, *The Primal Wound,* that when the adoptee begins to search for the birth mother he often feels he is searching for his sense of self. He is searching for the mirror in which he was discovering his own existence—the mirror that suddenly vanished, taking his sense of self along with it. Verrier states, "The search for Self is a mission for many adoptees who believe that their baby soul was annihilated upon the separation from the original mother. The search for Self, therefore, seems to be intimately connected to the search for the birthmother." Verrier calls this loss of the sense of self the *primal wound.*[1]

Verrier also warns parents to be aware that the adopted child may mask his more vulnerable feelings, including his feelings of defectiveness and the hole inside. Hiding his "true self" and wearing a "false front" may feel safer if the adoptee believes he was rejected by his birthmother because he is defective. Hiding his "true self" can create a wall that interferes with his ability to form secure attachments.[2]

2.2. Control

Many adopted children attempt to stay in control of their environment in order to avoid feeling vulnerable or anxious. By retaining a feeling of control they can ward off feelings of abandonment or rejection, shame, grief, or emptiness. When control has become a major issue to an adopted child, it is especially important to avoid making control the Holy Grail in the family. Give the child control whenever it is appropriate. Give him as many choices in his life as you can. Be firm about the important rules and don't nitpick about unimportant issues. Try to help him express the vulnerable feelings underlying the need to control by really listening to him and reflecting back your understanding of what he is saying to you without judging or evaluating his feelings.

3. TUNING IN TO YOUR CHILD

Although your child may have issues related to grief and loss you cannot fix, by becoming attuned to your child's feelings and issues and providing a secure environment for him to process his feelings, you *can* help your child. When a child feels he cannot share his feelings with his adoptive parents because they would become upset or rejecting, his feelings become much *more* powerful and overwhelming for him. When a parent can accept even the child's most negative feelings and continue to provide a steady safe environment for him, the child will naturally feel less overwhelmed and threatened by his own feelings. When a child feels safe expressing his feelings there becomes less of a need to repress them and act them out indirectly. When the child senses his parents are attuned with what he is going through he feels a more solid connection with them. This naturally increases the security of the attachment between the child and the parent.

4. TOSSING PEBBLES

Holly van Gulden and Lisa Bartels-Rabb, authors of *Real Parents, Real Children*, suggest using the "pebble method" to help the child know that it is O.K. for him to verbalize his feelings related to his adoption.[3] Just because a child is saying nothing does not mean he is not feeling or thinking about his adoption, and they suggest "throwing out a pebble" every few weeks or so. Pebbles are brief comments made in passing, not requiring a response, but just opening the door to the issue. For instance, an adoptive parent may think out loud, "Gee, I wonder if you inherited your athletic abilities from your birth mother or birth father." Or, after seeing a friend with a new baby, a parent may comment, "I've read that sometimes children who are adopted feel sad when they think about what they had to go through when they were babies."

5. KEEPING YOUR INNER CHILD OUT OF THE PARENTING ROLE

In order to be able to absorb your child's strong feelings it will be important to keep your own inner child safe and out of the parenting role so that you can stay in your adult wise mind. This becomes especially important when your child feels angry about his losses and when that anger is projected onto you. You are the safe, available target, after all, and the birth parent is not. A negative cycle can begin between the two of you if your child's rage triggers feeling memories for *you* related to rejection. Your inner hurt child may respond by "rejecting back" or becoming rageful. If this has happened to you, prepare yourself with a reminder card like the samples in Chapter Six. Use the inner child meditation from the end of Chapter Seven on a regular basis to keep your inner child out of the parenting role. It will be very therapeutic for your child if you can respond to his anger with an empathic, emotionally steady response such as, "You are very angry today. I wonder if you are feeling angry about losing your birth mother. I will not allow you to harm me or anyone else, but I understand your feelings and I'm here if you want to talk about it." Remember that the secure holding environment you provide will strengthen his attachment with you.

6. CLAIMING

Part of providing a secure holding environment for the child who has a core belief system that says, "I will always be rejected," is claiming the child. Claiming the child means demonstrating to the child that he belongs to this family and he is not going anywhere. Claiming does not mean denying the existence of the birth parents or the child's feelings of grief and loss or desire to find them someday. Claiming means acknowledging that although the adopted child has two sets of parents, he is a permanent member of his adoptive home. It is also important for the parents, as claiming acknowledges for them, their friends, and their family that they are entitled to be the parents to their adopted child. Adoptive parents often initially claim their child by sending out announcements to friends and relatives when the child joins the family. Religious rituals such as baptisms or self-designed rituals to welcome the child to the family can be important claiming events. Having family photographs taken to be hung on the wall, adding photographs of the child to the family album, or including the child in family videos help to claim the child as part of the family. Family rituals can be important in claiming, as your adopted child becomes part of the yearly holiday rituals in your family, birthday rituals, and religious rituals.

Sometimes adoptive parents' claim to their children is challenged by outsiders, such as the acquaintance or stranger who asks, "Now which ones are your real children?" Holly van Gulden suggests that responding with humor, such as "Well, these kids here are polyester," gives the parent and child a chance to share a good laugh over the insensitive questioner.[4]

7. DISCUSSING THE BIRTH PARENTS

It is very important to be aware of how closely an adopted child's identity is tied to the birth parents when discussing the birth parents with the child. It is important to sort out your own feelings and discuss them with someone so that your own feelings toward the birth parents do not interfere with being sensitive to your child's feelings. You may have angry feelings toward birth parents who conceive children without forethought. You may know of some neglect or abuse your child suffered in his birth parent's care and feel angry as a result. You may feel angry that your child has fantasies of perfect birth parents when you know they do not deserve a perfect image. Nevertheless, it will be important to work through your feelings so that you can talk with your child about his birth parents nonjudgmentally. If you judge your child's birth parents harshly, you risk causing your child to feel shame about who he is. You also risk putting your child in a position of divided loyalty between you and his birth parents which can create confusion and guilt.

Lois Ruskai Melina's book, *Making Sense of Adoption,* gives sound advice on how to talk to your child about his birth parents and other tough subjects related to adoption.[5]

8. THE UNATTACHED CHILD

Fortunately *most* adopted children *do not* enter their new families with severe attachment disorders, but there is a small minority of adopted children who are unattached or only barely attached. Adopting a child who has given up altogether on human relationships—who has lost the ability to attach—can be frightening and overwhelming to adoptive parents. It is especially difficult if the adoption workers did not recognize the disorder and did not prepare the parents for the severity of the problems they would be dealing with. Adoptive parents who adopt an unattached child can feel like their world has been turned upside down and they are all alone in it. The lack of conscience, destruction to property, cruelty to others and to animals, stealing, lying, fire setting, and preoccupation with blood and gore are behaviors that even the most skilled parent would find overwhelming.

The good news is that there is help for the unattached child. Normal parenting techniques do not work with the unattached child. Neither does typical play therapy, family therapy, or talk therapy. The therapy that is helpful with the unattached child is both intensive and intrusive enough to break through the defensive wall of control and help such a child release his pent-up rage and grief.

Parents of an unattached child must have a strategic approach to managing their child's behavior, developed with the help of an attachment therapist. They must avoid reacting to the unattached child's provocations or taking the child's behaviors personally, which means learning to view the child's behavior objectively, as a professional would. This means actually detaching emotionally from the child to a certain extent. This is not an easy task, even without parental misperceptions stemming from early experiences. Therefore, it is vital that parents be involved in the therapy, too.

Parents who can stay committed, however, and see their unattached child through the lengthy and tumultuous process of surrendering control and allowing himself to connect emotionally for the first time are rewarded with a child they can love and the knowledge that they helped to pull a child back from the abyss to save his life. Appendix D has a list of attachment resources and agencies.

9. IN CONCLUSION . . .

Adoptive parents who have overcome the influences of a difficult past and challenged their own misperceptions have the opportunity to take delight in getting to know their children for their own unique qualities. It's an exciting and curious thing to watch a child develop and grow to adulthood, and it's even more fun when we are not getting in the way with preconceived notions of who our child "should" be. It's fascinating to tune into the budding personalities of all of our children and to help them discover their own personal talents and interests. Adoption can add just a little more spice. In my own family, my husband and I have two children who were born to us, and like us tend to be into books and computers and such. Our middle child, Maddie, joined our family through adoption. The addition of Maddie to our family, with her preference for basketballs to books and her feisty, raucous nature was like adding salsa to the cheese dip. This evening, after she had rocketed through the kitchen creating a tremendous amount of clatter and cacophony, I asked aloud to no one in particular, "Did a tornado just go through here?" Without looking up from his book, my son Vince replied, "Yup. It's name was Maddie."

Although every child is unique, adoption can be even a little more like opening a surprise package. Adoptive families have the most fun when they are able to enjoy the unique flavor each child brings to the mix.

Chapter Fifteen

How to Strengthen Your Attachment with Your Child at Any Age

At this point you may believe there is some repair work to do in your relationship with your child. You may suspect that your child does not have a completely secure attachment with you and therefore you would like to strengthen that attachment relationship now. Or you may simply want to go the extra mile to make sure that your child is as securely attached as she can be to give her the best chance possible for optimum emotional health. This chapter will provide you with tools to help you either repair or maximize your attachment relationship with your child, from infancy through adulthood!

1. THE FIRST FEW MONTHS

1.1. Becoming Mindful with Your Infant

To strengthen your attachment relationship with your infant, one of the most important things you can do is to practice the skill of "one-mindfulness" taught in Chapter Seven while you are with her. To do this, simply practice focusing your attention on your infant as you hold her. Practice letting go of outside thoughts and let yourself enjoy "taking her in" through your senses. Pay attention to her eyes, her face, her hair, her small hands, and her tiny feet. Enjoy the smell of her as you nuzzle her neck. Take pleasure in the softness of her skin and her hair. Listen intently for the little soft coos and gurgles. Closely observe the movements and sounds she makes with her mouth and the expressions she shows on her face, and practice mirroring her expressions and sounds back to her. As you interact with your infant one-mindfully, it will be easy to pace your interactions with her without either overwhelming or overstimulating her. Try to match your voice to hers. She will sense your loving attunement with her. She will feel a sense of who she is mirrored in your gaze. Your focused, attuned presence will help her trust that you will be there for her and that she will not be abandoned. She will know that it is safe for her to fall completely in love with you.

Frequently, premature babies and sometimes full-term babies are born with an undeveloped nervous system and are extremely hypersensitive to external stimuli, even if it comes from you. They may cry at every noise. They may fuss or turn their heads away when talked to, picked up, or rocked. This can be very disheartening for parents. It is easy to misperceive the hypersensitive infant and think, "My child doesn't love me!" Dr. Brazelton recommends that parents of an infant who is hypersensitive connect with their infant through one kind of stimulus at a time to avoid overwhelming her.[1] The hypersensitive infant is overloaded when you rock her *and* talk with her *and* make eye contact all at the same time. To avoid overwhelming her nervous system, pick her up quietly without eye contact and wait until she has adjusted to that level of contact. When she's calm you can talk softly, but avoid looking at her eyes. When this level of contact has been mastered you can then try briefly looking her in the eyes. If she tolerates this, you can try making eye contact for a longer period.

Remember the skill of one-mindfulness: You consciously focus your attention on just what's in front of you, letting go of other distracting thoughts. With the hypersensitive infant one-mindfulness will be especially helpful as you observe each reaction closely and adjust the intensity of your stimulation to match what she is capable of handling. Your hypersensitive infant will thus feel safe and secure as she feels your attunement and learns to trust that you won't overwhelm her.

1.2. Infant Massage

Massage is a loving and gentle way to interact with your infant that will help strengthen the attachment through pleasurable touch, exchange of positive emotions, eye contact, and improved attunement. In addition, infant massage will improve circulation and help her feel relaxed and calm. Diane Moore has created a video called "Baby's First Touch" which I found very enjoyable and easy to follow.[2] The video demonstrates several types of massage strokes, and the best order to follow. Vimala Schneider McClure's book, *Infant Massage: A Handbook for Loving Parents*, also presents the techniques for infant massage, with numerous photographs, in a manner that is quite easy to follow.[3] I highly recommend that parents learn the proper way to massage their infants for optimal benefit. But even without specific massage instruction, any parent can very gently caress and massage his or her baby's legs and feet, tummy and chest, arms and hands, enhancing attachment. As long as your baby is not hypersensitive to too much stimulation, make eye contact, mirror her expressions and sounds, and talk softly and gently to her as you massage. With her face down, tummy across your lap, gently stroke and massage her back. Vimala Schneider McClure explains that "all of your strokes should be long, slow, and rhythmic, with just enough pressure to be comfortable but stimulating."[4]

For a colicky baby Diane Moore recommends massaging the tummy with small downward strokes from the top of the tummy paddling downward. Next she strokes the tummy clockwise in a circular motion around the tummy. Third, she gently pushes the knees up toward the tummy with several repetitions.[5]

Vimala Schneider McClure also describes massage techniques for ill, colicky, premature, and special-needs babies, and the older child.[6]

1.3. Floor Time

Stanley Greenspan, M.D., and Nancy Greenspan recommend an exercise they call "floor time" for strengthening the parent–child attachment relationship.[7] Floor time can be used with infants age three or four months up through elementary school age. Floor time can greatly increase the child's sense of attunement from the parent and provides a shared pleasurable experience, thereby increasing the security of the attachment relationship. It allows the child to feel a sense of control, removing control as the Holy Grail for the child. It allows her a way to express and work through fears and feelings of anger and sadness, and to feel affirmed by you. It gives the child another way to communicate with you, to interact with you, and to receive your attention without having to act out in a negative way!

Floor time *is* what it sounds like—it is time spent down on the floor with your child. During floor time the parent lets the child take the lead. To have effective floor time it is important for parents to dispute the misperception that "A parent should always have complete authority over the child." This is a good time to let go of control and just go with the flow! The skill of one-mindfulness will be helpful as you focus your mind on the play with your child. As distracting thoughts of the office or the household chores enter your mind, just notice the distracting thoughts and then gently bring your mind back to the here and now. Let yourself relax and enjoy observing your child in play. You can learn a tremendous amount about your child's thoughts and concerns and way of viewing the world as you get down on her level and observe her in play. As you get in synch with your child and become a part of her play world, she will feel your attunement with her.

During floor time, make comments to let her know that you are tuned in to her and that your role is not to critique her. For instance, instead of, "Don't put that block on there—your tower will fall!" you might say, "Wow! What a great crash that was!" Instead of, "Why are you coloring the girl's face green? Faces aren't green!" you might comment, "What a great color! I love green!" The purpose of floor time is to connect with your child by tuning in to her world and having fun with her. It's the time to prove to her that she is lovable just the way she is, not to correct her or judge her.

During floor time you can encourage your child to communicate with you by asking open-ended questions like, "I wonder where these cars are going?" or, "What are we building now?" You might ask for directions like, "Who should I be?" or, "Which hat do you think I should wear?" During floor time get involved with the fantasy, but don't try to take over or control the play.

With a baby, offer toys or offer yourself as the toy. Mirror your baby's expressions, imitate her silly noises, and applaud her as she discovers how to grab your nose or retrieves the block hidden under your shirt tail. Let your baby decide which toy she prefers and admire the toy along with your baby. Share her excitement and curiosity. Your interest and responsiveness will encourage her to become even more communicative and engaged with you. Her sense of connection with you will continue to strengthen.

As the child gets older she will use some of her floor time with you to work out fears, deal with her anger, and find mastery over her feelings of powerlessness. It is very important that you not censor or judge your child's play, but show her instead that you understand and accept all of her feelings. You will, however, want to set limits and be firm about destructive or hurtful behavior.

The toddler may turn you into her "baby." This role reversal is very common and allows her to learn about nurturing and to experience having the power in the relationship for a moment! Don't be surprised when your toddler sticks a bottle in your mouth or puts a bib on you. Humor her and have fun with it!

When my youngest began attending day care part time at age two we spent many an evening in floor time, playing—you guessed it—day care! I was the baby night after night as Hannah led me to day care, took off my coat, and said in a motherly way, "I go to work now. You stay here!" Off she would go, leaving me abandoned at the day care. I sensed it was very important for her to work through her separation fears by experiencing this situation in the more powerful role as the mother who was able to leave and return at will. She would next "switch hats" and become the day care provider, bedding me down for a nap, serving me lunch, and "running the show." I will never forget picking Hannah up from my parents' home one day only to find gramma and grampa lying on the floor covered with blankets under the firm and watchful eye of Miss Hannah, day-care provider!

As your preschooler or school-age child works out her fears or aggressive feelings with warriors, or by slaying a dragon with her bloody sword, stay calm! Try to avoid overreacting or judging this play. Instead, you might comment, "Wow, you're really strong and powerful!" Or you might ask, "What did the bad guy do that made you mad?" You can help her put words on her feelings with comments such as, "Wow, you are really mad at that monster!" Your child needs to know all of her feelings are accepted by you and that her feelings are not frightening or bad. You become the secure holding environment where she can safely express her feelings and find acceptance. As she "plays out" her feelings and finds feelings of mastery and control through her play, she will have less of a need to act out her feelings toward playmates or to find power and control through acting-out behaviors with you.

The child who has never experienced floor time with you may hold back from play with you. Or the child who has just spent a long day at the sitter's may angrily push you away. Watch out for the misperception, "My child doesn't love me." If she is pushing you away, it is only because she does love you and need you—but she is feeling insecure about you! Greenspan writes, "it is a rejection of himself and his sense of self-worth rather than a rejection of you." Greenspan explains that some children need to be wooed into a relationship with their parents.[8] The more uninterested a child appears to be in human relationships, the more help she needs to make a firm emotional connection with you. You can entice her into some playful fun on the floor with some interesting toys, figures, clay, or crayons. Use finger plays, patty-cake, or peek-a-boo games with the younger child. If you continue floor play on a daily basis, eventually your child will begin making playful overtures to you.

An important time for floor time is anytime you have had to be away from your child, or anytime you have had to set firm limits, withdraw privileges, or briefly scold your child. Floor time can help you firm up the relationship and balance the structure with feelings of love, nurturance, and acceptance.

Dr. Greenspan writes, "reserving special daily times, of 25 to 35 minutes or more of floor time, can be especially meaningful. This time with your child allows you to reaffirm that rhythm and sense of connection that you established at the beginning stages and enables you to elaborate your growing empathy and shared meanings."[9] Although this amount of time would be ideal, in many busy families it is impossible. Many parents would give up the idea altogether if they thought they had to participate for the full recommended time. Try to get down on the floor with your child for a little while each day, but be flexible—a minute or two here . . . and a few minutes there. Any period of time you spend engaged with your child counts and will increase the security of your attachment relationship.

1.4. Theraplay

Psychologist Ann Jernberg wrote a book in 1979 entitled, *Theraplay: A New Treatment Using Structured Play for Problem Children and Their Families,* outlining the treatment approach used by the Theraplay Institute in Chicago where Jernberg was clinical director. The Theraplay approach is different from floor time in that the therapist controls the activities and is in control of the play session. This approach has a slightly different type of objective in that it helps the child learn that she can relinquish control and *still* have fun and *still* be safe. Children needn't be made to believe that every time an adult takes charge it is to set limits, scold, or give consequences, and that the child is always left in a one-down position. Theraplay activities can be a complement to floor time, and can easily be incorporated into the schedule of a busy day. Like floor time, the activities promote closeness, touch, eye contact, and shared pleasure, enhancing parent–child attachment. Theraplay activities help the child feel she is special and important to the parent.

Theraplay activities are really not new. What is new for most parents is the idea of making a conscious effort to actively use these types of activities on a regular basis to strengthen attachment. If you have ever initiated a game of patty-cake with a child, you can do Theraplay. I have adapted many of the activities in the following list from ideas suggested in Jernberg's book,[11] but I've also thrown in a few of my own. You will probably come up with ideas of your own, perhaps some that you have already used in the past. The idea, of course, is to be the initiator of a little fun with your child throughout of the course of each day.

Suggestions

Make a game of counting freckles, eyes, ears, fingers, or toes, while admiring how special and beautiful your child is.[12]

Exchange "Eskimo kisses" (rub noses!)[13]

With a very young child initiate patty-cake or "This Little Piggie Went to Market."

Make a game of feeding your child with cherries, grapes, Cheerios, or M&Ms. You can let her pretend to be a baby bird while you're the mother bird. You can take turns and let her feed you as well. Or ask your child to close her eyes, and then hide the M&M somewhere in her clothes or yours for her to find.[14]

Draw a letter or shape on her back with your finger and ask her to guess what it is.

Hold her while you are standing, with her legs wrapped around your waist and her arms around your neck. Have her let go with her arms and fall slowly backward. She'll have fun walking around with her hands on your feet! This game promotes fun, closeness, and trust.[15]

Another trust game that can be fun is asking the child to close her eyes while you lead her somewhere—perhaps to her bed at bedtime. Take care not to let her get hurt in either of these games, as that certainly would not help her learn to trust!

A similar type of trust game my children enjoyed as toddlers or preschoolers is done by lying down on the floor, feet in the air, and knees bent. Your child stands at your feet facing you and then lies on your feet, holding your hands. Push her up and down in the air and let her pretend she is flying! Again, take care she doesn't get hurt or you'll cause her to become less likely to relinquish control the next time.

Rub lotion or powder on her arms and legs while she lies on the floor or bed and you sing or talk very softly to her. This is a nice calming bedtime activity with a child who is hyperactive.[16]

Put a pretzel or a doughnut on your finger and take turns taking a bite. The last one to take a bite without the pretzel or doughnut falling off your finger wins![17]

Wash, dry, and style your child's hair.

Polish your daughter's fingernails and toenails and allow her to polish yours.

Engage your child in a good-natured game of paper-scissors-rock, arm wrestling, thumb wrestling, or leg wrestling.

Offer a shoulder and neck massage at bedtime, or during a tedious hour of homework.

The last five activities can be enjoyed with older children—even teenagers. Although Jernberg suggests activities with few props so that you have plenty of touch and eye contact, pulling out a board game is also a great way to share a pleasurable activity with a teen or a younger child.

Jernberg also recommends plenty of cuddling, holding, and rocking while singing or feeding. She suggests the same kind of secure holding during a tantrum, maintaining a matter-of-fact attitude without judgment. She suggests offering reassuring messages such as, "I'll hold you here to keep you safe," and "We'll get through this together."[18] This type of holding is described in more detail later in this chapter.

1.5. Remediation Touching and Holding

Touch and eye contact are vital components in attachment. As a mother is nursing or cradling her infant in her arms as she feeds her, the child enjoys the pleasure of the sweet, warm milk as she feels the security of her mother's arms. As she gazes into her mother's eyes and listens to her talking softly and sweetly to her, the infant senses her mother's enjoyment and it becomes a shared pleasurable experience, bonding them together.

You may believe your child did not share enough blissful experiences with you as you held her in your arms as a baby or toddler. Perhaps you suffered from a postnatal depression, or you didn't have enough time to hold her because of stressful circumstances at the time. Perhaps you adopted your child and didn't get to spend those first few months with her. If you sense your child is not securely connected with you, is mistrustful or resentful, overreactive, or distancing with you, remediation holding may help to bridge the chasm and bring her closer to you. If your child has an emotional hole of some kind inside, remediation holding can help to fill it. Remediation holding is a fairly simple thing to do up to age nine or ten. Some children will accept remediation holding at an older age. For most parents and children, the ideal time for this kind of holding is just before bed. You might refer to it as "holding time" or "cuddle time." Wrap up together in a blanket and wrap your arms around your child. Cuddle her in a rocking chair or on her bed. It's O.K. to tell her, "We didn't get to do enough of this when you were a baby, so we need to do it now." Get into a position where you can get eye contact. The best position is with her across your lap, head on your arm, the way you would have held her to feed her as a baby. Ask her to tell you about the day's events. Sing, tell her stories about when she was a baby, or tell her stories about when you were little. Talk to her lovingly about her beautiful eyes, her wonderful curly hair, or her adorable freckles. It's best if you can spend 15 or 20 minutes together, but remember that any time spent holding is better than no time. If she is squirmy or uncomfortable, you can "jolly" her through it for as long as you can. You want to make it a pleasurable experience for both of you. A good way to encourage her cooperation and even further stimulate the infant attachment experience is by playfully offering her a popsicle which she can suck on while in the holding position. Or you may offer to feed her something sweet like grapes or cherries. If your child will not cooperate with any kind of remedial holding because she is too severely angry, mistrustful, or rejecting of you, it may be necessary to use rage reduction holding as described later.

For a child of any age, an illness is a good opportunity for strengthening attachment as you attentively nurse her back to health with a cold cloth on her forehead, chicken soup, and "T.L.C."

A younger child can be helped to become more securely attached by giving her comfort, touch, and reassurance when she is afraid from a nightmare or a thunderstorm, when her feelings have been hurt, or when she is injured. In fact, any time a child has experienced any kind of intense emotions she is more open and vulnerable to the attachment process than at any other time. So any time your child is feeling distressed you have an excellent opportunity for strengthening her sense of security, closeness, and trust with you.

If "closeness is unsafe" or "closeness is shameful" are problematic misperceptions for you, keep a cue card with you disputing these misperceptions and read it frequently. Repeat the inner child imagery from Chapter Eight each day. Practice "acting as if" you are comfortable with the closeness. Over time, if you continue touching or holding despite your discomfort, you will gradually begin to relax. In other words, try to "fake it 'till you make it!"

2. OLDER CHILDREN

For preteens and teenagers who find the idea of cuddling or rocking together too babyish you can start some regular rituals such as a big hug each night before bed, a bedside chat, or a nightly shoulder rub. Find every opportunity during the day to give her a passing squeeze or kiss on the forehead. Ruffle her hair as she's doing her homework. Offer to condition her hair for her or to dry and style it for her. Teens often lack touch because parents view them as big and independent, but everyone needs touch. A teen who is touch-deprived is naturally more likely to seek touch through sex than a teen who receives plenty of affectionate touch at home.

Taking time to make eye contact and really talk with your teen one on one is very important for strengthening and maintaining a secure attachment. It is important to make sure you are talking with your teen and not *only* talking *to* your teen. Listen nonjudgmentally to her views and opinions. Don't worry if she is experimenting with values and views that differ from yours. This is a normal part of adolescent development. It will be several years before she settles on the views and values that she will keep as an adult. I clearly remember in one adolescent phase I decided I would never marry or have children. In another phase I read Camus and decided I was an existentialist, and in another phase I became extremely dogmatic about religion.

Although it is extremely important that you show affection with your teenager, it is also very important to respect your teenager's boundaries.

Don't invade the privacy of her things and her room. Avoid lecturing your teenager about spending more time with the rest of the family. Your teen's needs for privacy and space are a very important part of her development as she moves toward separation and individuation. If you deny your teen privacy or her time alone she may withdraw from you further emotionally in order to retain her feelings of autonomy. This will have an adverse affect on your attachment relationship with her.

However, if you have serious suspicions that your teenager is using drugs and alcohol or has gang involvement, your teenager loses her right to space and privacy due to the dangerousness of the situation. When a child's emotional and physical health are at stake a parent must take charge to find out what is happening and obtain appropriate professional help for the child.

2.1. Rage Reduction Holding

Rage reduction holding is a method that accomplishes two tasks at the same time. It allows the child to express and discharge stored-up anger, and it provides an optimal condition for increasing attachment to the parent. Remember that following a state of heightened emotionality a child is psychologically more vulnerable and open to attaching as the parent steps in to calm and soothe. The infant who is crying and in distress is psychologically ready to attach to the parent who picks her up and gives her the comfort and nurturing she needs to feel better. The child who has bumped her knee is psychologically open to the parent who picks her up and takes care of her wounded knee. When our children are fearful, sad, in pain, or emotionally spent following a discharge of anger, they are psychologically vulnerable and more open to the attachment experience.

A child who has formed very strong defensive walls will not accept remediation holding or any other kind of touching or emotional nurturing. Her strong walls will keep her vulnerable feelings hidden, and will keep her parent at arms length. These walls are a protective device for the child who believes that closeness is not safe. She may have tight control over all of her feelings, or all of her feelings may simply get turned into anger, which gets expressed aggressively or passive-aggressively.

Rage reduction holding can be an effective way to break through the carefully maintained defensive walls of the angry child. It is highly recommended by many attachment specialists for children who have several symptoms of the unattached child such as lack of conscience, cruelty toward others or toward animals, constant lying, stealing, and lack of affection or eye contact except when it serves their own purposes. However, Dr. Martha Welch, Director of the Mothering Center and author of *Holding Time*, recommends that parents do holdings for any child to increase the security of the attachment relationship.[19] I used holdings with my youngest daughter when she had tantrums around two and three years of age, and I found the results remarkable in the closeness of the bond that developed between us following the holdings.

The easiest method of rage reduction holding for parents is to simply hold and contain the child securely when she has begun to go into a rage state. The most critical piece of this is that the parent must be able to hold the raging child without any hostility or derision. This is extremely difficult to do when you are holding a child who appears to be doing an imitation of Linda Blair in *The Exorcist*. She may be screaming hatefully, flailing about, perhaps even trying to bite or scratch you. It can be helpful to remind yourself that your child is actually quite miserable and is frightened by her overwhelming feelings.

Use your misperception cue cards to help you dispute any misperceptions that might interfere with your ability to provide a calm holding environment for your child's rage. To dispute such misperceptions as, "My child is abusive," or "My child doesn't love me enough," use your cue cards to remind yourself that your child is only a child and that she is actually extremely miserable and frightened by her out-of-control feelings. However, be realistic about what you can handle. If you do not believe you can hold your raging child without responding with anger yourself, don't attempt to hold without the presence of a trained professional.

The ideal position for holding is with your child across your lap, face up, and with her head in the crook of your left arm if you are right-handed. A pillow under your left arm will help. Keep her right arm tucked behind your back. You may also need to hold her left hand with your left hand and use your right hand to restrain kicking legs. A larger child may need a second parent at her feet. It is extremely important that you hold your child properly so that she can unleash her rage as strongly as she needs to without risk of any kind of injury to herself or to you.

When you begin to restrain the child who is having a tantrum, expect the intensity of her rage to increase because you are in control and she is not. She will likely become very resistant and try to get away. Even if a child is not already angry, if you pick up a child and begin holding her as described in the previous paragraph, you can expect the child to resist. Welch describes this as the "confrontation phase."[20]

During the next phase, the child typically rejects the parent. She may scream, cry, and vent her rage at you. You must be ready to accept all of her painful feelings at this time. Reflect her feelings back to her—let her know you understand how angry she is, how hurt, and how sad. Don't reprimand her for bad language or for anything she might say out of anger right now. Now is the time for her to vent. Reassure her that you won't let her hurt herself or you. Insist on eye contact, and express the depths of your own anger, sadness, or fears with her as well. Once your child has discharged her anger you may see tears. Welcome these, too. Cry with your child if you feel like it. This will help you connect with her on a genuine feeling level. Welch has described this release of pent-up emotions as the "rejection phase."[21]

As your child's body relaxes and lets go she will be open to bonding with you. Cuddle and talk quietly or just hold and rock. Welch describes this as the "resolution phase. She writes, "When both mother and child have reached to the depths of their feelings, a catharsis occurs and the resolution begins. . . . The child usually begins to caress the mother's face and to melt into her body. . . . The decidedly hurtful comments expressed during rejection are replaced by statements of love and affection: 'Momma, you are beautiful,' 'I love you,' and so forth."[22] Take plenty of time to enjoy this part of the holding, as it is a beautiful, loving, bonding experience for the two of you.

Allow plenty of time for a holding. It may take hours for a child with an insecure attachment to reach the point of resolution and bonding at first. If you cannot reach that point on the first try, you may reach it the second or third time you hold. Repeat the holdings as often as you need to, or each time your child goes into a rage if it is logistically possible to do so. In *Holding Time* Welch describes the holding technique in more detail and with numerous photographs, in a format that can be easily followed to use with any child for the purpose of increasing the security of her attachment to her parent.[23]

If your child is extremely rageful, or exhibits the severe symptoms of the unattached child, enlist the help of an attachment specialist trained in holding. Even older children with severe attachment disorders can be helped, although as a child gets older it becomes much more difficult to break through the defensive walls. In *Hope for High Risk and Rage Filled Children*, Cline describes the use of rage reduction holding in therapy along with other therapeutic techniques to help the unattached child.[24] *Adopting the Hurt Child*, by psychologist and attachment specialist Gregory Keck, offers advice for therapists and professionals including advice on holdings with the unattached child.[25] Josephine Anderson, a foster mother, describes how therapeutic holdings can be used to help unattached foster and adoptive children in an article entitled, "Holding Therapy: A Way of Helping Unattached Children."[26]

2.2. Staying Attached in a Disconnected Culture

Our culture presents many barriers to secure attachments within our families. Ours is a culture of "stuff." We have become accustomed to having lots of stuff, and we are used to getting our stuff right when we want it—with instant gratification. We are very attached to our stuff. We depend on our stuff. It makes us feel good, and it makes us feel good now. The comedian, George Carlin, performs a very insightful monologue called, "A Place for My Stuff," in which he says, "Everybody's gotta have a place for their stuff. That's what your house is—a place to keep your stuff—while you go out and get more stuff . . . Sometimes you gotta move—gotta get a bigger house. Why? No room for your stuff!"[27] Any of us, and any of our children, are at risk of forming stronger attachments to stuff than we have with people. We are at risk of spending more time earning money for stuff, buying stuff, and being with our stuff than with people.

Much of the stuff we are attached to is our electronic stuff. Psychologist Mary Pipher, in *The Shelter of Each Other: Rebuilding Our Families*, points out that our family time has been encroached upon by the time we spend with our technological devices. She writes, "Today family members are often living in the same house, but often they are not interacting . . . The outside world pours into the living room, the kitchen and the bedroom."[28] Both parents and children spend time off by themselves playing with the computer, watching television in their own rooms, and talking on the phone. Many children automatically turn to television or video games when they are feeling sad or lonely instead of turning to their family members—in other words, they are forming attachments to their electronic stuff!

Furthermore, our children spend so much time tuned into the media that the world of entertainment becomes a major source of learning about the world. Pipher writes, "There are televisions in birthing rooms so that literally, from birth on, children are exposed to media. Children see and hear information that is not appropriate to their developmental needs. Before they learn to ride tricycles, they are exposed to sexual and violent materials."[29] As soon as children are old enough to tune into the family television set the entertainers they see become all-important role models. Movies, television, and advertisements teach our children to solve problems through violence, to base relationships on physical attraction, to expect instant gratification, and to value the possession of "stuff" for a happy and fulfilling life. As parents trying to teach our children about the value of meaningful and genuine relationships with other human beings, we must compete with the very powerful voice of the media.

In my own experience another major challenge to keeping family members emotionally connected is the business of modern life with two-career families and the many activities now offered to children. Between swimming lessons, music lessons, dance lessons, softball, basketball, and volleyball, family life can become dizzying. Parents become stressed. Children become stressed. We can find ourselves with no time left to enjoy leisurely meals or quiet evenings as a family. It is all too easy for a parent to become caught up in the idea that the number of activities he gets his children involved in is equal to how responsible he is as a parent.

Even with all of the challenges that modern life presents to families, however, I do not sentimentally yearn for "the good old days." I believe that the incredible advances in technology over the last century will overall be more beneficial to mankind than harmful. We have made tremendous advances in caring about people of all races and ages and promoting equality for all men and women, even though we still have a long way to go.

However, to preserve our families in today's culture we need to become more protective of the time we spend together and, as Pipher says, "build walls that give the family definition, identity and power. These walls are built by making conscious choices about what will be accepted and rejected."[30] As parents we can make a decision to prioritize our activities and our children's activities and weed out all of those activities that are not at the very top of the list. We must compete with the electronic equipment in the house by tuning out the technology for part of each day and tuning into our children. When we turn off the T.V., the computer, and the phone and eat dinner together, discuss the day's events together, or play a board game we are encouraging attachments with each other instead of with our "stuff."

Pipher emphasizes the importance of rituals "to connect family to each other, to extended family, to family friends and to the community."[31] Rituals are losing their importance in modern life, and yet rituals have helped keep families connected for thousands of years. Children feel a sense of belonging, security, and consistency when they can count on the rituals that they have come to know and expect. The little daily rituals like the morning kiss, sitting down to dinner together, or the nightly bedside chat enhance a child's sense of a secure holding environment. My seven-year-old still sometimes asks me to sing the same song I used to sing to her when she was a baby. This has become a very important ritual to her because she knows that it is the same song my mother sang, and my grandmother sang, and my great-grandmother sang. It helps her feel connected—even to the grandmothers she never knew.

Family rituals repeated on holidays or birthdays are wonderful ways of keeping families connected to one another. If some of your old family rituals have dropped by the wayside, it can be a lot of fun to bring them back. You can consult with your parents or grandparents about their old family rituals and start them anew with your family. If there are no family rituals or you don't have good feelings about your family of origin, you can make up some new rituals that your family can start and pass on. When your children grow up and start reminiscing about their childhood they will remember first the rituals—the shared family activities they always knew they could count on.

2.3. Attachment through Language

Let us not forget the vital importance of simple conversation. Researchers Mary Maine, Nancy Kaplan, and Jude Cassidy found that more securely attached children have more fluid conversations with their parents. Parents and children who are less securely attached have awkward conversations that do not flow.[32] It's all about attunement. Begin talking with your youngster no matter what her age. Stop what you are doing when you can, and make eye contact. Touch her on the shoulder or the arm. Listen to what he is saying. Be interested. Really focus your mind—one-mindfully—on the conversation. You'll learn things about the way she feels and thinks that you never knew before. You will discover that your child is a fascinating creature when you really pay attention. If you're doing all the talking, then you're not listening. If the conversation is awkward, or she doesn't seem to have anything to say to you, don't force it. Just try again later, and keep trying. Ask her opinion about things. Ask about the things she is interested in. Keep listening. Do not make judgments about her opinions or thoughts. As she realizes you really want to know and you are *not* out to criticize what she has to say she'll begin to open up. It will be well worth the effort as your relationship with her grows.

3. FOR PARENTS WHOSE CHILDREN ARE GROWN

It's never too late to try to build a bridge, even when children are grown up and living on their own. Maybe your children are completely estranged from you. Perhaps your children just seem distant emotionally. Maybe you look back on your parenting when they were young and now see some major mistakes with 20/20 hindsight that you were unable to see at the time. Perhaps you were too harsh either verbally or physically. Perhaps you were distant emotionally. Maybe you were responding out of "feeling memories" from your own childhood. You may have been depressed, addicted, or in very stressful circumstances. Perhaps your child's inborn personality or temperament was a contributing factor to the problems between you. Nevertheless, it is important to repair the relationship. The most powerful way that you can do that is to simply acknowledge your mistakes and ask for forgiveness from your child. Repeatedly I have been told in some way, "If only I could hear from my parent the words, 'I'm sorry—I was wrong,' it would make a world of difference to me." The adults I have worked with in therapy who have felt they were mistreated by their parents in childhood have almost universally described a longing to have a better relationship with their parents in the present. Most adults yearn for signs of caring and affection from their parents. Most adults tell me in one way or another, "I would still give anything to feel loved by my parent." Your adult child is not too old to want to hear, "I love you," or to receive a hug from you. Ask yourself, "What would I wish for from my own parents now?" What you would wish for from your own parents may be exactly what your adult child wants and needs from you now.

Remember also, in your relationship with your adult child, that adult children are even more sensitive to criticism from their parents than they were as young children, because as adults, criticism from parents is an even greater insult. Be a nonjudgmental listener, not an advice giver. Your adult child is on her own now. Now is the time to follow the age-old proverb, "If you don't have anything good to say, don't say anything at all." Life is her best teacher now.

4. HEALING YOUR RELATIONSHIP WITH YOUR OWN PARENTS

For some adults, healing their relationships with their own parents is not possible. I have worked with many adults who suffered so much severe trauma at the hands of a parent that just being in the same vicinity as that parent triggers overwhelming panic. Many traumatized adults have had to cut off all contact with that parent in order to feel safe. Some adults I have worked with have a parent who was and is still afraid of or uncomfortable with closeness. The parent didn't want closeness then and doesn't want closeness now, and so he or she continues to reject any overtures for reconciliation.

On the other hand, I have worked with many adults who have discovered their parents have mellowed with age, or perhaps regret mistakes made in the past and want a better relationship with them in the present. Sometimes after processing their painful childhood memories of harsh discipline, verbal abuse, or emotional deprivation, adults become able to view their parents from an adult perspective instead of a child's perspective. This, in addition to increased understanding as to how one's upbringing can affect one's actions, helps many adults be more empathic to the parent's own difficult history and acknowledge any changes the older parent may have made. It has helped many adults to recognize that their parents were living during a period of time when help in the form of therapy or books was not accessible as it is now. With these insights many adults are able to find understanding and forgiveness, either partial or total, for the parent who hurt them in the past. There is no right or wrong way to handle your relationship with your parent. You will need to discover what measure of closeness or forgiveness will be possible for you.

Chapter Sixteen

The Ghosts Move Out ... Some Real-Life Stories Told by the Parents Themselves

Following are four courageous stories, as told through interviews with Melissa; with Gerard and his wife, Kay; with Ann; and with Joe. Their childhood experiences were quite painful. Whether your story was just as dramatic or less severe, your healing is just as important for your sake and for the sake of your relationship with your child. I hope these stories can be of help—both in understanding that you are not alone in the problems you have had in your parenting, and in giving you hope and courage to continue your own journey of healing.

1. GERARD AND KAY

The first story of courage belongs to Gerard. His hypervigilance and need to control almost broke up Gerard's family. However, Gerard's willingness to face his demons created healing and hope where there was none before.

His Story Begins ...

Gerard: I was raised by an alcoholic father and a mother who was very, very codependent. I wasn't nurtured. In fact, some of my memories are very frightening to me and very lonely. There were times that were really bad. I wish it could have been a happier time. I wish I could have learned things growing up that would have helped me to become a capable, nurturing parent.

One of my first memories is a memory of being locked in my room. If people came over my dad always locked me in my room. I was locked in my room often at night. I wasn't allowed out, even to go to the bathroom. There were also beatings with a belt, but the verbal abuse was worse than the physical abuse. Verbal abuse from an alcoholic can be crushing. The verbal abuse took any self-esteem I had and dissolved it. As a child I did everything I could not to experience that abuse. I daily, constantly, looked for approval so I would not get that abuse. I was not allowed to be a child. I was not allowed to make mistakes. I was expected to be perfect, to be quiet. I had all these expectations put on me that would be almost impossible for an adult to live up to, let alone a child. I didn't have a safe place. I didn't have a place where I could go and feel that everything would be O.K., because it just didn't exist.

Kay: He's talking about the blatant abuse that was so painful and apparent, but he isn't describing what to me has been so damaging for him: the neglect and deprivation. As an example, there is the picture of the baseball team where he is the only kid on the team that didn't get to have a uniform and shoes. He and his brother didn't even have proper clothes and shoes for school. They weren't ever taken to a doctor or a dentist for checkups. There was no protection or nurturing or love in their lives. In our home, life is always somewhat about the kids—their activities, their schooling, and so on. In *their* household it was all about Dad and Dad's moods. That was the central focus of the entire house. The attention they got from their mother was, "Shush! Don't make him mad! Quiet now! Quiet!"

Gerard: I remember the time when my brother had a terrible, terrible intestinal infection. I thought he had the flu. But he moaned in pain for days before my mother finally took him to the hospital. It turned out he had a severe intestinal infection. They were told that if they had waited one more day he would have died. When we did need some kind of medical attention like that we were made to feel guilty about it, like we weren't strong enough or tough enough.

On the weekends when my brother and I were somewhere between third and seventh grades, we were expected to take our jars of pennies we had saved and play poker with Dad. If he won, he'd keep it. I can remember many occasions when my brother, who was especially fond of his money, lost it all, and wound up in tears in the bedroom. Then Dad would yell at him and call him a big sissy.

Dad frequently made fun of my sexuality and of my body, making me feel dirty and ashamed. He also said terrible things about women—about their sexuality, and about how rotten and worthless they are.

I had to start paying rent to live in my house the day I started working when I was fifteen. Dad insisted I pay fifteen percent right off the top—not of my gross, but of my net.

My brother and I haven't talked for four or five years, and I do believe that's probably 90 percent childhood issues. When my brother was 16 years old, he worked hard and bought himself a car. He got caught skipping a couple days of school and my father told him he was going to take the car, sell it, and keep the money. My brother said go ahead, and he left. He didn't tell me. He didn't tell anybody. He just left. He couldn't take it anymore so he went to Boystown. It was probably one of the better things that happened to him. It absolutely enraged my dad, of course. He just about lost it. He came up to me, drunk, and said, "You pick a side right now. You're either on my side, or you're on his side." I remember how scared I was. I had this drunken, 40-year-old man in my face, and I said, "Your side." I thought I had to be true to that so when my brother was at Boystown I never contacted him. No one ever went to see him—not even my mother. I learned at that time that you can have somebody in your family and just throw them away. I didn't want to get thrown away. I had to survive. So I went through high school and I learned how to lie.

As funny as it may seem, I still love my mother very much. I want to take care of her, but at the same time there's this part of me inside that says, "How could you do that? How could you do those things to your own children? How could you just stand there and watch all those things happen?" It's a confusing thing that I experience.

The summer before my sophomore year I remember getting drunk on cherry vodka, and it felt great. It was the first time I had allowed myself to have fun. That continued throughout my high school years. I didn't study, and I was never at home. I was out trying to have fun. My object was to finish high school and get out of there. I moved out the day I graduated at age 17. From graduation until about two months before I met Kay my life was just wildness. I had no morals. I tried just about everything a guy could try. I bought myself a Harley—I still have it—and I just went nuts. I didn't have any ground base I could come back to. I was looking for something. I didn't know what I was looking for, but I was looking for something. I thought I was having a good time. I thought I was making lifelong friends. It was insanity.

I worked for a good man named John. He took me under his wing and pulled me back into reality when I started going out there too far. I believe he saved me. He'd invite me over to his home, and I'd see what he did for his family, and how he loved his wife and daughters. He wasn't even related to me and he offered to send me through college. He offered to help me buy my motorcycle. I am so grateful for what he did for me emotionally. There were some good people like that in my life. There was a teacher who offered to pay for my swimming lessons. There was a nun who paid for me to go to a chili feed at school. There were people out there who saw the need and tried to make up for it in some way.

The damage that has been done from my childhood has been like a snowball in my life. It started small, but as things didn't get repaired, the damage became a tremendous force in my life. As I went through my childhood I had what I have learned is a dissociative behavior. Many memories and just living everyday life was so painful that I disconnected from my feelings. That behavior continued into adulthood and allowed me to be an emotional cripple. I became dead inside. Things that affected other people tremendously didn't even bother me. I became the Ice Man. My childhood was a series of long periods of time where surviving was the key. Thank God I met Kay. Without her, I truly believe I never would have sobered up to begin with. I don't think it would even have occurred to me that I was an alcoholic. I certainly don't think I would have had the courage to go see a therapist.

I was still drinking when I met Kay. I was at a point in my drinking when I was tired of being around these losers and I knew there was something else in life, but I didn't know what it was. I was 30 years old and I was very lonely. I had friends, but they didn't do much for me.

I started having feelings toward Kay that I had never experienced before. There were some genuine feelings coming back at me. She did things for me without expecting anything in return. Every Tuesday she stopped by my house while I was at work and put a present in my mailbox. She did these little things for me that really touched me. I had never had a long-term relationship with a woman before I met Kay. I didn't think I was capable of having a real relationship. I loved Kay, but I couldn't identify it at the time. Sometimes when we had serious arguments I ended up actually feeling physically sick. I decided I wanted to marry her.

Kay: He told me not to have any expectations of being loved by him because he had determined that that was something that he could not do. He made it very clear that he could love his mother and he could love his brother, but that he could not love anyone else so not to expect that. It was about this time that I read an article in a women's magazine about adult children of alcoholics. In this magazine it had listed the symptomology and defined characteristics of adult children of alcoholics. I looked at that one day and said, "If this isn't Gerard, then this person doesn't exist."

Gerard: I agreed to go to some ACOA meetings, but they often had an alcoholic come in and speak. I would sit there and think, "I relate to *those* guys! Yeah, I feel that way!" There were times when I was drinking when I was very verbally abusive to Kay—very mean and cruel. Despite the fact that Kay was the mother of three at the time we married and ran a home day care, the house was always neat. And yet, if I came home and saw dirty dishes I'd jump all over her. It would get way out of hand. I was terrible. And I was in complete denial as to how my behavior was affecting the kids or Kay.

Kay: He was trying to be a parent to my three children and have a relationship with me, which was something he had never done before. He was trying to meet the responsibilities of a family of five when it had only been him. It got bad—fast.

Gerard: It came to the point where Kay had had it. By that time she recognized I had a drinking problem and she told me that if I didn't go to A.A., then I would have to leave. I remember crying and feeling totally abandoned. But she was right. I knew I needed help. Besides, if something didn't change at that moment in my life, I knew I was out of there. So I sobered up and started attending A.A. That was a big step for me. It changed things a lot. But unfortunately, it didn't stop all of my behaviors. Even after I sobered up, I was no longer abusive but I continued to be very controlling and very negative. And I always felt completely justified in my actions.

I can't believe Kay stayed with me. I can't imagine what it must have been like for her to live with somebody who doesn't give anything back. It must have been like looking at a pair of shark eyes with no emotions.

Kay: That isn't what I saw, though. I saw there were always emotions under the icy exterior. I saw just enough of that other side that I knew it was who he really was. The reason I stayed is that I have always seen a real desire to change in him. He has never been one to say, "It's all your fault, Kay," or "It's not me." He's always been willing to seek help, and to try to be better. That's a hard thing to walk away from—somebody that says, "I know I have problems. I want to be better." That made me want to stick it out. And he always has gotten better. It's not that he just talks about it. Over the last 14 years he has continued to make incredible changes—difficult, difficult changes.

For years, though, the parenting was just nuts. First of all, he was absolutely amazed that I didn't spank my kids. To him, spanking was parenting, although he did honor my view on that. However, he had this hypervigilance thing that was enough to make people insane. There was criticism for everything—for every little light that was left on, for every dish left in the sink, for every radio turned up too loud. I remember he used to get so angry when five-year-old Shea would go in and sleep with Kathleen. He would yell, "Shea has her own room! Why do we even have a room for her then?" It was so bizarre. I didn't even know what I was dealing with.

Gerard: I had made the kids their own rooms in the basement when I moved in. That had been a dream of mine as a child, to have my own room. I thought, how can you not appreciate having your own room? I couldn't understand.

I never thought the kids appreciated anything enough. If they got a bike for their birthday, and they said, "A bike! Thank you so much! I love my new bike!" and they weren't doing that a week later—or if they forgot to put it away one day—I thought they didn't appreciate that bike. Every normal kid behavior was evidence in my mind of a lack of respect, and a lack of appreciation. I was obsessed with the idea that they didn't have any gratitude. I couldn't see any gratitude, and I couldn't see any love. I couldn't see anything but being used. I definitely held the misperception, "My child doesn't love me enough."

I also held the misperception, "My child is invading me." If the kids got too close, I felt threatened. I maintained a certain distance from everyone in my life in order to protect myself. I had this push–pull relationship with anyone I ever met. I let others in as close as I could deal with, including the kids, and then I pushed them away.

Another problem perception was, "My child is too needy." When the kids needed attention I always thought they had some ulterior motive—that they wanted something. I was always suspicious of them. I couldn't see that they just needed affection.

The misperception, "My child doesn't have real feelings" was a problem, too. Feeling powerful and in control was very important to me. I couldn't risk empathizing with my children, because I couldn't risk tapping into my own feelings. It was just too painful for me.

Naturally I believed, "A parent should have complete authority over the children at all times." I didn't think the kids should even have the right to express any differences of opinion from mine.

When the kids weren't perfect, especially in public, I felt it was a negative reflection on me. For instance, Shea was a very shy child. If she wouldn't perform at the school programs, I felt embarrassed and very upset. I felt it was about me. If they performed well, then I felt worthwhile.

Kay: One of the biggest problems in parenting that I see Gerard still struggling with at times is taking things the kids say or do very personally. The philosophy that I have chosen in my parenting is to take nothing personally. When we take things personally, the normal human response is to have retribution—to fight back. If you don't take it personally, then you can deal with whatever the issue is objectively. It's not easy, and I don't do it perfectly, but it is the basic philosophy that I live by. Gerard still has a tendency to get so hurt by things they say. With his issues being what they are—the very essence of what a teenager is touches all his most vulnerable places. After all, who is more unappreciative of things or self-absorbed than a teenager?

Gerard: This is probably the toughest issue for me. It may be that I got so used to being mistreated, disrespected, and discounted when I was a child that I look for this kind of treatment from those I am closest to. It is so easy for me to perceive that my kids are purposely mistreating me. Hypervigilance is still a problem for me, too. Sometimes I still come in the house in this hyperalert state, like I'm expecting something bad to happen or looking for something to be wrong, or maybe expecting someone to mistreat me. Kay calls me "a man in search of a negative" when I do this. But they let me know what I'm doing in a joking way, and that helps. One of their favorite things to say is, "You're hypervigilating me!" They say that a lot.

I have learned, too, that I can't allow myself to get too stressed or too tired. For instance, last night I could feel it. It was like a dark veil was pulled over me. I could almost feel a change in myself and I knew that I needed to go to bed. I also know that when too much is going on in the house, when too many doorbells are ringing, and people are coming and going, I have to take time out. I am ultrasensitive to normal kinds of kid noise and commotion. I think I have some kind of built-in, ultrasensitive radar. I know then that if I don't remove myself, I will say something or do something hurtful.

Kay: The things that drive him so crazy are the things that I find most enjoyable—the hubbub and the bustle—birthday parties, Easter parties, Halloween parties—any excuse for a party with fun and friends. What we have tried to do is adapt to the problem. He'll just go on over and spend the night at my folks and let us have our fun. On a smaller scale if it gets too loud, he will retire to the bedroom and shut the door. Everybody totally accepts that. No one resents that or thinks he's weak for doing that. I'm so glad because it lets the rest of the household go on. He'll just say, "You know what. I think maybe it's time for me to go to our room." And I'll say, "O.K., I'll be in later." It's so very workable. He gets what he needs and we can go on with what we're doing.

Gerard: Whenever Kay and I run into some problems in our relationship I experience this overwhelming desire to go back to the way it was before—to go back to my old ways. It's something I know how to do. I can turn off everything and protect myself. It's always right there. There's never a lock on the door. There is a person who lives inside of me who can be so cruel and damaging and cold. I know he's in there, and he is a monster.

Kay: That product of his childhood is a monster. But this guy is not. He comes out so much less frequently now it's almost incredible to believe, because he fights it.

Gerard: In therapy I'm continuing to work on my ability to feel and manage my emotions. My childhood issues affect me every day, but the longer I'm in therapy, the easier it is for me to get more pleasure out of living. I'm still on a road of discovery, and I don't know where it will lead me. For years I just acted. I knew that I was supposed to be at the functions. I knew that I was supposed to cut the grass. I knew that I was supposed to clean up the house. I knew that I was supposed to feel, and to do these things just because. I went through the motions, but I could never feel it inside. I was never happy. I'm beginning to feel happy. I'm beginning to feel some joy throughout the day, and I'm losing some of the negativity.

Sometimes the guys at work will be talking about doing things with their kids, and I find myself thinking, "Yeah, they're just doing that naturally. They're doing that because that's what they learned." Sometimes it feels embarrassing to me that I have had to work so hard to learn how to do the things that most men do intuitively. I think I'm lucky, though, because I am a good person and I want to do better and I want to improve.

I am now experiencing a closeness with my kids that I never could have had with them before. Something as simple as spending the afternoon with Daniel yesterday, doing something he wanted to do instead of what I wanted to do, gave me such a feeling of connection with him. When I asked him to help me with the dishes this morning he hopped right up and started helping me. I think he felt like helping because he was feeling close to me. I used to tell Kay, "The kids don't love me," and she would say, "Yes they do, yes they do." I never really believed it, and then Kathleen gave me this wonderful, loving gift on Christmas that brought tears to my eyes. I thought to myself, "Yes, she loves me. They love me."

Just to enjoy today for today and to be able to have fun without experiencing all that other baggage is a remarkable thing. Yesterday, for instance, when I spent the morning with Alynn downtown and with Daniel in the afternoon I had a wonderful day. I enjoyed myself. Along with the pain of bringing up the past—reliving the memories that hurt me—is a freedom that I've never known. It's a new life. It gives me the opportunity to do the things in life that are supposed to be enjoyable, and to be able to actually feel the joy.

2. ANN

Ann's painful childhood, her alcoholism, and her relationship addiction all had tremendous impact on Ann's ability to be the kind of parent she had always wanted to be. But when Ann acknowledged what was happening to her children she became willing to go to any lengths to change the situation.

Her Story Begins . . .

My dad was an alcoholic. He played in a band and wasn't around too much. When he did come home he would often beat up my mother. We lived in a very small house. Me and my sisters slept in the same room and my parents' room was right next to ours, so I would hear a lot of it. One time I heard my dad tell my mom he was going to kill her and I ran in and found him poised, ready to hit her in the head with a rock. I came in between them and then he came to his senses. But it always seemed that if she would just say one word, he would snap. I was afraid every time he came home at night. I remember hearing it and getting in my bed, crying "When is he going to stop?" I remember how we would get up the next day to go to school, and she would have bruises and lumps all over. When we asked her what happened she lied to us, but I knew the truth. I didn't feel like I could talk to her about it, though. Now I know she was lying to protect us, but as a child I didn't understand because she always told us not to lie. I just thought my mom was a liar.

My mother never allowed me to talk about how I felt and never allowed me to have my own opinions about anything. If I told her something she'd say, "Oh, you're making that up" or "That's not right." I felt so much shame. She made me wear her clothes to school in junior high because I was heavy, and she said she couldn't afford to buy me my own clothes. I was constantly made fun of because of my clothes and because I was very overweight. I remember, too, that I wet the bed until I was 12 years old. My mother blamed it on medical reasons, but I think it was because I was so anxious all the time. I never felt safe. I couldn't talk to my mom or anyone about any of it.

I remember when I started my period at age 12, my mom hadn't prepared me for it. She always acted like anything that had to do with sex or bodies was dirty. I thought I was bleeding to death. I remember thinking, "Oh, my gosh, what is this?" I ran and told my dad what was happening, and he said, "Just stick some Kleenexes down there." Then when my mom got home she made me put a tampon in and it hurt. She still didn't explain anything and I was terrified.

I had a lot of criticism growing up and I had no one to talk to about it. I remember being spanked many times by my mom with a razor strap. She'd also make us pick a stick off the tree, and if it wasn't good enough, she'd go make us get another one.

My mom tried in other ways. She tried to bring us up in the church. Thank God for that, because I felt so peaceful there. It was a real sanctuary for me.

Dad left when I was 12. When I was 18 I felt the need to go see what my dad was like and find out more about him, so I went and moved to the town where he lived. I was able to talk to him at that time of his life and I liked him then. He was 55 when he died because of a combination of pills, pot, and alcohol. I don't know if it was accidental or not. He ended up in a vegetative state, on a respirator. I was the one who had to tell the doctors to go ahead and shut the machines off. That was very hard for me.

I started using alcohol at about age 18, and shortly after that I started dating Lilly's dad. There were signs that he was abusive right away. Even when we were dating he would get angry and push me. He even pushed my mom once. But then he'd come back and say, "I'm sorry, I'm sorry," and I would always take him back. I ended up marrying him. We moved to Hawaii because he was in the service. His drug and alcohol use began escalating there, whereas I became pregnant and stopped using alcohol or drugs during that time. After Lilly was born the abuse got very bad. When I got pregnant for the second time, he beat me so badly that I miscarried when I was five months along. Lilly would have had a brother. We were divorced when she was four.

A year later I met the boys' dad. When I dated him he was very nice. He lied to me just a couple of times, but I didn't think too much of it. We drank a lot together. After we got married he started cheating on me constantly. He also became very abusive physically, to the point where I ended up in the hospital several times from head injuries. He was also very mentally abusive. He called me all kinds of horrible names. I felt absolutely worthless.

The boys were four and five when I divorced their dad. He and his new wife used drugs very heavily. I think it was during about a three-month time period that the boys were sexually abused by their father and stepmother. I had noticed the boys acting out after the visits—touching each other's private parts, and kissing each other like they were making out, but they wouldn't tell me how they had learned these things. Finally John told my neighbor what his dad and his stepmother were doing to them, and Child Protective Services became involved.

After my divorce I started a relationship with Randall. Unfortunately, he was an active alcoholic and my own alcohol problem was also becoming more and more severe. The relationship worked for me because I had a lot of abandonment issues and with Randall I could say, "Get out of here." He would, but he would always come back, so I was comfortable with it. That relationship continued off and on for seven years. I once figured out that we broke up 200 and some times altogether. Randall was more mentally abusive than physically abusive, although he would rage, push me, break things, and punch holes in the walls. I often became so angry with him that I would become physically abusive toward him. I even went after him with knives once. I didn't even know myself at that point. Both of us continued to drink more and more alcohol until we were drinking heavily every single day. The boys hated him.

Four years ago when the boys were six and eight I got into recovery. The relationship with Randall lasted two more years after that. Getting out of that addictive relationship was more difficult than getting sober. When I was drinking, and when I was involved in addictive relationships, I didn't admit to myself how much my kids were affected. They always took a back seat to my addictions, and they rode those roller coaster rides right along with me.

When I was drinking, even though I continuously shouted at my kids, screamed at them, did not listen to them, and didn't show them love, I felt that putting a roof over their heads and food in their mouths was enough. I never spent any time with them. I was always in the bars, out with my friends, or out with my boyfriend. I made Lilly babysit all the time. She was practically the mother. There were a few times during the relationship with Randall that we fought so severely that the police wound up at the house. Finally they said, "Ma'am, if we have to come again, we're taking your kids." That's when I realized I had a problem, not only with Randall, but with alcohol, and that my parenting was completely out of whack. I was finally sick and tired of being sick and tired.

I didn't hit my kids very often because I always told myself I wouldn't act like my mom. I rationalized other things as O.K. because at least I wasn't consistently hitting the kids like my mom did with us.

I relate to the misperception, "My child doesn't love me enough." I have worked hard on not taking their behavior personally to keep myself from either overreacting, or giving in to them to make them love me. I have really come a long, long way on this one. I also used to interpret my boys' misbehavior as evidence that they were taking after their dad and acting like abusers. That also caused me to overreact to them. Sometimes I actually felt anxious and unsafe around them and I would have to leave the house and just drive around in my car or go to the bar.

I have changed so much in the way I view my boys and their behaviors now. It really helps when I don't take what they do personally. I try to be very consistent with them in using and following through with consequences and positive reinforcements. I rarely yell at my kids any more. I tell them, "This is it. This is your consequence." Then I follow through with it. I write it down so they can't manipulate me like they did when I was drinking and say, "No, mom, that's not what you said." I also spend a lot more time with my boys now. I used to spend all my time drinking or preoccupied with a man. I feel much closer to them than I ever did before. We have fun together. We go to the YMCA, and we play board games. Being consistent with the discipline and spending more quality time with them has made a tremendous positive change in their behavior.

I try not to have unrealistic expectations of my kids any more or look to them to make me feel good about myself. I know how it feels to be under that kind of pressure because that's how it was for me as a kid.

When I'm stressed out I still have to be careful not to blame my kids or turn to them to make me feel better. I remember all too well how anxious and responsible I felt for making everything O.K. with my mom and dad so they wouldn't get mad.

I set my mind to do whatever it took to better my home life and better my children. I have tried to find recovery in every way possible. I was so completely isolated from everyone. I felt so shameful. I was so disconnected, even from God. The combination of treatment, therapy, and the Twelve Step programs have helped tremendously. I attend both Alcoholics Anonymous and Codependency Anonymous. I have a sponsor who is a sponsor for both programs. In therapy, and with my sponsor, I began learning how to open up with others. I began learning how to trust other women in the program, too. This was a major change for me. I never had female relationships in the past. I definitely have always had the preoccupied attachment style with the men in my life. I was totally dependent on men to meet all of my emotional needs. I was totally preoccupied with my relationships, and then chose relationships that never could have worked. I knew Ed from the program, and we started dating about a year and a half ago. He treats me with respect. He doesn't criticize me or my children. He's respectful to my home and he doesn't yell at me or beat me. It's very different. He and I go to a recovering couple's Twelve Step meeting, too, and that really helps us to have a healthier relationship. Through everything I have become closer to God, which has been the most important change of all.

It took a lot of willingness. I really wanted to change, and I was willing to go to any lengths to get there.

3. MELISSA

Melissa's childhood abuse was severe, and left great hurdles for her to overcome as a parent. With courage and determination, Melissa persevered to get to where she is today.

Her Story Begins ...

My sisters and my brother and I were raised by my mother because my father was gone most of the time and eventually left us for good. Our home had an angry, chaotic atmosphere. My mother wasn't capable of any kind of nurturing. As a small child when I tried to get hugs from her, she would push me away and get angry with me. When she did touch me, it was never with affection. It always involved some sort of inappropriate touching of a sexual nature. She also talked about sex a lot, and made it sound like a very dirty thing. She consistently made very rude and inappropriate comments about my body parts and about the sexual parts of other people. She talked about things that weren't supposed to be sexual in a dirty way, like breastfeeding.

My father was a sex addict, although I didn't know what that was as a child. He also did speed and other drugs to stay awake because he was a trucker. I knew even as a child that he had a woman in every city that he went to because my mother always talked to me about his sexual antics as if I were a peer. I remember one incident when I was four or five and my father had returned from a truck trip. I watched as my mother angrily stripped him and washed him in the tub while berating him for being with other women. Afterward she sent him to sleep with me and I comforted him and told him it would be all right. At the same time I remember longing for him to comfort me instead. I often cried for him when he wasn't there, which was most of the time. I cried for him even into my adult years. I've always longed to have a father, and I've always longed for a mother who didn't make me feel dirty and ashamed.

Sexual abuse was an integral part of my childhood experience, as I was not only molested by my mother, but I was also molested by more than one extended family member, and by a neighbor named Donald. Mother insisted I go to church every Sunday with Donald and his wife and children. He would sit me in his lap in the front row of the church and molest me under my dress. After church we would go back to his house and my mother would come over for dinner. Then he and I would go upstairs for games. He would tie me up to the four-poster bed, and tell his children to stay out of the room because I was the prisoner and he was the interrogator. Then he would come in and molest me. He told me that if I told anybody he would do the same thing to my two younger sisters. I don't have any idea how many times this happened. I know I would stare up at the window at the color of the yellow sunshine and pretend I wasn't there. I somehow imagined I was a part of the yellow color. I now know that this is called dissociation. To this day it still haunts me when it looks that way outside. I have been almost crippled at times because of a certain yellow color in the sunshine.

After I'd been molested I would often go walking around the neighborhood aimlessly feeling like there was nothing to live for and nowhere that was safe. I lived in pure shame.

I remember when I started kindergarten I hid in the school one day and stole a bunch of clay and art supplies. I told my mother someone gave me the things, and ended up getting in a lot of trouble for it. That didn't stop me, though. Throughout kindergarten and first grade I continued to steal things. When I was older I realized why I did it. At ages three, four, and five my father would carry me around the five and ten store and encourage me to steal things by hiding them under my dress. I thought it was fun. Somehow stealing became a connection to my father, and so I had a lot of problems with it when I first started school.

I was lonely almost every minute of my childhood. I didn't have any friends at all. The kids at school made fun of me and degraded me. I was frequently beat up on the way to school and beat up on the way home from school. I had long braids and the kids pulled my hair and spit on me. They made fun of me because I lived in the projects. They also taunted and teased me because I was chubby, and because my father was always in and out of jail. I had so much shame. It wasn't safe for me to be in school, and on the way home it wasn't safe. I was always afraid, too, that Donald would be out in his yard, lurking there behind the tree waiting for me. I remember running past his house to my door, terrified, feeling like there was a monster behind me. And when I got home it wasn't safe because my mother was there.

After school I would lay on my bed and listen to the other kids in the neighborhood playing. I was so lonely I just wanted to die. I felt like I was completely disconnected from my family. It felt like there was no true connection for me anywhere. I couldn't even find a connection to God, because the God I was taught to believe in was a punishing God. I felt that there would never be anything I could do that would be good enough for me to be with Him or for Him to love me. I thought the physical and sexual abuse I endured was my fault—that somehow I had caused it because I was bad. I felt I was a terrible sinner. The loneliness was so deep it cut right through my soul.

To this day as an adult, after-school hours are hard for me. When I hear kids in the neighborhood playing and having a good time, I grieve for those lost years.

I've always been hypervigilant. That is because I never knew when I was going to be attacked when I was younger. I never knew when I was going to be beaten by the strap in the middle of my sleep by my mother or assaulted sexually by someone. I had to stay superalert—just in case. It depletes your energy to stay in that hypervigilant state all the time.

When I learned about the "fearful attachment style" I knew that was me. I have always wanted to be close to others, but have been too afraid of getting hurt to let anyone in. For me there has always been an additional aspect to this problem. Because of all the sexual abuse I've experienced, when I meet someone the first thing I do is evaluate whether or not he or she could be a sexual perpetrator. If I feel the least bit unsafe, I will avoid that person at all costs. I'm sure that often I imagine someone is a perpetrator who is not. On the other hand, I don't think anyone who is a perpetrator could get by me.

I married young, but I was 29 when we adopted our oldest son, Matthew. He was an infant when he came to us, and I had no problem getting close to him and nurturing him. When he was three we adopted Christine, also an infant, but right from the start it just was never really as comfortable as it was with my son. I never understood why. I didn't talk about it, and I didn't deal with it or look at it. When my two youngest sons were born, I breastfed them because I knew it was a healthy thing to do. But the whole time I was breastfeeding I had a lot of feelings of shame about it.

I first began attending Adult Children of Alcoholics and therapy when my mother was dying. I was suffering from symptoms of severe post-traumatic stress disorder—anxiety, depression, and flashback episodes.

Eventually in therapy I realized that I had a problem being intimate with my daughter because of my experiences when I was a little girl. I held the misperception that being close was dirty and shameful. It had nothing to do with her, of course. It was my stuff. It felt shameful, and I just never let her in the way I let my boys in. As she got older my daughter would run up to me and lay a kiss on my cheek or try to hug me and I was just so uncomfortable. If her arm accidentally brushed across my chest I flipped out and wanted to slap her. These were just body flashbacks that she was triggering. I wanted to be close to her, though, because she was my only girl. And she was exhibiting many symptoms of severe attachment problems and needed holding therapy.

I've made a lot of progress. I began holding therapy with my daughter, and when we first started I could barely hold her. I can hold my daughter now. I have talked to her, though, and explained that it's not O.K. to come up and catch me off guard real suddenly. I don't tell her much detail but I have explained that it startles me. She understands that she has to approach me more slowly or give me warning and let me approach her first. Then I'm fine holding her and snuggling her. I've finally reached the point that I can nurture her like I nurture the boys and not feel dirty or ashamed.

I wish I had worked through my issues about my mom before breastfeeding my youngest two. My problem with breastfeeding was of course related to my mother's attitudes. I still feel angry that she made what could have been a wonderful experience less enjoyable for me.

One of the tools my therapist used to resolve my past traumas was EMDR, which really helped me. I don't understand how it works, but I know it works because it has helped me make connections that I never had before, and implant new positive beliefs that have stayed with me.

I also identified the unlivable agreement that I had made unconsciously with my mother. I identified all the ways of thinking and behaving that I thought I had to have in order to get my mother to stay with me. I couldn't believe it after I wrote them down. I thought, "Oh, my God. This agreement is not about me! I agreed to live this way to please my mother." It was truly an unlivable agreement, and I realized that no child could or should have to fulfill this agreement. I lived with it because I feared that if I didn't, I would be abandoned, and if I was abandoned, I would die.

I made a new agreement and took back my power so that I could be whole—not to do anything against her or to blame her. I hold her accountable, but I don't hate her. I read my new contract over a lot and it really helped me to leave behind the enmeshment state that I had with my mother for my whole life and become my own person.

I was also lucky enough to do inner child therapy. I incorporate every skill that I've learned. I've absorbed it all like a sponge. I'm so hungry to be whole I call on all my skills, not just one. I don't think any one skill can be the one that does it all. I believe in using whatever it takes and I go through different combinations. It's all about healing.

I had always wanted to be a nurse. After my divorce when my youngest son was almost two, I made the decision that I was not going to be a welfare statistic any longer. My mother became kind of a burden after we all moved out of the house because she had nothing and she just clung to us. I didn't want to do that to my kids, and I didn't want to live my life the way I was brought up. So on the spur of the moment one day I signed up for college, and here I am. In only two more semesters I'll have my B.S. in nursing. I was really intimidated the first semester, but I did well in my classes and that built my self-esteem. It's been like food for the soul ever since. My achievements have given me encouragement. I don't think I had ever actually experienced the feeling of achieving before. And now I can use everything I have learned in my Twelve Step groups and in my therapy, and apply it in my career. I really excel in my ability to be supportive to my patients emotionally because of what I've been through.

After my divorce I began to admit to myself that I am gay. I had a hard time coming to terms with this because it's a lifestyle that is not generally accepted, especially for mothers. I was sure about my sexuality for several years before I sat down and talked with my older two children about it. They had a lot of questions which I tried to answer in a way they would understand. I don't want them to get hurt because of it, so I explained to them we need to have boundaries about who we talk to about it because it's a private matter, and because many people don't accept it. I have told them who knows so they can talk openly about it with those people.

I told my kids they have permission to hate that part of me, but they don't seem to. We have never had any prejudice in our home toward any kind of minority group. I think my kids are more open to all kinds of people because of that. We talk about how God likes variety, and that's why he made us all so different.

I am very protective of my children, and although I have dated, I will never have anyone move in with me unless they are very good with my children. I have no shame about my sexuality now, but I do feel guilty because I will never be able to provide another father for my children. I also feel guilty that it could be hard on them. Recently my son had to deal with rumors at his school about me after a babysitter had seen some posters in my room of some well-known gay entertainers.

Anger is another problem that has affected my parenting. The anger started becoming a problem after I got into school. I never had an explosive anger problem like that before. I was just too stressed trying to manage my class work, keep up the house, and raise four children by myself. Two of my children are special needs. David is hearing impaired and has chronic asthma, and Nathan has ADHD and bounces all over the place. My ex-husband helps financially, but he does not spend time with the children or offer any kind of support emotionally. When I became overwhelmed I began screaming and yelling like my mother did. I hated acting like her. I desperately needed to find some ways to relieve my stress. My therapist helped my get lined up for respite care through a social services agency. I had a lady who came in two evenings a week for almost a year.

That really helped me a lot because I had two evenings a week to get away and do my homework or just do whatever I wanted to do. I got out of the responsibility of the dinnertime thing and the bathtime thing and the bedtime thing on those two nights. It was almost like having a partner there for awhile. It was a tremendous relief. Currently, she only comes one night a week, but that's enough for me now.

I have also learned to give myself timeouts with my anger. When I feel myself losing my temper I go in my bedroom and shut the door, and the kids know that I'm taking a timeout.

The misperception, "My child is invading me" has been a trigger for my anger quite frequently. I felt like my children were invading me when they got into my belongings or entered my room, and I really overreacted to it. When I was growing up the environment was too chaotic to allow for any privacy. My siblings used to go through my things and give my stuff away. My mother would laugh when I got upset about it. So I still have this little girl need of, "It's mine and you can't have it." It gets triggered pretty badly with my children. I know, now, they are just being typical kids. Probably all kids poke around in their parents' things once in a while. Now I stop and remind myself that it's normal, and think about why I'm reacting the way I am. Then I set limits with them calmly, but firmly.

I definitely held the misperception, "The parent should have complete authority at all times." My mother had all the power in the house and the children had absolutely none. I thought it was my turn to have the power when I had kids. When they would ask me if they could do something like go outside and play or go to someone's house my answer was always automatically a vehement, "No!" I never really considered the request. I was obsessed with the idea that I had to maintain complete authority!

I have always had the problem of getting caught up in overwhelming feelings. Sometimes I have been caught up in the anger, but other times it has been an anxious feeling. When I get anxious I have always felt I needed something—fast—to make the feeling go away. That's usually when I have binged. One time I even tried gambling and lost a large amount of money because of it. What I'm learning about myself is I get caught up in a feeling and I can't think logically about what I'm doing. I can't analyze what I'm doing. I just get caught up in a feeling and can't step aside long enough to work my way out of it. I have learned that this is called emotion-focused coping, a common problem for people who have experienced trauma. It's like I'm only about four or five years old when

I'm caught in these feelings, and my whole focus becomes escaping the feelings. I am now trying to become more at home with my feelings. I am learning mindfulness and distress tolerance skills. I have a little code for myself. When I realize I'm stuck in my anxiety I think STOP and get back into my adult to do some problem-focused coping instead. And I am trying to fill that void inside spiritually instead of filling it up with quick-fix things like food or gambling—things which only made me feel worse about myself.

I screw up a lot and probably always will—probably more than many mothers. I've hurt my kids with things I've done, or not done, said, or not said. But one good thing about being in recovery is that I always go back to them and talk to them. I admit to them when I'm wrong. I tell them I'm sorry, and I explain why I acted the way I did if I understand it. That's a big difference I think between a household that is recovering and one that's not. I will tell them, "It's not your fault that this happened." I also assure my children, "It's not your fault that your father's gone. It had nothing to do with you." I am telling them all the things that should have been told to me so that they don't carry the kind of self-blaming that I carried for all those years.

4. JOE

Traumatic childhood experiences and addictions had a tremendous impact on Joe's ability to form trusting relationships with his wife and children. His is yet another story of courage and determination to throw out the ghosts and become a "whole" and healed parent today.

His Story Begins . . .

I grew up in a very orthodox, Christian home. My mom was an alcoholic. My dad was on the road a lot. I was kind of in charge of my mom from the earliest time I can remember—helping her when she was choking on bacon because she was drunk, or covering for her, or just being left completely alone. I was also shamed sexually and abused sexually by her. I was cut off, very alone, and depressed. I spent a lot of time sitting up on the roof of the house where I'd be all alone. I would often sit up there at night. I had a lot of physical punishment, with belts and yardsticks. Sometimes I didn't even understand what I was being punished for. I remember being scared all the time. I remember trying to separate myself from my life. Even at a very early age I remember sneaking into the liquor cabinet and finding a little relief in alcohol. I had suicidal thoughts by seven or eight years old, which continued on and off into my adult life.

When I was 12 years old I was raped by an older male friend. I couldn't tell my parents. I completely hid it from my family. It was a very violent, life-threatening thing, but I was able to hide it because I spent so much time alone. I didn't tell my parents because I felt like it was my fault. I didn't feel like there would be any protection from them anyway. My dad was gone all the time, and my mom certainly wasn't there to protect me. I had already experienced so much sexual shame that when the rape happened it was just too much. I couldn't talk about it to anyone.

I left home at 12 to go away to school. During that time I found solace in alcohol, and later in marijuana and other drugs. The drugs and alcohol helped me as a teenager to survive—to hold things together, although just barely.

My first really serious suicide attempt was probably at age 14. I tried to hang myself in a closet but the rod broke. So I straightened everything up and I covered up my tracks. Everything I did was a coverup. I had this false front I showed the rest of the world. Nobody saw beneath it. I didn't even see beneath it after awhile. I hid everything, but only with the help of my alcohol and my drugs. With the help of chemicals I could talk to people, and I could do things. I was very much into medicating myself—into blurring my consciousness in any way I could.

When I was 19 I married the first woman I ever slept with. It turned into a real nightmare. It was just a very empty relationship. There was no love. My alcoholism and my drug use were full-blown. I was in college at the time, and I didn't like going to school, so I skipped most of my classes and became kind of a hippie, hitchhiking and traveling around. The marriage didn't last very long, but we had two beautiful girls early on who were terribly hurt by the whole thing.

As time went on I did manage to begin a creative kind of career. I started achieving some things, and I had some neat opportunities come my way. But I still had to have my drugs and my alcohol. Still, there was no one who really knew me. I didn't have any real friends—no one that I really told anything to. It was all a front—just a front.

Then I met this really different woman. Grace was just really different. For the first time I fell in love, and I started letting her see just a little bit of

the real me—not everything—but it was the closest thing to a real relationship I ever had. Then we got married, and I brought hell into that relationship because I was still drinking and using drugs, and I was afraid of
the closeness. I was still continually seeking some kind of high, emotional
or chemical or something. There would be periods of real intimacy punc-
tuated by periods of real withdrawal. I would just start running away
from it out of fear. I very much fit the fearful attachment model. I have always been very uncomfortable with closeness. With Grace it was the first
time I ever tried it. I believe maybe I tried it a little bit with my paternal
grandparents, who were pretty extraordinary, earthy Danish people. I did
have some positive experiences of closeness with them. In fact, all of my
good memories are with them, and those memories are very vivid,
whereas my memories of being at home with my parents are foggier, and
primarily negative. When I found this relationship with Grace I discovered I really needed the emotional closeness with her, but at the same time
it frightened the hell out of me. I would run away or do something to sabotage it, and then come back because I had to have it. I would think to myself, "Don't do this. Don't have this relationship because you're just going
to get clobbered." But I couldn't not have it. It was the first light I ever saw
in my adult life.

Then the drugs and the alcohol, which had helped me survive for
such a long time, just stopped working for me. And the rape, which I had
suppressed for such a long time with the help of the chemicals, was gradually surfacing. I became very suicidal, and at last sought some help.

I went to treatment for my chemical dependency, and for the first time
in my life I found some spirituality. For several years following treatment,
I managed really well with the help of Alcoholics Anonymous, but the fear
was still lurking underneath. I just could not get rid of the fear. I would always think, "My wife's going to leave tomorrow," or "My wife's with this
man or with that man." I thought if she found out about the rape, it would
be too much for her. And then I told her about the rape and it wasn't too
much for her. But I was sure that after awhile it would be too much because it did stunt my skills for intimacy. All that fear I lived in was really
hard on her and hard on a relationship. I was in this circle knowing that
my fear was creating what I feared, but I couldn't get out of the circle. And
then it hit me—a massive, massive depression. I completely broke down.
I just wanted to die. I lost my sobriety and lost my spirituality. The only
thing I kept was my fear. I lost touch with reality and had to be hospitalized. Due to the circumstances, I was forced to work through the rape. I

had some very intensive therapy, and I looked at all of these things I hadn't looked at before. I had thought of the rape as the really defining moment of my life, but it really wasn't. I was already totally cut off way before that even happened due to the abuse from my mother that began early on. The rape was just the coffin lid. I had to get past that and the deeper issues as well. The fear about tackling those things was tremendous. But through all this my wife stayed with me, and gradually the security of my attachment to her increased.

I've always had trouble feeling human. I've always felt like this small threatened creature in this world of strangers—like a whole different race. I felt like I was an alien—like the title of Robert Heinlein's book, *A Stranger in a Strange Land*. It wasn't just a question of connecting with another person—I couldn't connect with the world. I couldn't connect with nature, I couldn't connect with God, I couldn't connect with any kind of spiritual center in myself. I couldn't even connect with myself in the final analysis. I was disconnected inside myself. The technical word is dissociation. There were parts of me I was not connected to. These parts of myself were completely separated. I wasn't even hooked up to me. My whole life had been fear—fear my mom would leave me alone, fear my mom wouldn't leave me alone, fear my dad would come home, fear that he wouldn't come home, fear about emotional relationships, sexual relationships, and fear about my own children. I had always lived in fear—complete fear. That kind of fearfulness prevents one from having a spiritual basis. I couldn't have a spiritual basis and be fearful like that—I just couldn't. But I just couldn't tell anyone about any of it until I absolutely had to—until I had no choice. It came down to, I had to tell somebody or kill myself.

Through all of this my wife and I had these wonderful boys. Obviously when I was drinking and using and in denial, I wasn't capable of being a good parent to them. But even after I went to treatment I was lucky Grace was with me, because if I'd been with a woman who didn't have this innate skill and instinct with children, God knows what kind of damage I would have caused. I never really knew how to be a parent—to be a dad. Luckily I was kind of supervised in the sense that I was attached to her as close as I could be to anybody and she was pretty straightforward in protecting the children and letting me know what was going on. She would tell me, "That was wrong," or "That behavior is hurting them."

I had the same fears with my children that I had about my wife. I feared they didn't love me, which caused me to be oversensitive to things they would say and take their behaviors personally. I also feared that something terrible would happen to them, and then at other times when they had needs I resented them because I was so totally absorbed in my own problems. When they were easy and they were happy they were wonderful. When they had trouble I just wanted it to be over. It wasn't all right for them to have any problems or negative feelings. When they had needs I would say to them things like, "Just get over it. Forget about it. It's O.K. Stop crying. It's all O.K. Everything's just O.K." I was teaching them that it's not all right to tell the truth about what's going on. I was teaching them to put on a front like I did. I was unconsciously laying that on them a lot. It put a wall between me and the kids. It prevented me from being attuned with their feelings. It prevented them from being able to stay connected to me, or me to them. Throughout all this, though, the walls would go up and they'd come down. The walls would go up and they'd come down between my wife and me and between my kids and me. There were periods of great intimacy, and there were periods of wonderful love and companionship. There were periods of nurturing going both ways and every way, and then the walls would come up again and my behavior would sabotage because the fear would grow. Intimacy created some sort of Newtonian reaction where so much impact would create so much rebound in response.

I say this with some hesitation, but I believe I have finally reached a point in my therapy where I have come to realize that no matter what, I can't hide from my problems and I can't be passive. No matter what my fears—I need to address my issues squarely. I'm also learning that I can't control everything. I have to take risks. I am learning to let go of trying to control my wife and my children. I have found that when I don't control, good things come back to me—freely. When I don't control the kids they do more of the things I like them to do. When I tune in to them instead of control them I enjoy the feeling of closeness I have with them. When I don't control my wife she feels happier and I'm happier. When I don't control all of my feelings so rigidly I feel more human. I am especially trying to stop controlling my fear. I'm trying to take the risk of allowing myself to just acknowledge and feel whatever I'm feeling. So now I can be afraid, but I don't have to live out of my fear. I can have fear, but I don't have to be run by it. I can talk about it instead of hiding it, and as a result it no longer has power over me.

I have found there is real freedom in letting go. I am enjoying my family, and experiencing real happiness in my life for the first time.

5. IN CONCLUSION . . .

All of the parents in these examples at one time felt trapped by unconscious forces they could not understand. Using the keys offered in this book, they faced their ghosts and identified their parental misperceptions, thereby coming to understand their broken instincts. As they created a new wellspring of nurturing experiences, resolved past traumas, changed their negative beliefs, and learned to manage their emotions they found healing and freedom from the bondage of the past. As they became more attuned and developed stronger attachment relationships with their children they experienced a newfound joy in sharing their lives with them.

Whether your difficulties have been more subtle than those experienced by the parents in these stories or just as severe, you share a common thread with many, many other parents with difficult pasts—the desire for a better life for yourself and for your family. Remember that none of the parents in these stories did it alone. They found the courage to reach out and let others help them—professionals, pastors, support groups, friends, and significant others. God can work through many people in our lives. So let some people in. Share this book with them. Work together. Laugh together. I have always found any journey to be much more enjoyable and more meaningful when it is shared.

Epilogue

Yes, you *can* become a terrific parent even if you didn't have one! If you have read this far, you are a parent with the courage to examine your own actions, thoughts, and feelings, and the motivation to take action for personal growth and recovery. By facing the ghosts head on you can overcome the effects of your difficult past, learn to manage difficulties in the present, and become the parent you have always wanted to be.

1. THE REWARDS TO YOU AND YOUR CHILDREN

Parents who have healed the past and mended their broken instincts have discovered an increased capacity to form secure attachments with other adults and with children. They find they experience more enjoyment of their children and more enjoyment of their lives. "Whole" parents have increased ability to manage anxious feelings and therefore have less need to control events or people around them. They have improved self-esteem and more self-confidence. "Whole" parents are *not perfect* parents, as perfect parents do not exist. But they are more comfortable with feelings and more effective in the manner in which they respond to their children's emotional needs. They are better able to tune in to their children's feelings, allow them to have their feelings, and provide the reassurance their children need. They are better able to stay "adult" as they interact with their children and less likely to respond to their children out of the feelings of the "hurt child." As they overcome their parental misperceptions, "whole" parents are better able to provide effectively the structure their children need in terms of consistency and clear limits.

The children of parents who have overcome the effects of a difficult past develop more secure attachments. As their parents heal, the children get their emotional needs met with greater consistency and discover they

can count on their parents when they need them, increasing their sense of
security. They also feel more secure in that they know what to expect in
terms of limits and consequences. As they become more secure, the children develop more self-confidence and more self-esteem. No, the children
of "whole" parents do *not* become *perfect*, as perfect children, like perfect
parents, do not exist. But they do tend to be more cooperative with their
parents, less aggressive at home and outside the home, and to develop
more satisfying relationships with peers and teachers.

2. THE REWARDS PASSED ON

Now imagine what happens as the children of healing, more "whole"
parents grow up and become parents themselves. They will naturally
draw upon their wellspring of nurturing experiences with their own
healed and "whole" parents to nurture their own children. Their own
comfort level with feelings will allow them to tune in to their children's
feelings and give them the nurturing and reassurance they need. They will
be able to parent from their adult ego states and will be less likely to experience hurt-child feelings in their interactions with their children. Their
sense of security will allow them to respond to their children in a manner
that is effective, as they will be less likely to take misbehaviors personally
and overreact.

The healing work you do as a parent now will improve your own life
and impact the emotional well-being of your children for the rest of their
lives. I cannot imagine anything that could be more important.

3. YOUR CAPACITY FOR A DEEPER EMPATHY

Adults who had a painful past and who have begun to get in touch
with and heal their feelings are often capable of a deeper empathy toward
the struggles of children that adults with easy childhoods may not be capable of having. Many parents who have allowed themselves to remember
their own pain become strongly proactive not only in giving their own
children the support and encouragement they need, but in helping children in the greater community. I have observed many recovering adults
become passionate about causes that are beneficial to children. I have noticed that adults recovering from a difficult past often become involved in

jobs or volunteer activities that involve children and they show a deep sensitivity to the needs of the children in their care as day care providers, teachers, Scout leaders, and counselors.

Eric is a counselor in his late 30s who now works with families and children in a small town. His story is an example of how a difficult childhood can inspire a deeper empathy for the feelings of children and a desire to help them:

Eric: I am the second of four boys born within five years to professional parents in their late 20s. My mother is very devoted to her professional career and she had not had much nurturing or play from her parents when she was growing up. Subsequently she didn't know how to play with her own children or meet them at their own emotional level. My father is extremely shy and has very low self-esteem due to his own childhood under a very strict and nonnurturing father. In addition, my parents had to expend most of the time and energy they had caring for and getting specialized services for my youngest brother, who has severe physical disabilities from cerebral palsy as well as learning disabilities.

I clearly remember feeling very lonely as a child, desperately wanting someone to understand me and feeling a lot of pain around not feeling a strong emotional connection with anyone. I longed for someone with whom I could talk about my feelings. Neither of my parents was ever available or ever supported the discussion of feelings. I did not experience that I had anyone in my childhood to help me process my pain and confusion, and therefore as a child I had no way of healing from those hurts. While I am very clear that my parents did the absolute very best that they could raising us four boys, I am also clear that all four of us grew up with a lot of emotional deficits.

My emotional ability to connect with others was deeply impacted by my upbringing. I came to believe that I could not ever really depend on anyone in this world, subsequently I did not wish to be very vulnerable with others. Other people were bound to let me down, it was just a question of when and how they would do it. Looking back I recognize that I unconsciously did many things to prevent relationships from starting, and if one did start, then I would sabotage it.

I have done a lot of hard work to overcome the walls which I had erected to protect myself from all of the pain I felt in my childhood. It has taken a lot of work for me to change some of my old, deeply entrenched beliefs. When I embarked on a serious program of personal recovery, however, I started developing the discipline to not act on my scared feelings and run away (in all of my very creative and unhealthy ways!) from the possibility of a long-term committed relationship.

When I met Patti, who later became my wife, I recognized that here was a person with values and ethics and the ability to work hard that could possibly lead to a long-term relationship. I now had the opportunity and the awareness to work toward a healthy relationship, something that I had so desperately wanted for so many years.

Patti did not have a desire to have children and I was very relieved about this. Because Patti and I have not worked out all of our issues in this relationship, I have felt that it would be unfair to bring a child into the situation. While I know that no marriage or family can be perfect, I definitely did not want to contribute to *any* child having the painful feelings and experiences that I had as a child. I decided that I wanted to help some of the kids out there who desperately need someone to take the time to be with and understand them. I felt what could be described as a spiritual calling to be there and to support the children who are already on this planet to get the emotional support that I believe all children deserve. In many ways as a counselor I act as "a guide who has been through this before" to assist the children and teenagers I work with along their journeys of healing and growing. Because of what I went through growing up I feel I can connect with the kids in a way I might not have been able to had my life been different. As I have continued to do the hard work of my own healing, I feel even more committed to do whatever I can to be an advocate for children. I am working very hard to make a difference in the lives of many children, far more than I could have if I had just focused on my own birth or adopted children.

Eric's childhood experiences have contributed significantly toward a profound understanding of the pain, confusion, and the desire for and struggle to have meaningful relationships that many of his child and adolescent clients are grappling with. His path to recovery has allowed him to be more effective in his chosen field and make a difference in the lives of many children.

4. FOR THE LOVE OF A CHILD

Parents who love their children, but want to provide a safer, more nurturing environment than the one they had often seem to have enormous courage in healing their pasts and overcoming the obstacles to becoming a "whole parent." There is probably no greater motivator to accomplish great feats than a parent's love for a child. Occasionally I read in the paper a story about a mom or a dad who suddenly had a surge of incredible strength brought on by a situation where a child was in peril. I have read about parents lifting whole automobiles to free a child trapped under a tire. I have read about moms and dads who have stopped a car from rolling down a hill with nothing but the force of their own strength when a child was trapped inside. A parent's love for a child can be a source of inhuman strength when that child's physical or emotional welfare is at stake.

5. BE PATIENT WITH YOURSELF

There are many stories out there. They all have both differences and similarities to one another. Your story is just as important as every other story. As you continue your journey remember that you are human. Give yourself permission to get scared, to stumble, to backslide, and to lose your courage and conviction at times. As parents, we must allow for our own humanness. If we can laugh at ourselves and forgive ourselves when we make mistakes, then we can pick up and keep on trying. Avoid becoming immobilized by perfectionism.

Keep this book handy so that you can go back to it and reread whatever sections you need at the moment as many times as you need to. Keep your notebook handy and continue looking back at the many exercises you have completed. Continue documenting your journey, both your successes and your mistakes. Take the risk to reach out and let others help you on your way. Recovery should never be a solitary venture.

As you grow and you become more healed and "whole," may you find joy in your relationship with your children and tremendous satisfaction in knowing that the joy you feel you are also giving to your children to be passed on by them to their children and to their children's children. There can be no greater miracle than this!

Recommended Books and Tapes

PARENTING SKILLS

Parenting with Love and Logic: Teaching Children Responsibility by Foster Cline and Jim Fay. Pinon, Colorado Springs, CO, 1990.

Parenting Teens with Love and Logic: Preparing Adolescents for Responsible Adulthood by Foster Cline and Jim Fay. Pinon, Colorado Springs, CO, 1992.

The Sixty Second Scolding [audiotape] by Foster Cline. Love and Logic Institute, Golden, CO, 1989. (Other tapes are available through Love and Logic Institute, phone 800-338-4065, www.loveandlogic.com)

Touchpoints: Your Child's Emotional and Behavioral Development by T. Berry Brazelton. Addison-Wesley, Reading, MA, 1992.

Listen to a Child: Understanding the Normal Problems of Growing Up by T. Berry Brazelton. Addison-Wesley, Reading, MA, 1984.

The Essential Partnership: How Parents and Children Can Meet the Emotional Challenges of Infancy and Childhood by Stanley Greenspan and Nancy Greenspan. Viking Penguin, New York, 1989.

Raising Your Spirited Child by Mary Sheedy Kurcinka. Harper Perennial, New York, 1991.

The Difficult Child by Stanley Turecki with Leslie Tonner. Bantam Books, New York, 1989.

A Parent's Guide to Attention Deficit Disorders by Lisa Bain. Dell, New York, 1991.

Holding Time by Martha Welch. Simon and Schuster, New York, 1988.

INFANT MASSAGE

Infant Massage: A Handbook for Loving Parents, by Vimala McClure. Bantam Books, New York, 1989.

Baby's First Touch: Step-By-Step Instruction for Infant Massage [videotape] by Diane Moore. International Loving Touch Foundation, Portland, OR, 1992. (International Loving Touch Foundation, P.O. Box 16374, Portland, Oregon 92716)

INNER CHILD

Inside Out: Rebuilding Self and Personality through Inner Child Therapy [workbook] by Ann Potter. Accelerated Development, Muncie, IN, 1994.
Inside Out: Visualization Tape by Ann Potter. Accelerated Development, Muncie, IN, 1994. (Accelerated Development, Inc., phone 317-284-7511)
Homecoming: Reclaiming and Championing Your Inner Child by John Bradshaw. Bantam Books, New York, 1990.

MENTAL HEALTH

Cognitive–Behavioral Treatment of Borderline Pesonality Disorder [for therapists] by Marsha Linehan. Guilford Press, New York, 1993.
Coping with Trauma: A Guide to Self-Understanding by Jon Allen. American Psychiatric Press, Washington, D.C., 1995.
Feeling Good: The New Mood Therapy by David Burns. Signet Books, New York, 1980.
Skills Training Manual for Treating Borderline Personality Disorder by Marsha Linehan. Guilford Press, New York, 1993. (Intended to be used with a therapist.)
Transforming Trauma: EMDR the Revolutionary New Therapy for Freeing the Mind, Clearing the Body, and Opening the Heart by Laurell Parnell. Norton, New York, 1977.

ADOPTION

Adopting the Hurt Child: Hope for Families with Special-Needs Kids by Gregory C. Keck and Regina Kupecky. Pinon, Colorado Springs, CO, 1995.
Real Parents, Real Children by Holly van Gulden and Lisa Bartels-Rabb. Crossroad Publishing, New York, 1993.
Making Sense of Adoption by Lois R. Melina. Harper and Row, New York, 1989.
The Primal Wound: Understanding the Adopted Child by Nancy N. Verrier. Gateway, Baltimore, MD, 1996.

National Organizations

EMDR

EMDR Institute, Inc.
P.O. Box 51010, Pacific Grove, CA 93950-6010
Phone 831 372-3900
Fax 831 647-9881
http://www.emdr.com
e-mail: inst@emdr.com
(Information about Eye Movement Desensitization and Reprocessing for trauma resolution)

ATTENTION DEFICIT HYPERACTIVITY DISORDER

CHADD (Children and Adults with Attention Deficit Disorders)
499 Northwest 70th Ave., Ste. 101, Plantation, FL 33317
Phone 954 587-3700
(Up-to-date information about ADHD and support meetings throughout the country)

ADDA (Attention Deficit Disorders Association)
P.O. Box 972, Mentor, OH 44061
Phone 800 487-2282
(Up-to-date information about ADHD)

SINGLE PARENTING

Parents Without Partners
International, Inc.
401 N. Michigan Avenue
Chicago, IL 60611-4267
Phone 800 637-7974
http://www.parentswithoutpartners.org

INFERTILITY

Resolve, Inc.
1310 Broadway, Somerville, MA 02144-1731
Phone 617 623-1156
Helpline 617 623-0744
Fax 617 623-0252
http://www.resolve.org
(For support, information, local chapter meetings, and doctor referrals;
may send a self-addressed stamped envelope)

MENTAL HEALTH

National Institute of Mental Health
Public Inquiries, Room 7C-02
5600 Fishers Lane, Bethesda, MD 20892-8030
http://www.nimh.nih.gov/
e-mail: nimhinfo@nih.gov
(Up-to-date mental health information)

National Mental Health Association
1201 Prince Street, Alexandria, VA 22314-2971
Phone 703 684-7722, 703 684-5968
Fax 800 969-6942
(Up-to-date mental health information)

National Depressive and Manic Depressive Association
730 Franklin Street, Ste. 501, Chicago, IL 60610
Phone 312 642-0049, 312 642-7243
Toll-free 800 826-3632
(Up-to-date information about depression and Bipolar Disorder)

National Alliance for the Mentally Ill
200 North Glebe Road, Ste. 1015, Arlington, VA 22203-3754
Phone 703 524-7600, 703 524-9094
Helpline 800 950-6264 10 AM until 5 PM EST M–F
(For information, doctor and support group referrals)

National Foundation for Depressive Illness
P.O. Box 2257, New York, NY 10016
Phone 212 268-4260, 212 268-4434
Helpline 800 248-4344

POSTPARTUM DEPRESSION

Postpartum Support International
927 N. Kellogg Ave., Santa Barbara, CA 93111
Phone 805 967-7636
Fax 805 967-0608
www.iup.edu/an/postpartum
e-mail: thonikman@compuserve.com
(International network for individuals and groups interested in increasing awareness about the emotional reactions women experience during pregnancy and the first year after the baby arrives)

The Association for Post-Natal Illness (APNI)
25 Jerdan Place, Fulham, London SW6 IBE, England
(Send a self-addressed envelope for information)

Twelve Step Self-Help Groups

TWELVE STEP GROUPS

Alcoholics Anonymous
A.A. General Service Office
475 Riverside Drive, New York, NY 10015
Phone 212 870-3400
Fax 212 870-3003
http://www.alcoholics-anonymous.org/
(For information about meetings in the United States, Canada, and around the world)

Al-Anon Family Group Headquarters, Inc.
1600 Corporate Landing Parkway, Virginia Beach, VA 23454-5617
Phone 800 344-2666
www.al-anon.org/
(Information about Al-Anon and Alateen meetings for families of alcoholics in the United States and Canada)

Adult Children of Alcoholics Central Service Board
P.O. Box 3216, Torrance, CA 90515
Phone 310 534-1815
http://www.recovery.org/acoa/acoa.html
(Send self-addressed stamped #10 envelope for information and list of meetings in your area)

ACA General Service Network
P.O. Box 25166, Minneapolis, MN 55458-6166
http://www.talamasca.org/avatar/aca.html

Narcotics Anonymous
World Service Office
P.O. Box 9999, Van Nuys, CA 91409
Phone 818 773-9999
Fax 818 700-0700
(Information about meetings in the United States, Canada, and around the world)

Cocaine Anonymous World Service Office (CAWSO)
P.O. Box 2000, Los Angeles, CA 90049-8000
Phone 310 559-5833
Fax 310 559-2554
Referral line 800 347-8998
(Information about meetings in the United States, Canada, and England)

Sex Addicts Anonymous
ISO of SAA
P.O. Box 70949, Houston, TX 77270
Phone 713 869-4902 (M–F, 10 AM–6 PM)
http://www.saa-recovery.org/
e-mail: info@saa-recovery.org
(Information about meetings world-wide)

Organizations and Agencies for Information and Treatment of Children with Attachment Problems

Association for Treatment and Training in the Attachment of Children (ATTACh)
3900 E. Camelback Rd., Ste. 200, Phoenix, AZ 85018
Phone 602 912-5340

Attachment Center at Evergreen
P.O. Box 2764, Evergreen, CO 80437
Phone 303 674-1910

ABC
Attachment Bonding Center of Ohio
12608 State Road, North Royalton, OH 44133
Phone 440 230-1960

Attachment and Bonding Center of Nebraska
302 S. 74th, Omaha, NE 68114
Phone 402 392-8949

Attachment Center Northwest
8011 118th Ave., Kirkland, WA 98033
Phone 425 889-8524

Attachment Disorder Parents Network
P.O. Box 18475, Boulder, CO 80308

Attachment Parents Network of CT
16 Heritage Circle, Clinton, CT 06413
Phone 860 669-2750

Center for Attachment Therapy, Training, and Education (CATTE)
101 Nawk Point Court, Folsom, CA 95630
Phone 916 988-6233

Attachment Resource Center
410 Avenue N South, Saskatoon, SK S7M2N4
Phone 306 652-8588

Beech Brook
3737 Lander Rd., Cleveland, OH 44124
Phone 216 831-2255

Children Unlimited
P.O. Box 11463, Columbia, SC 29211
Phone 803 799-8311

Eden Prairie Psychological Resources
5500 Lincoln Dr. #160, Edina, MN 55436

Evergreen Consultants in Human Behavior
2800 Meadow Drive #206, Evergreen, CO 80439-8345
Phone 303 674-5503

Association for Pre- and Perinatal Psychology and Health (APPAH)
340 Colony Road, Box 994, Geyserville, CA 95441-0994
Phone 707 857-4041

Mothering Center
Martha Welch, MD
952 5th Ave., New York, NY 10021
Phone 212 861-6816, 203 661-1413

Intermountain Children's Home
500 S. Lamborn, Helena, MT 59601
Phone 406 442-7920

KC ATTACh
6500 W. 183rd St., Stilwell, KS 66085
Phone 913 897-4774

Keys Attachment Center
Haslingen Old Road, Rawtenstall BB4 8RS, Rossendale, Lancs, England

National Adoption Information Clearinghouse
11426 Rockville Pike, Ste. 410, Rockville, MD 20852
Phone 202 842-1919

Notes

CHAPTER ONE

1. Selma Fraiberg, Edna Adelson, and Vivian Shapiro, "Ghosts in the Nursery: A Psychoanalytic Approach to the Problems of Impaired Infant–Mother Relationships," in *Selected Writings of Selma Fraiberg*. Ed. Louis Fraiberg. Columbus, OH: Ohio State University Press, 1987, pp. 100–143.

CHAPTER TWO

1. Daniel N. Stern, *The Motherhood Constellation: A Unified View of Parent–Infant Psychotherapy*. New York: Basic Books, 1995, p. 58.
2. *Ibid.*, p. 51. I am indebted to the research and writing of Daniel Stern for the concept of the remembering context and the layers of the mind, so important to the conceptualization of this book.
3. *Ibid.*, p. 51.
4. Endel Tulving, "How Many Memory Systems Are There?" *American Psychologist* 40(1985):385–398.
5. Lenore Terr, *Too Scared to Cry: How Trauma Affects Children . . . and Ultimately Us All*. New York: Basic Books, 1990, pp. 181–182.
6. Daniel N. Stern, *The Motherhood Constellation: A Unified View of Parent–Infant Psychotherapy*. New York: Basic Books, 1995, pp. 50–54.
7. Eric Berne, *Transactional Analysis in Psychotherapy: A Systematic Individual and Social Psychiatry*. New York: Grove Press, 1961.
8. John Dusay, *Egograms: How I See You and You See Me*. New York: Harper and Row, 1977. I gratefully acknowledge John Dusay's concept of the egogram as a valuable contribution to understanding how ego states affect our responses and interactions with others. The egogram image in Figures 3 and 4 has been reprinted with the permission of the publisher.

CHAPTER THREE

1. John Bowlby, "The Role of Attachment in Personality Development and Psychopathology," in *The Course of Life. Volume One: Infancy*. Eds. Stanley I. Greenspan and George H. Pollock. Madison, CT: International Universities Press, 1989, pp. 229–270.

2. Harry F. Harlow and Robert R. Zimmermann, "Affectional Responses in the Infant Monkey," *Science* 130(1959):421–432.
3. John Bowlby, "The Role of Attachment in Personality Development and Psychopathology," in *The Course of Life. Volume One: Infancy*. Eds. Stanley I. Greenspan and George H. Pollock. Madison, CT: International Universities Press, 1989, pp. 229–270.
4. *Ibid.*
5. Donald W. Winnicott, *Home is Where We Start From: Essays by a Psychoanalyst*. New York: Viking Penguin, 1986, p. 28.
6. Donald W. Winnicott, *The Family and Individual Development*. New York: Basic Books, 1965, pp. 148–149.
7. *Ibid.*, pp. 17–19
8. John Bowlby, "The Role of Attachment in Personality Development and Psychopathology," in *The Course of Life. Volume One: Infancy*. Eds. Stanley I. Greenspan and George H. Pollock. Madison, CT: International Universities Press, 1989, pp. 229–270.
9. Bertrand G. Cramer, *The Importance of Being Baby: The Scripts Parents Write and the Roles Babies Play*. Reading, MA: Addison-Wesley, 1992, pp. 182–183.

CHAPTER FOUR

1. Kim Bartholomew and Leonard M. Horowitz, "Attachment Styles among Young Adults: A Test of a Four-Category Model," *Journal of Personality and Social Psychology* 61(1991):226–244.
2. *Ibid.*
3. *Ibid.*
4. Judith A. Feeney, Patricia Noller, and Mary Hanrahan, "Assessing Adult Attachment," in *Attachment in Adults: Clinical and Developmental Perspectives*. Eds. Michael B. Sperling and William H. Berman. New York: Guilford Press, 1994, p. 131. The definitions of the four adult attachment styles have been reprinted with permission of the publisher.
5. Alicia F. Lieberman and Jeree H. Pawl, "Clinical Applications of Attachment Theory," in *Clinical Implications of Attachment Theory*. Eds. Jay Belsky and Teresa Nezworski. Hillsdale, NJ: Erlbaum, 1988, pp. 327–351.
6. *Ibid.*
7. Foster W. Cline, *Hope for High Risk and Rage Filled Children: Reactive Attachment Disorder*. Evergreen, CO: EC Publications, 1992, pp. 29–49.
8. Colin M. Turnbull, *The Mountain People*. New York: Simon and Schuster, 1972.
9. *Ibid.*, pp. 294–295.

CHAPTER FIVE

1. Bertrand G. Cramer, *The Importance of Being Baby: The Scripts Parents Write and the Roles Babies Play*. Reading, MA: Addison-Wesley, 1992, p. 76.
2. Ann E. Potter, *Inside Out: Rebuilding Self and Personality through Inner Child Therapy* [workbook]. Muncie, IN: Accelerated Development, 1994, p. 56.
3. Daniel N. Stern, *The Motherhood Constellation: A Unified View of Parent–Infant Psychotherapy*. New York: Basic Books, 1995, p. 58.

4. *Marvin's Room,* movie featuring Meryl Streep, Leonardo DiCaprio, Diane Keaton, and Robert DeNiro, Buena Vista Pictures, 1996.

5. Bessel van der Kolk, "The Psychological and Biological Processing of Traumatic Experience: Clinical Implications," Lecture, Ninth Annual International Conference on Attachment and Bonding. Omaha, NE, 18 October 1997.

6. Bertrand G. Cramer, *The Importance of Being Baby; The Scripts Parents Write and the Roles Babies Play.* Reading, MA: Addison-Wesley, 1992, p. 121.

CHAPTER SIX

1. Albert Ellis, *A New Guide to Rational Living.* North Hollywood, CA: Wilshire, 1975.

2. Aaron T. Beck, *Cognitive Therapy and the Emotional Disorders.* New York: International Universities Press, 1976.

3. David D. Burns, *Feeling Good: The New Mood Therapy.* New York: Signet, 1981.

CHAPTER SEVEN

1. Bessel van der Kolk, "The Psychological and Biological Processing of Traumatic Experience: Clinical Implications," Lecture, Ninth Annual International Conference on Attachment and Bonding. Omaha, NE, 18 October 1997.

2. Marsha M. Linehan, *Skills Training Manual for Treating Borderline Personality Disorder.* New York: Guilford Press, 1993, p. 3. The group of practitioners with which I am affiliated offers the Dialectical Behavioral Therapy approach through group and individuals for clients who can benefit. The therapists involved meet weekly primarily to study Linehan's approach. This study has proven invaluable as a source of ideas for this chapter. I would like to gratefully acknowledge Linehan's concepts for emotion regulation, distress tolerance, and mindfulness from which I drew heavily in the writing of this chapter. I refer the reader to Linehan's workbook for further study, although the workbook is designed to be used with the help of a professional therapist.

3. *Ibid.*

4. *Ibid.,* p. 109.

5. *Ibid.,* p. 65.

6. *Ibid.,* p. 65.

7. *Ibid.,* p. 66.

8. *Ibid.,* pp. 63–69.

9. *Ibid.,* p. 113.

10. *Ibid.,* p. 93.

11. *Ibid.,* p. 160.

12. *Ibid.,* p. 93.

13. *Ibid.,* pp. 98–100.

14. *Ibid.,* p. 167.

15. *Ibid.,* p. 100.

16. *Ibid.,* p. 113.

17. *Ibid.,* p. 161.

18. *Alcoholics Anonymous.* New York: Alcoholics Anonymous, 1955, p. 59.

CHAPTER NINE

1. Scott Henderson, "The Significance of Social Relationships in the Etiology of Neurosis," in *The Place of Attachment in Human Behavior*. Eds. Colin Murray Parkes and Joan Stevenson-Hinde. New York: Tavistock, 1982, pp. 205–231.
2. Craig Nakken, *The Addictive Personality*. Center City, MN: Hazelden, 1988, pp. 3–18.
3. *Ibid.*, pp. 13–18.
4. David D. Burns, *Intimate Connections: The Clinically Proven Program for Making Close Friends and Finding a Loving Partner*. New York: Signet, 1985.
5. *Ibid.*, pp. 84–135. I gratefully credit Dr. Burns for his straightforward commonsense ideas for helping people make friends as a primary source for this section of the chapter.
6. *Ibid.*, p. 108. I gratefully acknowledge Dr. Burns' helpful suggestions for combating thinking errors associated with social anxiety which I have adapted for this section.
7. David D. Burns, *Feeling Good: The New Mood Therapy*. New York: Signet, 1981, p. 38. This guide for helping mood through changing self-defeating thought patterns is the source for this thinking error. I refer the reader to Dr. Burns' book for further help in changing other self-defeating thoughts.
8. Marsha M. Linehan, *Skills Training Manual for Treating Borderline Personality Disorder*. New York: Guilford, 1993, pp. 115–133. I am indebted to Linehan's work in the area of relationship skills as the central source for this section of the chapter. I refer the reader to the workbook for further study of these helpful skills.
9. *Ibid.*, p. 116.
10. *Ibid.*, pp. 73–75.
11. *Ibid.*, pp. 121–122.
12. *Ibid.*, pp. 121–122.
13. *Ibid.*, pp. 125–126.
14. *Ibid.*, p. 127.
15. *Ibid.*, p. 128.

CHAPTER TEN

1. Landry Wildwind, Unpublished manuscript. 1996, p. 1.
2. *Ibid.*, p. 2.
3. Bertrand G. Cramer, *The Importance of Being Baby: The Scripts Parents Write and the Roles Babies Play*. Reading, MA: Addison-Wesley, 1992, p. 61.
4. Mary Main, Nancy Kaplan, and Jude Cassidy, "Security in Infancy, Childhood, and Adulthood: A Move to the Level of Representation," *Monographs of the Society for Research in Child Development* 50(1–2; 1985):66–104.

CHAPTER ELEVEN

1. Joy D. Osofsky, Della M. Hann, and Claire Peebles, "Adolescent Parenthood: Risks and Opportunities for Mothers and Infants," in *Handbook of Infant Mental Health*. Ed. Charles H. Zeanah, Jr. New York: Guilford Press, 1993, pp. 107–118. The ideas presented in Osofsky's material were very helpful to the development of this section of the chapter.
2. *Ibid.*

3. Marsha M. Linehan, *Skills Training Manual for Treating Borderline Personality Disorder.* New York: Guilford Press, 1993.

4. Claudia Black, *It Will Never Happen to Me!* New York: Ballentine, 1981, pp. 24–48.

CHAPTER TWELVE

1. Stanley Greenspan and Nancy Thorndike Greenspan, *The Essential Partnership: How Parents and Children Can Meet the Emotional Challenges of Infancy and Childhood.* New York: Viking Penguin, 1989, pp. 52–54.

2. T. Berry Brazelton, *Touchpoints: Your Child's Emotional and Behavioral Development.* Reading, MA: Addison-Wesley, 1992, p. 253.

3. Murray A. Strauss, *Beating the Devil out of Them: Corporal Punishment in American Families.* New York: Lexington Books, 1994.

4. Foster W. Cline and Jim Fay, *Parenting with Love and Logic: Teaching Children Responsibility.* Colorado Springs, CO: Pinon, 1990, p. 94.

5. *Ibid.,* p. 49.

6. *Ibid.,* p. 51.

7. Foster Cline, *The Sixty Second Scolding* [Audiotape]. Golden, CO: Love and Logic Institute, 1989.

8. Foster W. Cline and Jim Fay, *Parenting with Love and Logic: Teaching Children Responsibility.* Colorado Springs, CO: Pinon, 1990, pp. 77–78.

9. *Ibid.,* pp. 60–69.

CHAPTER THIRTEEN

1. Stella Chess and Alexander Thomas, *Temperament in Clinical Practice.* New York: Guilford Press, 1986, pp. xi–xiv.

2. *Ibid.,* p. 27.

3. *Ibid.,* p. 12.

4. From pp. 16–17 of *The Difficult Child* by Stanley Turecki, M.D., and Leslie Tonner. © 1989 by Stanley Turecki, M.D., and Leslie Tonner. Used by permission of Bantam Books, a division of Bantam Doubleday Dell Publishing Group, Inc.

5. From pp. 107–108 of *The Difficult Child* by Stanley Turecki, M.D., and Leslie Tonner. © 1989 by Stanley Turecki, M.D., and Leslie Tonner. Used by permission of Bantam Books, a division of Bantam Doubleday Dell Publishing Group, Inc.

6. *Ibid.,* p. 106. I am indebted to Dr. Turecki's book as a primary source for many of the ideas in this chapter. His ideas for identifying behaviors related to temperament and labeling the child's difficulties for him are vital to the management of the behavior of the difficult child and became a primary concept around which this chapter was organized.

7. *Ibid.,* pp. 106–110.

8. *Ibid.,* pp. 114.

9. *Ibid.,* pp. 114–120.

10. Stella Chess and Alexander Thomas, *Temperament in Clinical Practice.* New York: Guilford Press, 1986, pp. 39–40.

11. T. Berry Brazelton, *Touchpoints: Your Child's Emotional and Behavioral Development.* Reading, MA: Addison-Wesley, 1992, p. 287.

12. Stanley Turecki with Leslie Tonner, *The Difficult Child*. New York: Bantam Books, 1989, p. 143
13. *Ibid.*, p. 146.
14. *Ibid.*, p. 154.
15. *Ibid.*, p. 162.
16. *Ibid.*, p. 153.
17. *Ibid.*, p. 168.
18. *Ibid.*, p. 165.
19. *Ibid.*, pp. 190–193.
20. *Ibid.*, pp. 151–152.
21. Paul H. Wender, *Attention-Deficit Hyperactivity Disorder in Adults*. New York: Oxford University Press, 1995, pp. 76–121.
22. Lisa J. Bain, *A Parent's Guide to Attention Deficit Disorders*. New York: Dell, 1991, pp. 19–40.
23. Reprinted with permission from the *Diagnostic and Statistical Manual of Mental Disorders, Fourth Edition*. Copyright 1994 American Psychiatric Association.
24. Soleil Gregg, *Preventing Antisocial Behavior in Disabled and At-Risk Students*. Policy Briefs. Charleston, WV: Appalachia Educational Laboratories, 1996.

CHAPTER FOURTEEN

1. Nancy Newton Verrier, *The Primal Wound: Understanding the Adopted Child*. Baltimore, MD: Gateway, 1996, p. 33.
2. *Ibid.*, pp. 33–35.
3. Holly van Gulden and Lisa M. Bartels-Rabb, *Real Parents, Real Children: Parenting the Adopted Child*. New York: Crossroad, 1993, pp. 200–201.
4. Holly van Gulden, "Keys to Successful Adoptive Parenting Workshop," Lecture, Boystown, NE, 30 September 1994.
5. Lois Ruskai Melina, *Making Sense of Adoption*. New York: Harper and Row, 1989.

CHAPTER FIFTEEN

1. T. Berry Brazelton, *Touchpoints: Your Child's Emotional and Behavioral Development*. Reading, MA: Addison-Wesley, 1992, pp. 26–27.
2. Diana Moore, *Baby's First Touch: Step-by-Step Instruction for Infant Massage* [Videotape]. Portland, OR: International Loving Touch Foundation, 1992.
3. Vimala Schneider McClure, *Infant Massage: A Handbook for Loving Parents*. New York: Bantam, 1989.
4. *Ibid.*, p. 65.
5. Diana Moore, *Baby's First Touch: Step-by-Step Instruction for Infant Massage* [Videotape]. Portland, OR: International Loving Touch Foundation, 1992.
6. Vimala Schneider McClure, *Infant Massage: A Handbook for Loving Parents*. New York: Bantam, 1989, pp. 135–177.
7. Stanley Greenspan and Nancy Thornkike Greenspan, *The Essential Partnership: How Parents and Children Can Meet the Emotional Challenges of Infancy and Childhood*. New York: Viking Penguin, 1989, pp. 19–62. I refer the reader to this book for a more detailed de-

scription of the use of floor time, an idea originated by the authors which I have gratefully drawn upon for this section. I have found floor time to be extremely useful for parents in strengthening their attachments with their youngsters.

8. *Ibid.*, p. 76.
9. *Ibid.*, p. 20.
10. Ann M. Jernberg, *Theraplay: A New Treatment Using Structured Play for Problem Children and Their Families.* San Francisco: Jossey-Bass, 1979.
11. *Ibid.*
12. *Ibid.*, p. 115. I gratefully credit Ann Jernberg for the several Theraplay ideas which I have adapted here for use by parents. Although Jernberg does not specifically discuss her techniques in relation to attachment, I have found these ideas extremely helpful to parents in building a stronger bond with their youngsters.
13. *Ibid.*, p. 119.
14. *Ibid.*, p. 113.
15. *Ibid.*, p. 120.
16. *Ibid.*, p. 113.
17. *Ibid.*, p. 123.
18. *Ibid.*, pp. 58–59.
19. Martha G. Welch, *Holding Time.* New York: Simon and Schuster, 1988, p. 17.
20. *Ibid.*, p. 49.
21. *Ibid.*, p. 51.
22. *Ibid.*, p. 56.
23. *Ibid.*
24. Foster W. Cline, *Hope for High Risk and Rage Filled Children: Reactive Attachment Disorder.* Evergreen, CO: EC Publications, 1992.
25. Gregory C. Keck, *Adopting the Hurt Child: Hope for Families for Special Needs Kids.* Colorado Springs, CO: Pinon, 1995, pp. 153–161.
26. Josephine Anderson, "Holding Therapy: A Way of Helping Unattached Children," in *Adoption Resources for Mental Health Professionals.* Ed. Pamela V. Grabe. New Brunswick, NJ: Transaction, 1990, pp. 87–97.
27. George Carlin, "A Place for My Stuff!" [Audiotape]. New York: Atlantic Recording Corporation, 1981.
28. Mary Pipher, *The Shelter of Each Other: Rebuilding Our Families.* New York: Grossett/Putnam, 1996, p. 230.
29. *Ibid.*, p. 14.
30. *Ibid.*, p. 230.
31. *Ibid.*, p. 240.
32. Mary Main, Nancy Kaplan, and Jude Cassidy, "Security in Infancy, Childhood, and Adulthood: A Move to the Level of Representation," *Monographs of the Society for Research in Child Development* 50(1–2; 1985):66–104.

Bibliography

Aber, J. Lawrence, and Amy J. L. Baker, "Security of Attachment in Toddlerhood," in *Attachment in the Preschool Years: Theory, Research and Intervention*. Eds. Mark T. Greenberg, Dante Cichetti, and Mark E. Cummings. Chicago: University of Chicago Press, 1990, pp. 427–460.

Adam, Kenneth S., "Suicidal Behavior and Attachment: A Developmental Model," in *Attachment in Adults*. Eds. Michael B. Sperling and William H. Berman. New York: Guilford Press, 1994, pp. 275–298.

Ainsworth, Mary D. Salter, "Attachment: Retrospect and Prospect," in *The Place of Attachment in Human Behavior*. Eds. Collin Murray Parkes and Joan Stevenson-Hinde. New York: Tavistock, 1982, pp. 3–29.

Ainsworth, Mary D. Salter, "Attachments beyond Infancy," *American Psychologist* 44(1989):709–716.

Alcoholics Anonymous. New York: Alcoholics Anonymous, 1955.

Allen, Jon G., *Coping with Trauma*. Washington, DC: American Psychiatric Press, 1995.

Amen, Antony J., and Sharon R. Johnson with Daniel G. Amen, *A Teenager's Guide to A.D.D.: Understanding and Treating Attention Deficit Disorders through the Teenage Years*. Fairfield, CA: MindWorks, 1996.

American Psychiatric Association, *Diagnostic and Statistical Manual of Mental Disorders. Fourth Edition*. Washington, DC: American Psychiatric Association, 1994.

Anderson, Josephine, "Holding Therapy: A Way of Helping Unattached Children," in *Adoption Resources for Mental Health Professionals*. Ed. Pamela V. Grabe. New Brunswick, NJ: Transaction, 1990, pp. 87–97.

Bain, Lisa J., *A Parent's Guide to Attention Deficit Disorders*. New York: Dell, 1991.

Bartholomew, Kim, and Horowitz, Leonard M., "Attachment Styles among Young Adults: A Test of a Four-Category Model," *Journal of Personality and Social Psychology* 61(1991):226–244.

Batgos, Joanna, and Bonnie J. Leadbeater, "Parental Attachment, Peer Relations, and Dysphoria in Adolescence," in *Attachment in Adults*. Eds. Michael B. Sperling and William H. Berman. New York: Guilford Press, 1994, pp. 155–178.

Beck, Aaron T., *Cognitive Therapy and the Emotional Disorders*. New York: International Universities Press, 1996.

Belsky, Jay, and Russell Isabella, "Maternal, Infant, and Social-Contextual Determinants of Attachment Security," in *Clinical Implications of Attachment*. Eds. Jay Belsky and Teresa Nezworski. Hillsdale, NJ: Erlbaum, 1988, pp.41–93.

Berne, Eric, *Transactional Analysis in Psychotherapy: A Systematic Individual and Social Psychiatry*. New York: Grove Press, 1961.

Black, Claudia, *It Will Never Happen to Me!* New York: Ballentine, 1981.

Bowlby, John, *Attachment*. New York: Basic Books, 1982.

Bowlby, John, *A Secure Base*. New York: Basic Books, 1988.

Bowlby, John, "Developmental Psychiatry Comes of Age," *American Journal of Psychiatry* 145(1989):1–9.

Bowlby, John, "The Role of Attachment in Personality Development and Psychopathology," in *The Course of Life. Volume One: Infancy*. Eds. Stanley I. Greenspan and George H. Pollock. Madison, CT: International Universities Press, 1989, pp. 229–270.

Bradford, Evan, and William J. Lyddon, "Assessing Adolescent and Adult Attachment: an Update," *Journal of Counseling and Development* 73(1994):215–219.

Bradshaw, John, *Healing the Shame that Binds You*. Deerfield Beach, FL: Health Communications, 1988.

Bradshaw, John, *Homecoming: Reclaiming and Championing Your Inner Child*. New York: Bantam, 1990.

Brazelton, T. Berry, *Touchpoints: Your Child's Emotional and Behavioral Development*. Reading, MA: Addison-Wesley, 1992.

Brazelton, T. Berry, *Listen to a Child: Understanding the Normal Problems of Growing Up*. Reading, MA: Addison-Wesley, 1994.

Brazelton, T. Berry, and Bertrand G. Cramer, *The Earliest Relationship*. Reading, MA: Addison-Wesley, 1990.

Burns, David D., *Feeling Good: The New Mood Therapy*. New York: Signet Books, 1980.

Burns, David D., *Intimate Connections: The Clinically Proven Program for Making Close Friends and Finding a Loving Partner*. New York: Signet Books, 1985.

Chess, Stella, and Alexander Thomas, *Temperament in Clinical Practice*. New York: Guilford Press, 1986.

Cicchetti, Dante, and Douglas Barnett, "Attachment Organization in Maltreated Preschoolers," *Development and Psychopathology* 3(1991):397–411.

Cicchetti, Dante, Mark E. Cummings, Mark T. Greenberg, and Robert S. Marvin, "An Organizational Perspective on Attachment Beyond Infancy," in *Attachment in the Pre-School Years*. Eds. Mark T. Greenberg, Dante Cicchetti, and Mark E. Cummings. Chicago: University of Chicago Press, 1990, pp. 3–49.

Cicchetti, Dante, and Mark T. Greenberg, "The Legacy of John Bowlby," *Development and Psychopathology* 3(1991):347–350.

Cline, Foster W., "Understanding and Treating the Severely Disturbed Child," in *Adoption Resources for Mental Health Professionals*. Ed. P. V. Grabe. New Brunswick, NJ: Transaction, 1990, pp. 137–150.

Cline, Foster W., *Hope for High Risk and Rage Filled Children: Reactive Attachment Disorder*. Evergreen, CO: EC Publications, 1992.

Cline, Foster W., and Jim Fay. *Parenting with Love and Logic: Teaching Children Responsibility*. Colorado Springs, CO: Pinon, 1990.

Cline, Foster W., and Jim Fay, *Parenting Teens with Love and Logic*. Colorado Springs, CO: Pinon, 1992.

Cohn, Jeffrey F., Susan B. Campbell, and Shelley Ross, "Infant Response in the Still-Face Paradigm at 6 Months Predicts Avoidant and Secure Attachment at 12 Months," *Development and Psychopathology* 3(1991):367–376.

Collins, Nancy L., and Stephen J. Read, "Adult Attachment, Working Models, and Relationship Quality in Dating Couples," *Journal of Personality and Social Psychology* 58(1990):644–663.

Cramer, Bertrand G., *The Importance of Being Baby: The Scripts Parents Write and the Roles Babies Play*. Reading, MA: Addison-Wesley, 1992.

Crittenden, Patricia M., "Relationships at Risk," in *Clinical Implications of Attachment*. Eds. Jay Belsky and Teresa Nezworski. Hillsdale, NJ: Erlbaum, 1988, pp. 136–174.

Crittenden, Patricia M., "Treatment of Anxious Attachment in Infancy and Early Childhood," *Development and Psychopathology* 4(1992):575–602.

Crittenden, Patricia M., Mary F. Partridge, and Angelika H. Claussen, "Family Patterns of Relationship in Normative and Dysfunctional Families," *Development and Psychopathology* 3(1991):491–512.

Crowell, Judith A., Elizabeth O'Connor, Gretchen Wollmers, Joyce Sprafkin, and Uma Rao, "Mothers' Conceptualizations of Parent–Child Relationships: Relation to Mother–Child Interaction and Child Behavior Problems," *Development and Psychopathology* 3(1991):431–444.

DeLozier, Pauline P., "Attachment Theory and Child Abuse," in *The Place of Attachment in Human Behavior.* Eds. C. M. Parkes and J. Stevenson-Hinde. New York: Tavistock, 1982, pp. 95–117.

Dozier, Mary, Andrea L. Stevenson, Spring W. Lee, and Dawn I. Velligan, "Attachment Organization and Familial Overinvolvement for Adults with Serious Psychopathological Disorders," *Development and Psychopathology* 3(1991):475–489.

Dusay, John, *Egograms: How I See You and You See Me.* New York: Harper and Row, 1977.

Ellis, Albert, *A New Guide to Rational Living.* North Hollywood, CA: Wilshire, 1975.

Erickson, Martha Farrell, Jon Korfmacher, and Byron R. Egeland, "Attachments Past and Present: Implications for Therapeutic Intervention with Mother–Infant Dyads," *Development and Psychopathology* 4(1992):495–507.

Fahlberg, Vera I., *A Child's Journey through Placement.* Indianapolis, IN: Perspectives Press, 1991.

Feeney, Judith A., and Patricia Noller, "Attachment Style as a Predictor of Adult Romantic Relationships," *Journal of Personality and Social Psychology* 2(1990):281–291.

Feeney, Judith A., Patricia Noller, and Mary Hanrahan, "Assessing Adult Attachment," in *Attachment in Adults: Clinical and Developmental Perspectives.* Eds. Michael B. Sperling and William H. Berman. New York: Guilford Press, 1994, pp. 128–152.

Fraiberg, Selma, Edna Adelson, and Vivian Shapiro, "Ghosts in the Nursery: A Psychoanalytic Approach to the Problems of Impaired Infant–Mother Relationships," in *Selected Writings of Selma Fraiberg.* Ed. Louis Fraiberg. Columbus, OH: Ohio State University Press, 1987, pp. 100–136.

Greenberg, Mark T., Matthew L. Speltz, Michelle Deklyen, and Marya C. Endriga, "Attachment Security in Preschoolers with and without Externalizing Behavior Problems: A Replication," *Development and Psychopathology* 3(1991):413–430.

Greenspan, Stanley, and N. T. Greenspan, *The Essential Partnership: How Parents and Children Can Meet the Emotional Challenges of Infancy and Childhood.* New York: Viking Penguin, 1989.

Greenspan, Stanley, and Alicia F. Lieberman, "A Clinical Approach to Attachment," in *Clinical Implications of Attachment.* Eds. Jay Belsky and T. Nezworski. Hillsdale, NJ: Erlbaum, 1988, pp. 387–424.

Gregg, Soleil, *Preventing Antisocial Behavior in Disabled and At-Risk Students. Policy Briefs.* Charleston, WV: Appalachia Educational Laboratory, 1996.

Grossman, Karin, Elisabeth Fremmer-Bombik, Joseph Rudolph, and Klaus E. Grossmann, "Maternal Attachment Representations as Related to Patterns of Infant–Mother Attachment and Maternal Care during the First Year," in *Relationships within Families: Mutual Influences.* Eds. R. A. Hinde and Joan Stevenson-Hinde. Oxford: Clarenden Press, 1988, pp. 241–260.

Harlow, Harry F., and Robert R. Zimmermann, "Affectional Responses in the Infant Monkey," *Science* 21(1959):421–432.

Hazan, Cindy, and Phillip Shaver, "Romantic Love Conceptualized as an Attachment Process," *Journal of Personality and Social Psychology* 52(1987):511–524.

Henderson, Scott, "The Significance of Social Relationships in the Etiology of Neurosis," in *The Place of Attachment in Human Behavior.* Eds. Colin Murray Parkes and Joan Stevenson-Hinde. New York: Tavistock, 1982, pp. 205–231.

Herman, Judith L., *Trauma and Recovery.* New York: Basic Books, 1992.

Hindy, Carl G., and J. Conrad Schwarz, "Anxious Romantic Attachment in Adult Relationships," in *Attachment in Adults.* Eds. Michael B. Sperling and William H. Berman. New York: Guilford Press, 1994, pp. 179–203.

Holmes, Jeremy, *John Bowlby and Attachment Theory.* New York: Routledge, 1993.

Jacobvitz, Deborah B., Elizabeth Morgan, Molly D. Kretchmar, and Yvonne Morgan, "The Transmission of Mother–Child Boundary Disturbances across Three Generations," *Development and Psychopathology* 3(1991):513–527.

Jernberg, Ann M., *Theraplay: A New Treatment Using Structured Play for Problem Children and Their Families.* San Francisco: Jossey-Bass, 1979.

Jernberg, Ann M., "Attachment Enhancing for Adopted Children," in *Adoption Resources for Mental Health Professionals.* Ed. P. V. Grabe. New Brunswick, NJ: Transaction, 1990, pp. 271–279.

Keck, Gregory C., *Adopting the Hurt Child: Hope for Families for Special Needs Kids.* Colorado Springs, CO: Pinon, 1995.

Kobak, R. Rogers, Nanette Sudler, and Wendy Gamble, "Attachment and Depressive Symptoms during Adolescence: A Developmental Pathways Analysis," *Development and Psychopathology* 3(1991):462–474.

Kurcinka, Mary Sheedy, *Raising Your Spirited Child.* New York: Harper Collins, 1991.

Leach, Penelope, *Your Baby and Child: From Birth to Age Five.* New York: Knopf, 1981.

Levine, Lauren V., Steven B. Tuber, Arietta Slade, and Mary J. Ward, "Mothers' Mental Representations and Their Relationship to Mother–Infant Attachment," *Bulletin of the Menninger Clinic* 55(1991):454–469.

Lieberman, Alicia F., "Infant–Parent Psychotherapy with Toddlers," *Development and Psychopathology* 4(1992):559–574.

Lieberman, Alicia F., and Jeree H. Pawl, "Clinical Applications of Attachment Theory," in *Clinical Implications of Attachment Theory.* Eds. Jay Belsky and Teresa Nezworski. Hillsdale, NJ: Erlbaum, 1988.

Lieberman, Alicia F., and Jeree H. Pawl, "Disorders of Attachment and Secure Base Behavior in the Second Year of Life," in *Attachment in the Preschool Years: Theory, Research and Intervention.* Eds. Mark T. Greenberg, Dante Cicchetti, and Mark E. Cummings. Chicago: University of Chicago Press, 1990, pp. 375–397.

Linehan, Marsha M., *Cognitive Behavioral Treatment of Borderline Personality Disorder.* New York: Guilford Press, 1993.

Linehan, Marsha M., *Skills Training Manual for Treating Borderline Personality Disorder.* New York: Guilford Press, 1993.

Lifton, Betty J., *Lost and Found: The Adoption Experience.* New York: Harper and Row, 1988.

Lyons-Ruth, Karlen, Betty Repacholi, Sara McLeod, and Eugenia Silva, "Disorganized Attachment Behavior in Infancy: Short-Term Stability, Maternal and Infant Correlates, and Risk-Related Subtypes," *Development and Psychopathology* 3(1991):377–396.

Main, Mary, and Erik Hesse, "Parents' Unresolved Traumatic Experiences Are Related to Infant Disorganized Attachment Status," in *Attachment in the Preschool Years: Theory, Research and Intervention.* Eds. Mark T. Greenberg, Dante Cicchetti, and Mark E. Cummings. Chicago: University of Chicago Press, 1990, pp. 161–182.

Main, Mary, Nancy Kaplan, and Jude Cassidy, "Security in Infancy, Childhood, and Adulthood: A Move to the Level of Representation," *Monographs of the Society for Research in Child Development* 50(1–2; 1985):66–104.

Main, Mary, and Judith Solomon, "Procedures for Identifying Infants as Disorganized/Disoriented during the Ainsworth Strange Situation," in *Attachment in the Preschool Years: Theory, Research and Intervention*. Eds. Mark T. Greenberg, Dante Cichetti, and Mark E. Cummings. Chicago: University of Chicago Press, 1990, pp. 121–159.

Main, Mary, and Judith Solomon, "Discovery of an Insecure-Disorganized/Disoriented Attachment Pattern," in *Affective Development in Infancy*. Eds. T. Berry Brazelton and M. Yogman. Norwood, NJ: Ablex, 1986, pp. 95–124.

Main, Mary, and Donna R. Weston, "Avoidance of the Attachment Figure in Infancy: Descriptions and Interpretations," in *The Place of Attachment in Human Behavior*. Eds. Collin Murray Parkes and Joan Stevenson-Hinde. New York: Tavistock, 1982, pp. 31–59.

McClure, Vimala Schneider, *Infant Massage: A Handbook for Loving Parents*. New York: Bantam Books, 1989.

Melina, Lois Ruskai, *Making Sense of Adoption*. New York: Harper and Row, 1989.

Moore, Diana, *Baby's First Touch: Step-by-Step Instruction for Infant Massage* [Videotape]. Portland, OR: International Loving Touch Foundation, 1992.

Nakken, Craig, *The Addictive Personality*. Center City, MN: Hazelden, 1988.

Nezworski, Teresa, William J. Tolan, and Jay Belsky, "Intervention in Insecure Infant Attachment," in *Clinical Implications of Attachment*. Eds. Jay Belsky and Teresa Nezworski. Hillsdale, NJ: Erlbaum, 1988, pp. 352–386.

Osofsky, Joy D., Della M. Hann, and Claire Peebles, "Adolescent Parenthood: Risks and Opportunities for Mothers and Infants," in *Handbook of Infant Mental Health*. Ed. Charles H. Zeanah, Jr. New York: Guilford Press, 1993, pp. 107–118.

Parker, Gordon, "Parental 'Affectionless Control' as an Antecedent to Adult Depression," *Archives of General Psychiatry* 40(1993):956–960.

Parker, Gordon, "Parental Bonding and Depressive Disorders," in *Attachment in Adults*. Eds. Michael B. Sperling and William H. Berman. New York: Tavistock, 1994, pp. 299–312.

Parker, Harvey C., *The ADD Hyperactivity Workbook for Parents, Teachers, and Kids: Second Edition*. Plantation, FL: Specialty Press, 1994.

Parkes, Collin Murray, "Attachment and the Prevention of Mental Disorders," in *The Place of Attachment in Human Behavior*. Eds. Collin Murray Parkes and Joan Stevenson-Hinde. New York: Tavistock, 1992, pp. 295–309.

Pipher, Mary, *The Shelter of Each Other: Rebuilding Our Families*. New York: Grosset/Putnam, 1996.

Potter, Ann E., *Inside Out: Rebuilding Self and Personality through Inner Child Therapy* [Workbook]. Muncie, IN: Accelerated Development, 1994.

Pound, Andrea, "Attachment and Maternal Depression," in *The Place of Attachment in Human Behavior*. Eds. Collin Murray Parkes and Joan Stevenson-Hinde. New York: Tavistock, 1982, pp. 118–130.

Rodning, Carol, Leila Beckwith, and Judy Howard, "Quality of Attachment and Home Environments in Children Prenatally Exposed to PCP and Cocaine," *Development and Psychopathology* 3(1982):351–366.

Schaffer, J., and Lindstrom, C., *How to Raise an Adopted Child: A Guide to Help Your Child Flourish from Infancy through Adolescence*. New York: Plume, 1991.

Shapiro, Francine, *Eye Movement Desensitization and Reprocessing: Basic Principles, Protocols, and Procedures*. New York: Guilford Press, 1995.

Sperling, Michael B., and Lisa Sandow Lyons, "Representations of Attachment and Psychotherapeutic Change," in *Attachment in Adults*. Eds. Michael B. Sperling and William H. Berman. New York: Guilford Press, 1994, pp. 331–348.

Spieker, Susan J., and Catherine L. Booth, "Maternal Antecedents of Attachment Quality," in *Clinical Implications of Attachment*. Eds. Jay Belsky and Teresa Nezworski. Hillsdale, NJ: Erlbaum, 1988, pp. 95–135.

Sroufe, L. Alan, "The Role of Infant–Caregiver Attachment in Development," in *Clinical Implications of Attachment*. Eds. Jay Belsky and Teresa Nezworski. Hillsdale, NJ: Erlbaum, 1988, pp. 13–38.

Sroufe, L. Alan, Robert G. Cooper, Ganie B. Dettart, and Mary E. Marshall, *Child Development: Its Nature and Course: Second Edition*. New York: McGraw-Hill, 1992.

Stern, Daniel N., *The Motherhood Constellation: A Unified View of Parent–Infant Psychotherapy*. New York: Basic Books, 1995.

Strauss, Murray A., *Beating the Devil out of Them: Corporal Punishment in American Families*. New York: Lexington Books, 1994.

Terr, Lenore, *Too Scared to Cry: How Trauma Affects Children . . . and Ultimately Us All*. New York: Basic Books, 1990.

Terr, Lenore, *Unchained Memories: True Stories of Traumatic Memories, Lost and Found*. New York: Basic Books, 1994.

Tulving, Endel, "How Many Memory Systems Are There?" *American Psychologist* 44(1985):385–398.

Turecki, Stanley, with Leslie Tonner, *The Difficult Child*. New York: Bantam Books, 1989.

Turnbull, Colin M., *The Mountain People*. New York: Simon and Schuster, 1972.

Urban, Joan, Elizabeth Carlson, Byron Egeland, and L. Alan Sroufe, "Patterns of Individual Adaptation across Childhood," *Development and Psychopathology* 3(1991):445–460.

van Gulden, Holly, and Lisa M. Bartels-Rabb, *Real Parents, Real Children: Parenting the Adopted Child*. New York: Crossroad, 1993.

Van Ijzendoorn, Marinus H., "Intergenerational Transmission of Parenting: A Review of Studies in Nonclinical Populations," *Developmental Review* 12(1992):76–99.

Vaughn, Brian E., Gretchen B. Lefever, Ronald Seifer, and Peter Barglow, "Attachment Behavior, Attachment Security, and Temperament During Infancy," *Child Development* 60(1989):728–737.

Verrier, Nancy Newton, *The Primal Wound: Understanding the Adopted Child*. Baltimore, MD: Gateway, 1996.

Weiss, Robert S., "Attachment in Adult Life," in *The Place of Attachment in Human Behavior*. Eds. Collin Murray Parkes and Joan Stevenson-Hinde. New York: Tavistock, 1982, pp. 171–184.

Welch, Martha G., *Holding Time*. New York: Simon and Schuster, 1988.

Wender, Paul. H., *Attention-Deficit Hyperactivity Disorder in Adults*. New York: Oxford University Press, 1995.

West, Malcolm, and Adrienne Keller, "Psychotherapy Strategies for Insecure Attachment in Personality Disorders," in *Attachment in Adults*. Eds. Collin Murray Parkes and Joan Stevenson-Hinde. New York: Guilford Press, 1994, pp. 313–330.

Winnicott, Donald W., *The Family and Individual Development*. New York: Basic Books, 1965.

Winnicott, Donald W., *Home Is Where We Start From: Essays by a Psychoanalyst*. New York: Viking Penguin, 1986.

Index

The Whole Parent

How to Become a Terrific Parent
Even if You Didn't Have One